A

Economic Development in Action:
Theories, Problems, and Procedures as Applied in the Middle East

This book is part of the
WORLD SERIES IN ECONOMICS
E. E. Liebhafsky, *Consulting Editor*

Other books in this series

MONOGRAPHS

THE CLASSICAL THEORY OF ECONOMIC POLICY
Warren J. Samuels

TECHNOLOGY, MANPOWER, AND RETIREMENT POLICY
Edited by Juanita Kreps

Economic Development in Action:
Theories, Problems, and Procedures
as Applied in the Middle East

TAGHI T. KERMANI
The Youngstown University

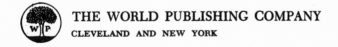

THE WORLD PUBLISHING COMPANY
CLEVELAND AND NEW YORK

Published by THE WORLD PUBLISHING COMPANY
2231 West 110th Street, Cleveland, Ohio 44102

Published simultaneously in Canada by
Nelson, Foster & Scott Ltd.

Library of Congress Catalog Card Number: 67–11436

PRINTED IN THE UNITED STATES OF AMERICA

To the People of the Middle East

ACKNOWLEDGMENTS

A number of people have helped me in this endeavor. I should like to thank them for their efforts. Among these are my wife Shirley and my daughter Venus, who deserve a special thanks for putting up with me during the time I was involved in writing this book. The other person is Mr. John Sumansky, my student assistant, who helped gather certain information.

PREFACE

Theories of economic growth, especially those dealing with economic development in underdeveloped areas, have aroused worldwide interest during the past twenty years. This has happened for two reasons: (1) the social awakening in underdeveloped countries and their striving toward an economic development comparable to that in advanced Western areas and (2) the new strategic position that the present underdeveloped countries hold in shaping the world's balance of power.

However, most existing theories of economic growth lack contact with the exact economic, social, and political reality that exists in underdeveloped countries. Usually these theories are based on the past records of the developing nations or have sought to analyze growth in a well-established, progressive economy. The present underdeveloped countries differ from the nations upon which these theories are based in background, location, social structure, and even propensities. Nor do the existing underdeveloped countries in the world share common problems. A theory of economic development, regardless of its comprehensiveness, often fails to treat specific problems in a particular area. A theory of economic development to be effective, must therefore be tailor-made.

This book is designed to teach students the major theories of economic development and their application in a designated area. The Middle East has been selected because there one can find most major economic, political, and social symptoms of economic backwardness. In particular, this book seeks to bring most existing theories of economic development into contact with reality as it exists in the Middle East. The book, furthermore, aims to broaden the students' understanding by introducing the role of foreign assistance in the process of economic development in the area.

Two problems have limited the comprehensiveness of this book. The first is the fact that the Middle Eastern countries have only recently begun their quest for progress; it is not possible to place these countries in a proper classification or fit them to a neatly designed theory. Though one might easily determine their accomplishments, it is not possible reasonably to predict their direction. Although everything may look good now, events such as a revolution or even an orderly change of government may alter the entire future outlook. The second obstacle has been the lack of adequate and comprehensive data. The available data on the Middle East are either scattered, incomprehensive, incomplete, or inaccurate. It may sound strange, but while these conditions have limited the book's comprehensiveness to some extent, they have actually increased its usefulness. But they are inherent in a situation dealing with underdeveloped areas, and the use of such data from certain Middle Eastern countries made it possible to bring together existing theories of economic development with reality as it exists today in the Middle East.

TAGHI T. KERMANI

Pahlavi University
January 1967

CONTENTS

LIST OF TABLES

Chapter 1

THE GEOGRAPHY AND THE SOCIAL AND ECONOMIC STRUCTURE OF THE MIDDLE EAST

Since we cannot properly discuss or evaluate a subject without some basic knowledge of its construction, function, or behavior, any discussion of economic problems or development in the Middle East must be prefaced by certain information about the region itself. This chapter therefore examines the Middle Eastern physical, social, and economic structure.

MIDDLE EAST DEFINED

Historically speaking, the term "Near East" was first used during the fifteenth century to describe the area toward the eastern and southern parts of the Mediterranean. The term "Middle East" was introduced later to include countries between the Ottoman Empire and the Far East—Iran, Afghanistan, and India. During the nineteenth century, however, both terms were used freely and often interchangeably.[1]

[1] For instance, while the American Oriental Society refers to Iran and Iraq as the Middle East, according to the monthly *Journal of Middle Eastern Affairs*, the term *Middle East* includes Turkey, Syria, Lebanon, Iraq, Iran, Israel, Jordan, The U.A.R., Saudi Arabia, Yemen, Aden, Oman, and Somaliland. The UN statistical paper, on the other hand, adds Sudan, Cyprus, and Ethiopia to the above list. The *Encyclopedia Americana* (1956) goes even further, including Greece (and Crete) in Europe, Afghanistan and Western Pakistan in Asia, and Morocco, Algeria, and Libya in Africa within the confines of the Middle East. Finally, according to the United States 1945 *Government Manual*, the Division of Near Eastern Affairs included Egypt, Greece, Iraq, Lebanon, Palestine, Jordan, Saudi Arabia, other countries in the Arabian Peninsula, Syria, and Turkey; the Division of Middle Eastern Affairs included Afghanistan, Burma, Ceylon, India, and Iran.

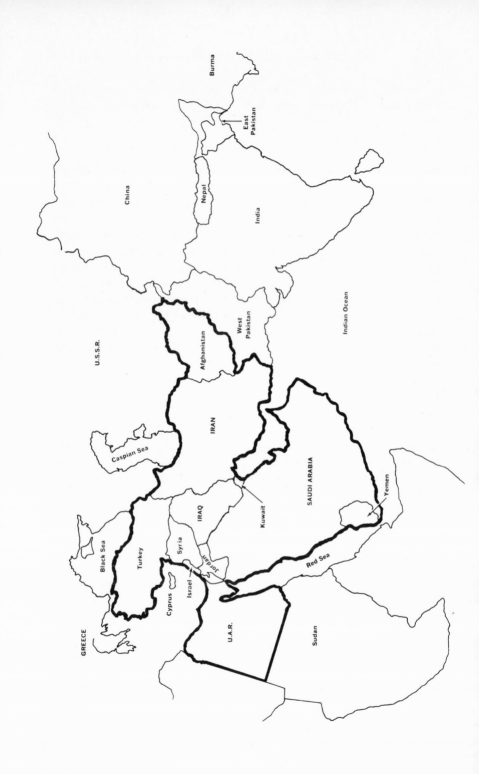

Generally speaking, "Middle East" and "Near East" are political rather than geographic terms. Neither has been consistently used to describe a specific geographic area, as have such terms as "Central America" or "the Far East."

For the purposes of this book the terms "Near East" and "Middle East" will be restricted to Iran, Iraq, Jordan, Syria, Lebanon, Israel, Saudi Arabia, and all the countries of the Arabian Peninsula. Afghanistan and the United Arab Republic may conceivably fall into this category and are occasionally referred to in this book. Turkey, which definitely shares some of the major geographic and social characteristics of the Middle East, has been excluded from our discussion for two reasons. First, because of her exceptional strategic position, Turkey has become a focus of Western attention and therefore has received (and probably will continue to receive) a relatively larger share of foreign economic and noneconomic assistance than have other countries in the Middle East. Second, because of her geographic location, Turkey has achieved far more social and economic integration with Europe and therefore possesses a more balanced social institution than do other areas in the Middle East. Lebanon and Israel have been excluded from analysis here for similar reasons.

Although the area of the Middle East has been defined and the countries therein have been specified, this book will not treat all sections of the Middle East uniformly, to avoid unnecessary length and duplication. Our discussion will concentrate on three Middle Eastern countries representative of the region in economic, social, and political conditions: Iran, Iraq, and Jordan. (Turkey, Israel, and to some extent Lebanon are excluded as noted because their social, economic, and political positions differ significantly from those of the rest of the region. Saudi Arabia, Syria, and other countries of the Arabian Peninsula have been excluded because of inadequate data, and because their economic, social, and political situations are represented in our discussion of Iran, Iraq, and Jordan. However, all of these countries are occasionally referred to for comparison.)

A combined study of Iran, Iraq, and Jordan should be adequate to illustrate the economic and social conditions that exist in the Middle East. Jordan, for instance, suffers from extreme economic poverty and the lack of adequate resources. These factors strongly limit her ability to plan and operate the economic development programs necessary to keep pace with the rapidly growing population.

Iran enjoys a relatively adequate supply of natural resources, but they are underdeveloped and underutilized. Iran's resources, fully utilized, could easily yield a higher national income, but thus far their development has been limited by certain institutional and economic obstacles. Iran provides a good case study of some of the most critical economic and social problems in the region: land distribution and ownership, poor utilization of resources, inadequate technology, and institutional maladjustments.

Iraq, in every way, has more than it needs. She is blessed with large and profitable oil fields, abundant fresh water, good land, and a small population. She can be a classic example of a nation blessed with wealth but plagued by political disturbances and social insecurity.

LAND AND CLIMATE

The Middle East, as defined in this book, lies between 12.5 and 40 degrees north latitude and between 34 and 63 degrees east longitude. More specifically, Jordan extends from 35 to 39 degrees longitude and 28.5 to 33.5 degrees latitude. It is bounded by Syria on the north, Iraq on the east, Saudi Arabia on the south, and Israel on the west. Jordan's total land area is 37,000 square miles, of which only 13 per cent is arable.

Iraq extends from 28.5 to 35.5 degrees latitude and 39 to 48.5 degrees longitude. She is bounded by Turkey and Syria on the north, Syria and Jordan on the northwest and west, Saudi Arabia on the south, and by the Persian Gulf and Iran on the east. Of Iraq's total area of 168,000 square miles, 26 per cent is arable.

Iran lies between 25 and 40 degrees latitude and 44 and 63 degrees longitude. She is bounded by the U.S.S.R. on the north, Afghanistan and Pakistan on the east, the Oman Sea and Persian Gulf on the south, and Iraq and Turkey on the west. The total area of Iran is 629,000 square miles; only 11 per cent is arable.[2]

---

[2] Statistics and Reports Division, Agency for International Development, *Selected Economic Data for the Less Developed Countries* (Washington, D.C., June 1965), p. 20.

The climate in different parts of the Middle East varies according to land structure and geographic location. Roughly speaking, the Middle East's climate may be divided into three categories: Mediterranean, desert, and continental. Mediterranean climate covers the northern parts of the U.A.R., around the Mediterranean and the Black seas, and the northern and southern parts of Iran; it has hot and rainless summers and cool and rainy winters. Desert climate covers the central and eastern parts of Iran, all Saudi Arabia, and other countries of the Arabian Peninsula except the lower shores of the Red Sea. This climate is very hot and dry with little (or no) rainfall, which either evaporates or seeps into the ground, thus making the area poor for cultivation. Continental climate covers the western parts of Iran, northern parts of Iraq, and southeastern and eastern parts of Turkey. This climate is more humid than the desert climate and has cold winters and hot summers.

Rainfall in the Middle East also varies in different sections, with the highest rate in the north and northwest, averaging as much as 30 inches a year, and lower rates toward the southern and eastern sections, averaging from 5.5 inches in central Iraq to 1.7 inches in western Iraq to nearly zero in central Iran and the Arabian Desert. Generally speaking, at least three-fourths of the region's total area receives fewer than ten inches of rainfall annually.

NATURAL RESOURCES

The resources of the Middle East, as in other parts of the world, may be classified into three categories: natural, human, and technical and/or capital. Except for oil, the Middle East is not very prosperous in natural resources, and the existing resources are poorly and uneconomically distributed and utilized.

OIL

Petroleum is the most important natural resource of the Middle East, not only in relation to the supply of other resources in the area but also in relation to the world's oil supply. In 1964, about 68 per cent of the world's total proven oil reserve was known to be in the Middle East, but the area produced only 34 per cent of total world oil.

The countries of the Middle East, however, do not all enjoy an equal share of oil deposits. Within the Middle East, Kuwait accounts for about 20 per cent of the world reserve, Saudi Arabia 19 per cent, Iran 12 per cent, and Iraq 8 per cent (see Figure 1.1).

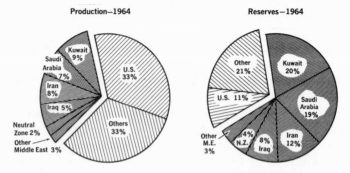

Source: Statistics and Reports Division, Agency for International Development, *Near East and South Asia Economic Growth Trend* (Washington, D.C., Sept. 1965), p. 10.

FIGURE 1.1. Oil Reserves and Production: World and Middle East

Table 1.1.   Crude Oil Production in 1000 Metric Tons*

	1950	1960	1962	1963	1964
Turkey	17	360	508	728	800
Iraq	6,457	47,500	49,190	56,465	61,500
Iran	32,259	52,050	65,405	72,684	83,300
S.A.	26,179	61,500	75,746	81,000	86,000
Kuwait	17,291	81,863	92,200	96,200	106,000
Kuwait, S.A. .... Neutral Zone		7,284	13,050	16,400	19,000
Bahrain	1,510	2,250	2,250	2,260	2,400
Qatar	1,632	8,212	8,800	9,100	8,943
Abu Dhalii			800	2,483	9,000
Egypt	2,349	3,272	4,670	5,600	6,500
Israel		129	133	150	200
U.S.A.	271,081	347,121	360,769	371,087	379,000
U.S.S.R.	37,800	147,000	186,000	206,100	223,600

* Oil production by various countries of the Middle East.
Source: *Statesman's Year Book* (1965–1966), p. xxvii.

MINERALS, FORESTS, AND LIVESTOCK

Various mineral resources exist in modest quantities in parts of the Middle East. But, other than oil, the only minerals produced and exported in any quantity are red iron oxide and turquoise in Iran and potash in Jordan. Coal, iron ore, and chromium also exist in Turkey, Iran, and Egypt. Rock salt is mined in Iran and some is exported to other countries in the region. Other minerals such as lead and nickel, copper, alum, arsenic, calcium, potash, borate, sulfur, and fuller's earth have been discovered and are being exploited in different sections, but production is not presently sufficient for major export.

The Middle East is not rich in forest lands, and those that do exist have long been abused or are exhausted. The region's total forest land has been estimated to be about 145 million acres, or about 10.9 per cent of the area's total land—approximately 3.6 per cent of the world's total forest lands. The forest areas in the Middle East are located chiefly around the Caspian littoral, the north-western parts of Iraq, and the shores of the Mediterranean. Iran's forest lands have been estimated at about 19 million acres, 11.7 per cent of the country's total area. Iraq has about 1.77 million acres of forest, 4 per cent of its total land, and Jordan has about 525,000 acres of forest land, or 5.4 per cent of the country's total area.

Livestock is raised in the Middle East by two groups: farmers, who put emphasis on breeding cattle for use in agricultural production; and the nomadic tribes, who breed sheep and goats and possess about 80 per cent of the total sheep and goats in the region. In 1953–1954, about 30 per cent of the world's sheep and goats were owned by the people of the Middle East. During the same period, the Middle Eastern people owned about 32.3 per cent of the world's donkeys, 23.1 per cent of the world's mules, 15.9 per cent of the world's horses, and 11.3 per cent of the world's camels.[3]

---

[3] U.N. Food and Agriculture Organization, *Year Book of Food and Agriculture Statistics* (Lake Success, N. Y., 1955), pp. 114–46.

HUMAN RESOURCES

In 1964 the Middle East's total population was an estimated 122 million, or 50 persons per square mile.[4] Comparing the average population density of the Middle East with that of Western industrialized nations, the region can be considered underpopulated. But because of the traditional population immobility caused by poor transportation as well as by political and other barriers, the existing population is not uniformly distributed throughout the region. For

Table 1.2. **Population and Population Density in the Middle East, 1964**

Region & Countries	Population (in 1,000,000)	Population Density (persons per sq mi)	Population Growth Rate (per cent)
Free world	2,200	55	2.1
Middle East	122	50	2.5
Iran	22.9	35	2.5
Iraq	7.0	40	2.0
Jordan	1.9	50	3.0
Lebanon	2.4	475	3.0
Saudi Arabia ...	6.5	10	1.0
Syria	5.9	76	3.0
Turkey	30.8	103	2.9
U.A.R.	28.9	73	3.0
Yemen	4.0	67	n.a.
Greece	8.5	165	0.9
Cyprus	0.6	165	1.0
Israel	2.5	310	4.0

Source: *Selected Economic Data for the Less Developed Countries,* Statistics and Reports Division, Agency for International Development (Washington, D.C., June 1965), pp. 20–21.

example, while the average population density in Saudi Arabia is only 10 persons per square mile, there are about 310 persons per square mile in Israel and 475 in Lebanon. This unbalanced population distribution is also noticeable within the individual countries of the Middle East.

[4] Includes Cyprus, Greece, Iran, Iraq, Israel, Jordan, Kuwait, Lebanon, Saudi Arabia, Syria, Turkey, the U.A.R., and Yemen.

Iran and Iraq in particular can be considered underpopulated, in respect to both total area and available natural resources. Jordan holds a peculiar position in this regard. After the annexation of Arab Palestine and the inflow of a large number of Arab refugees into Jordan, the population of the country increased from 464,680 to 1,410,000, or from 17.8 to 38 persons per square mile.[5] Today, Jordan suffers from almost all the symptoms of population pressure, not in relation to its total area but in relation to the supply of natural resources.

Middle Eastern people vary in race and language, but the greatest majority adhere to a similar religious faith. Islam is the predominant religion in the Middle East and has undoubtedly influenced the social, political, and even the economic institutions of the area. About 98 per cent of the Iranian people, 93 per cent of the Iraqi population, and 99 per cent of the people in Saudi Arabia are followers of Islam. In most Middle Eastern countries, the civil law is based on the Koran. Not all countries of the Middle East are predominantly Moslem, however. Christianity and Judaism are the two most important religious minorities in the area, with Christians concentrated primarily in Cyprus (82 per cent) and in Lebanon (54 per cent) and the followers of the Jewish faith mostly concentrated in Israel (93 per cent of population).

MIDDLE EASTERN SOCIAL STRUCTURE

The social structure of the Middle East is on the whole extremely unbalanced. The vast majority of the population, despite recent reform efforts, own very little wealth and have little or no political power. On the other hand, a small minority, composed of wealthy merchants, landlords, the clergy, and the high-ranking military officers, own most of the region's wealth, live in great luxury, and are in complete control of the majority, politically and economically. The middle class of craftsmen, shopkeepers, and smaller merchants is so small and powerless that its members have often found it to their advantage to join the forces of the powerful minorities rather than resist.

---

[5] Nation Associates, *Security in the Middle East, The Problem and Its Solution*. Proposals submitted to the President of the United States (Washington, D.C., April 1954), p. 7.

A new front has also been forming during the last decade or two. This is the new group of so-called intelligentsia, composed of students returning from foreign universities, students attending local colleges and high schools, and at times smaller businessmen and even civil servants. This group, despite its small size, has shown signs of strength on many occasions and has created a force for progress or—in many cases—social and political disturbance.

THE STRUCTURE OF GOVERNMENT

The Middle Eastern countries may be classified into three groups with respect to governmental structure: (1) Those countries that have established a republican form of government, such as Turkey, the United Arab Republic, the Syrian Arab Republic, Lebanon, Iraq, and Israel (democracy nevertheless does not necessarily exist in all these countries). (2) Those countries that have combined their traditional form of government with modern democracy and accepted a form of constitutional monarchy. Among these are Iran, Jordan, Afghanistan, and Saudi Arabia. (3) The sheikdoms and smaller countries that are either independent or to some extent under foreign protection, such as Aden, Masqat, Oman, Gatar, Kuwait, and Bahrain.

Regardless of the form or method of operation, most Middle Eastern governments are controlled by a small minority of the population and seem to change hands from one such group into another. As a result, public officials are generally disliked and mistrusted.[6]

LIVING CONDITIONS

In general, most attempts at comprehensive analysis of living conditions in the Middle East have been restricted by the lack of adequate information. In the first place, a good number of the Middle East's people are still nomadic tribes. Registration of events or transactions does not exist among these people, and they seldom cooperate with the central government in supplying such information. In the second place, because of the extent of ignorance and illiteracy among most Middle Eastern populations—especially among those living in isolated sections—the benefits of record-keeping and registration have not yet been realized. Among these

---

[6] *Ibid.*, pp. 50–52.

people are those who "don't know even that World War I is over."[7]

Accordingly, most of the existing information on the region's living conditions, especially that supplied by the local governments, is either incomplete or of doubtful accuracy. The data are incomplete because of the local government's lack of the ability and technical knowledge to collect and process accurate information. They are doubtful because of the general tendency of such national governments to show the situation better than it is— minimizing the problems, but exaggerating the good points.

The level of income in most Middle Eastern countries is still among the lowest in the world, although this low income level is not shared equally by all Middle Eastern countries. In 1963, when the U.S. had $3080 per capita gross national product, Kuwait's per capita GNP stood at $3300, Afghanistan's at $80 (see Table 1.3).

Table 1.3. Gross National Product for 1963
(in U.S. Dollars)

	GNP in $100,000	GNP in dollars per capita		GNP in $100,000	GNP in dollars per capita
U.S.A.	584,000	3,080	Lebanon	750	319
Middle East ..	29,290	240	Saudi Arabia ..1,120		175
Iran	4,790	216	Syria	800	145
Iraq	1,645	235	Turkey 6,975		233
Jordan	360	199	UAR 3,900		139
Israel	2,688	1,131	Yemen	360	90
Kuwait	1,122	3,300	Afghanistan ...1,100		80

Source: Statistics and Reports Division, Agency for International Development, *Selected Economic Data for the Less Developed Countries* (Washington, D.C., June 1965), pp. 20–21.

Since 1955, however, most Middle Eastern countries have shown a relatively rapid rate of economic growth. This has been partly because of extensive oil production and partly a result of the implementation of many development projects, supplemented by a vast inflow of foreign assistance (see Table 1.4).

[7] "Hunt Spread into Pakistan," Omaha (Nebraska) *World-Herald*, March 28, 1957, p. 1.

Table 1.4.   Gross National Product, 1957 and 1964,
for the U.S.A. and Selected Middle Eastern Countries
(in U.S. dollars per capita)

	GNP for 1957	GNP for 1964E*	% Growth
U.S.A.	2,572	3,080	16.5
Iran	186	220	18.2
Iraq	188	254	35.0
Jordan	139	223	60.4
Israel	708	1,116	36.5
Turkey	205	222	8.3
Pakistan	72	82	13.9

* Estimated
Source: Statistics and Reports Division, Agency for International Development, *Selected Economic Data for the Less Developed Countries* (Washington, D.C., June 1965), pp. 20–21.

Finally, it is necessary to keep in mind that the increased GNP in various sections of the Middle East does not necessarily mean a better living for the majority of the population. These increases in income are not uniformly distributed in the area or among different class groups. The majority of the population, who have received little or no increase in money income, may actually be in a worse situation than before due to the increase in the cost of living and a consequent decline in real income.

HEALTH AND EDUCATION

Food and Agricultural Organization cites 2390 calories as the daily requirement for a normal human body; the average daily caloric intake per person in the Middle East in the most recent account was 2400, compared with 2200 for 1955 in that area (see Table 1.5).

Except for a few regions, the conditions of health and sanitation in the Middle East, are still among the worst in the world. Such diseases as tuberculosis, malaria, typhoid, bilharzia, trachoma, and hookworm are dominant among the majority of the lower-income population. The number of qualified physicians is only one for every 3900 persons in Iran, one for every 4900 in Iraq, and one for every

4700 in Jordan. For the region as a whole, there is one physician for every 2000 persons, as compared with one physician for every 740 persons in the U.S.A. (see Table 1.5).

The level of education in most parts of the Middle East is also among the lowest in the world, with the majority of educated persons concentrated in certain areas or among certain groups. According to the latest available report, the over-all rate of literacy in the region was about 35 per cent of the total population, compared with 98 per cent in the U.S.A. Israel and Lebanon, with 90 per cent and 80 per cent, respectively, have the region's highest literacy rates. Afghanistan and Saudi Arabia, with 5 to 10 per cent and 5 to 15 per cent, respectively, hold the lowest rates (see Table 1.5).

Table 1.5. Health and Education in the Middle East
(latest figures)

	Number of persons for each qualified physician	Daily caloric intake per person	Literacy rate (%)	Population enrolled in elementary and secondary schools (%)
U.S.A.	740	3,090	98	24
Middle East ..	2,000	2,400	35	12
Iran	3,900	2,160	15–20	9
Iraq	4,900	2,280	20	15
Israel	400	2,840	90	22
Jordan	4,700	2,200	35–40	17
Kuwait	1,000	n.a.	34	15
Lebanon	1,200	2,550	80	18
Saudi Arabia ..	12,600	2,000	5–15	2
Syria	5,100	2,300	35	12
Turkey	2,000	2,600	44	13
U.A.R.	2,600	2,330	30	13
Yemen	68,000	n.a.	25	2
Afghanistan ...	33,500	n.a.	5–10	2

Source: Statistics and Reports Division, Agency for International Development, *Selected Economic Data for the Less Developed Countries* (Washington, D.C., June 1965), pp. 20–21.

In most parts of the Middle East, facilities for improving the educational level of the people are not yet adequate. In addition, in many Middle Eastern countries education has been delayed by either the lack of a compulsory education law or the difficulty of enforcing one. Only 12 per cent of the Middle Eastern population is enrolled in elementary and secondary schools, compared with 24 per cent in the U.S.A. (see Table 1.5).

ECONOMIC STRUCTURE

Seventy to 80 per cent of the working population in the Middle East is engaged in agricultural production, leaving 20 to 30 per cent of the working population for other forms of activity. This does not necessarily mean that a similar share of the area's gross national product (GNP) is also derived from agriculture, however. In many countries of the Middle East, the industrial origin of the GNP is larger than that from agriculture. In other parts of the area, the share of the GNP from agriculture is much smaller than

**Table 1.6.   Industrial Origin of Gross Domestic Product
in the Middle East: Percentage of Total, 1963**

	Iran	Iraq	Jordan(*)	Israel	Turkey
Agriculture, fishing, and forestry	25	17	18	10	41
Manufacturing, mining, and utilities	33(a)	47(d)	10	26	17
Construction	3	3	4	8	6
Transportation and communication	(b)	7	12	8	7
Wholesale and retail	12	5	23	18(e)	9
Defense and public administration	9(c)	10	16	19(f)	10(c)
Others	18	11	17	11	10

(*) 1962. (a) 15% oil. (b) Included in others. (c) Include government services. (d) 36% oil. (e) Include private services. (f) Include government services and nonprofit organizations.

Source: Statistics and Reports Division, Agency for International Development, *Selected Economic Data for the Less Developed Countries* (Washington, D.C., June 1965), p. 25.

the ratio of working people employed in agriculture. This is mainly the result of two factors. First, the production of oil has been included in industrial origin of GNP. This especially accounts for the largest share of industrial production in Iran, Iraq, Kuwait, and Saudi Arabia. Second, most industries in the Middle East are new and have thus utilized advanced technology, while the methods of agricultural production are usually primitive, failing to exploit land to its optimum potential.

In Iran, about 33 per cent of the 1963 GNP originated in industrial sectors, only 25 per cent in agriculture. Iraq's industrial origin of 1963 GNP, on the other hand, was 47 per cent, compared with 17 per cent from agriculture. Jordan's industrial origin of 1963 GNP was 10 per cent, compared with 18 per cent from agriculture (see Table 1.6). Considering that the majority of Jordan's working population is engaged in agricultural production, an 18 per cent contribution seems insignificant.

AGRICULTURE

Agriculture plays a vital role in the Middle Eastern economy. Excluding the oil revenue, the largest single part of the GNP in most Middle Eastern countries is derived from agricultural activities.

Many sections of the Middle East enjoy fertile soil, adequate water, and good climate. But these favorable conditions are limited to only 34 per cent of the region's total area, or about 4.3 acres per capita, and the distribution is far from balanced.

In Iran, 11 per cent of the total land—2 acres per capita—is being cultivated. Iraq cultivates 26 per cent of its land—4.1 acres per capita. Jordan, on the other hand, cultivates 13 per cent of its land—1.6 acres per capita (see Table 1.7).

Except for the Euphrates and Tigris rivers in Iraq, the Nile in Egypt, and the Karun in Iran, most Middle Eastern rivers are small and the lakes are salty. Except for the rain-fed areas of the Mediterranean shores, northern Iran, and Iraq, agricultural production in most parts of the region depend on the amount of water that can be brought to the field by means of irrigation. In many areas, where rainfall is inadequate and irrigation is absent, a system of two- or three-year rotation of land is customary.

16   Middle East Economy

Table 1.7.   World and Middle East Agricultural Land

	—Agricultural Land—			—Agricultural Land—	
	Per cent of the area	Acres per capita		Per cent of the area	Acres per capita
Free World ..	31	3.7	Syria	70	5.7
Middle East ..	34	4.3	Turkey	69	4.3
Iran	11	2.0	U.A.R.	3	.2
Iraq	26	4.1	Afghanistan ..	19	2.2
Jordan	13	1.6	Saudi Arabia .	58	35.6
Israel	53	1.1	Lebanon	27	.4

Source: Nation Associates, *Security in the Middle East, The Problem and Its Solution.* Proposals submitted to the President of the United States (Washington, D.C., Sept. 1954), p. 7.

By the end of 1964, Iraq had more than 9 million acres of land under irrigation. However, about 20 to 30 per cent of her cultivable land has been "abandoned in recent years as a result of salinization caused by irrigation without drainage."[8] In Iran about two fifths of the cultivated area has been irrigated. It is expected that with proper irrigation about 30 per cent of the land can be cultivated.[9] Jordan's major irrigation projects have, so far, been delayed by either the lack of funds or the absence of a proper agreement with Syria and Israel for utilization of the waters of the Jordan and Yarmuh rivers. According to the government's official report, about 30 per cent of Jordan's total agricultural products comes from the irrigated lands. Jordanian officials expect this to increase to 40 per cent by 1970.[10]

Agricultural production methods are still primitive in most parts of the Middle East, as already noted. Modern farm equipment is scarce and in most cases is being used only for demonstration. The use of chemical fertilizers is limited; modern methods of grazing and harvesting are almost unknown. In 1954, for instance, less than

[8] Data from U.S. Department of State, *Iraq*, Revision #195, p. 3.

[9] Data from U.S. Department of State, *Iran*, Revision #201, p. 2.

[10] *Seven-Year Economic Development Programs*, 1964–1970. Presented to Jordan's Development Committee, Amman, October 1965.

1 per cent of the total world's tractor supply was being used in the Middle East (excluding Israel), as compared with 60.5 per cent of the world's total supply in the U.S.A. Most tools for cultivation are still handmade and manually employed.

Wheat and barley are the two most important types of grain crops in the Middle East; they are cultivated in almost every part of the region and form the major diet of the population. In 1955, about 69.3 per cent of the total crop lands in the Middle East were in barley and wheat, which accounted for 65.1 per cent of the region's total grain production. The same year, about 17.5 per cent of the region's crop lands were in millet and sorghum. Rice, rye, oats, and maize are produced for local consumption. Dates are another important agricultural product (see Table 1.8).

Table 1.8. Summary of Major Crop and Cropped Area in the World and in the Middle East, 1955

	Cultivated Area (in million hectares)				Production (in million metric tons)			
	World total	M. E. total	% of world	% of M. E.	World total	M. E. total	% of world	% of M. E.
Wheat	135.5	15.3	11.3	47.8	151.5	13.3	8.8	44.0
Barley	44.7	6.9	15.4	21.5	55.8	6.4	11.5	21.1
Millet & Sorghum ..	83.5	5.6	6.7	17.5	59.2	4.2	7.1	13.9
Maize	86.9	2.3	2.6	7.2	137.3	3.2	2.3	10.6
Rice and Paddy	97.4	.9	1.0	2.8	162.2	2.3	1.4	7.8
Rye	14.7	.6	4.1	1.9	20.3	.5	2.5	1.6
Oats	37.2	.4	1.1	1.2	49.4	.3	.6	1.0
TOTAL GRAINS .	499.4	32.0	6.4	100.0	635.7	30.2	4.8	100.0
Dates (1954) .					1.5	1.17	78.0	
Potatoes	12.9	.2	1.6		166.9	1.5	.9	
Pulses	38.6	1.9	4.9		24.4	1.4	5.7	
Oilseeds	81.4	3.0	3.7		54.6	2.0	3.7	
Cotton	30.4	2.1	6.9		7.2	.8	11.1	

Source: *FOA Yearbook* (1955), p. 43. (Percentages calculated from original figures.)

INDUSTRY

Except for oil production, modern industries in most parts of the Middle East are still limited in size and number. The existing industries, however, fall into three groups: (1) the oil industry, (2) recent large-scale industries initiated by government projects or by foreign investments, and (3) industries engaged in meeting the primary local needs, such as construction, textile manufacturing, and food-processing.

The oil industry is undoubtedly the most important industry in the Middle East. In 1964, oil accounted for about 93 per cent of Iran's total exports and for about 90 to 95 per cent of Iraq's total export.[11]

Some of the most important types of industries in the Middle East that deal solely with agricultural products are: flour milling, fruit drying, date packing, and oil extracting and distilling. Among the most important types of industries for consumption purposes are the textile, tobacco, soap, and sugar industries. Two of the most important industries for production of construction materials are those that manufacture cement and bricks. Other industries include carpet-weaving, dairying, tanning, shoemaking, nail manufacturing, hardware production, and the traditional handicraft industries. As a result of the recent surge for industrialization in the Middle East, a new working class has been created. This group, though still small, is gradually gaining power by organizing labor unions and influencing legislators to enact protective laws pertaining to workmen's compensation, minimum wages, maximum working hours, working conditions, and the like.

TERTIARY, FINANCIAL, AND PUBLIC UTILITIES

Tertiary occupations, especially those in commerce, have long been regarded respectable fields of employment in the Middle East. The partnership and corporation, however, are not yet well established forms of business structure in the region. The attitude of most businessmen toward accepting a partner in business can be illustrated by an Iranian proverb: "If a partner was a good thing, God

---

[11] Department of State, *Economic Background Highlights, Iraq*, Revision #195 (Washington, D.C.), and for *Iran*, Revision #201 (March 1965).

would have one." Consequently, most businesses in the Middle East are either individual proprietorships or very limited partnerships.

Import, export, and wholesale trade in the region is usually concentrated in the hands of a few merchants, who seek profit not through expanding the volume of their business but by speculation. Retail trade in the Middle East is usually carried on by two different groups: the petty merchants, who own shops and tools and often collaborate with the richer merchants or clergy; and the very poor retailers, who own very little capital and usually sell their commodities on street corners or from donkey-pulled carriages.

Most financial organizations of medium or large size in the Middle East are controlled or subsidized by the national governments or are branches of foreign institutions. On July 14, 1964, the government of Iraq nationalized all banks, insurance corporations, and 32 of its largest industrial and commercial firms. In Iran, there were 9 government-controlled banks, 5 modern private banks, and 1 foreign bank in 1954. As a result of recent government encouragement several private banking institutions have been organized since.

Transportation and communication facilities are primitive in most parts of the Middle East. Improvement in such facilities has been limited by the size of the national budget and by political instability, but transportation and communication development is top on the list of all development programs in the region.

In 1964, for every 1000 square miles in the area, there were 19 miles of improved road in Iran, 40 in Iraq, and 52 in Jordan—compared with 890 in the U.S.A. (see Table 1.9). The Middle Eastern railway system is even less developed. In 1964, the total railway mileage was 2300 miles or 3.6 miles per 1000 square miles in Iran, and 1050 miles or 6 miles per 1000 square miles in Iraq.[12]

Because of limited internal waterways and strong competition by foreign merchant vessels in external waterways, water transportation in the Middle East is in general even less developed than the roads and railways on land. Small and often old-fashioned commercial boats, seldom equipped with motors, are used in northern parts of the Nile in Egypt, in southern sections of the Tigris and the Euphrates in Iraq, on the Karun River, and also in the Caspian

---

[12] *Ibid.*

Sea in Iran, the Persian Gulf, the Red Sea, and the eastern portion of the Mediterranean.

As a bridge between three continents many eastbound airliners from the West traverse and eventually offer service to most Middle Eastern countries—BOAC, Air France, KLM, TWA, Pan American, SAS, and LAT among them. Besides the services received from foreign airline systems, several national and regional air transport companies have been established and are rendering service on local, regional, and even international levels.

Communications facilities in the Middle East are either nationalized, subsidized, or controlled by the national governments. Telephone service was nationalized in Iran in 1952 and is publicly controlled in Iraq and Jordan. Almost all radio, wireless, and television stations are owned and operated by the national governments. Administration of the telegraph service in most countries of the Middle East falls within the jurisdiction of the Ministry of Post and Telegraph.

Electric power output in the Middle East is among the lowest in the world, despite a sharp increase in the region's power production during the decade 1955–65. In 1963, the electric power output per capita in the Middle East was 157 KWH, compared with 5320 KWH for the U.S.A. In the same year, the per capita electric power output was 67 KWH in Iran, 155 KWH in Iraq, and 63 KWH in Jordan (see Table 1.9).

Table 1.9.   Road and Electric Output in the Middle East

	Roads—miles per 1000 sq mi, 1964	Electric output per capita 1963		Roads—miles per 1000 sq mi, 1964	Electric output per capita 1963
U.S.A.	890	5,320	Lebanon ...1,006		255
Middle East .	50	157	Saudi Arabia	6	n.a.
Iran	19	67	Turkey	107	132
Iraq	40	155	U.A.R.	36	152
Jordan	52	63	Kuwait	530	1,320
Israel	530	1,320	Syria	60	98

Source: Same as Table 1.6.

PUBLIC FINANCE AND FOREIGN TRADE

Except for the oil-producing countries, the financial position of most Middle Eastern countries is weak, and government budgets are characterized by continuous deficit. Public revenue in these countries is limited not only by the low level of the national income but also by poorly adapted and administered taxes and other sources of revenue.

In Iran, Iraq, and a few other oil-producing countries, the large oil revenue contributes toward financing of budget deficit. Jordan, lacking this source of revenue, has had to depend largely on foreign aid and subsidies to cover part of its deficits. For instance, it is the primary goal of Jordan's most recent Seven-Year Development Plan (1964–1970) to reduce Jordan's dependence on foreign subsidy from 14 million J.D. in 1963 to 6 million J.D. in 1970.[13]

The greater portion of the public revenue in the Middle Eastern countries is generally devoted to the most essential functions of government, leaving only a small share to be spent for such social services as health and education. In Iran, for instance, about 66.2 per cent of the 1965 budget was allocated for national defense and current government expenditures.[14]

Except for the four major oil-producing countries—Iran, Iraq, Kuwait, and Saudi Arabia—all other countries of the Middle East suffer from chronic balance-of-trade deficits (see Table 1.10). This is because, except for oil, the supply of surplus goods for export is limited and the demand for imports of both capital and consumer goods is high. This tendency to underexport and overimport has been especially aggravated by the recent increases in the demand for capital equipments for development purposes.

---

[13] *Seven-Year Development Programs,* 1964–1970. Presented to Jordan's Development Committee, (Amman, October 1965).

[14] Department of State, *Economic Background Highlights, Iran,* Revision No. 195 (Washington, D.C., Nov. 1964), p. 9.

Table 1.10. Balance of Foreign Trade in the Middle East
(in million U.S. dollars)

	1953	1958	1960	1961	1962	1963	1964	Major Export—% of 1961–63 exports
Middle East ..	+ 81	+420	+389	+104	+318	+268	+658	
Oil-Producing Countries								
Iran	− 79	+169	+220	+163	+451	+410	+581	Oil 85%
Iraq	+200	+260	+263	+254	+329	+462	+421	Oil 93%
Kuwait	+422	+720	+718	+691	+765	+786	+896	Oil 98%
Saudi Arabia ..	+350	+510	+585	+619	+632	+732	+855	Oil 96%
Non-Oil-Prod. Countries								
Jordan	− 46	− 85	−109	−102	−111	−134	−114	Phosphates 26%
Lebanon	−119	−181	−262	−291	−299	−282	−341	Fruit 23%
Syria	− 15	− 77	−119	− 89	− 67	− 46	− 59	Cotton 47%
Turkey	−136	− 68	−147	−162	−241	−322	−131	Tobacco 23%
U.A.R.	−106	−190	−100	−215	−340	−394	−394	Cotton 56%
Afghanistan ..	n.a.	− 27	− 37	− 46	− 57	− 56	− 52	Skins 24%/Fruits 23%
Israel	−221	−282	−286	−347	−356	−322	−456	Polished Diamonds 32% / Citrus Fruits 19%

Source: Statistics and Reports Division, Agency for International Development, *Near East and South Asia, Economic Growth Trends* (Washington, D.C., Sept. 1965), pp. 32–33.

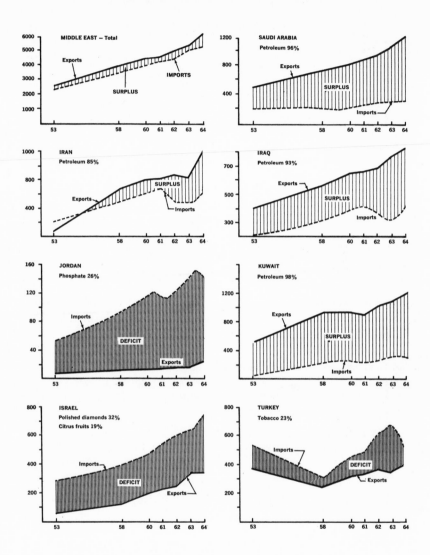

Figures from Statistics and Report Division, Agency for International Development, *Near East and South Asia Economic Growth Trend* (1965), pp. 32–33.

FIGURE 1.2. Balance of Foreign Trade for Selected Middle Eastern Countries

Chapter 2

SOME THEORIES OF ECONOMIC
DEVELOPMENT AND THEIR APPLICATION
IN THE MIDDLE EAST

Discussions and theories of growth are not new. Many economists and writers, even before the classical economists, dealt with economic growth in one way or another because economic growth was associated with human welfare and was thus treated as an individual or social goal. But the theories of economic growth, especially those related to the economic development in underdeveloped countries, are rather new and have mushroomed during the post-World War II period. This has been true for two reasons: (1) the social awakening in underdeveloped countries and their striving toward an economic development comparable to that in Western developed areas and (2) the new strategic position that the present underdeveloped countries hold in shaping the world's balance of power.

Some of the major theories of economic growth and their application in the Middle East will be treated in this chapter. This will be done in four sections: the meaning of economic growth, some selective theories of economic growth, application of some growth theories in the Middle East, and the role of rich nations in bringing economic growth to underdeveloped areas.

THE MEANINGS OF ECONOMIC DEVELOPMENT

The word *underdeveloped*, a product of the United Nations, has been widely used in recent years to define economic conditions in certain areas of the world relative to other parts which are considered developed or advanced. No exact criteria for economic backwardness exist and no universal factor has yet been designated the principal cause for underdevelopment. Economic backwardness in an area has been attributed to one or more economic and/or social elements—among them low per capita income, low productivity per worker, inadequate industrialization, unbalanced socioeconomic structure, even the difference in the nation's propensities.[1] However, the closest definition of economic underdevelopment, for the purposes of this book, is that in UNESCO's *International Social Science Bulletin*: ". . . the difference in the economy as it now exists and as it might be with the full application in both agriculture and industry of scientific knowledge, skills and techniques already in use in advanced countries."

The United States, Canada, the countries of Western Europe, and Australia are usually used to illustrate a standard for development. But it must be remembered that such a selection can represent only a relative state of economic development, not an absolute one. In other words, these countries are considered advanced not because they are assumed to have utilized all their potentialities for development, but because they have made greater progress than certain others. Thus the term *underdevelopment*, or similar ones such as *economic backwardness, less advanced,* and *less developed,* are merely expressions of a relative economic condition between two or more countries. The degree of underdevelopment in a country may therefore vary according to the standard with which the country is being compared. The Middle East, for instance, may be considered less backward compared with Australia than when compared with the United States—and may even be considered advanced when compared with certain parts of Africa.

Descriptions of the process of economic development also vary, depending on the factors held to be responsible for economic backwardness. In most of the United Nations' literature, *development* is defined as "the process of increasing real capital and improving techniques of production."[2] E. P. Reuben requires "increase in national product per capita"[3] and eventually a better utilization

---

[1] See W. W. Rostow, *The Process of Economic Growth* (New York: W. W. Norton Co., Inc., 1962), p. 70.

[2] Gunnar Myrdal, *An International Economy, Problems and Prospects* (New York: Harper & Row, Publishers, Inc., 1956), p. 15.

[3] United Nations, *Methods of Financing Economic Development in Underdeveloped Countries* (Lake Success, N. Y., 1949), p. 90.

of resources. According to R. G. Hawtry, economic development is achieved through a widening and deepening of capital. Finally, W. W. Rostow defines the process of *take off* as "an increase in the volume and productivity of investment in a society, such that a sustained increase in per capita real income results."[4]

Despite the large number of definitions presented for economic backwardness, they all in one way or another deal with one common condition: social discomfort. Accordingly, a country may be considered underdeveloped if it shows a considerably lower standard of living and a lower degree of social comfort than other countries of the world. The process of economic development, on the other hand, may be explained as the process of promoting higher standards of living through more efficient and fuller utilization of manpower, natural resources, and capital. It is necessary to keep in mind, however, that mere change or growth in an economy caused by changes in population, utilization of extracting industries, or the inflow of capital is only a change in data, not economic progress. To be progressive, an economy must create within itself a self-generating, self-sustaining, cumulative force leading the economy toward betterment.

BRIEF REFERENCES TO SELECTED THEORIES OF ECONOMIC GROWTH

Generally speaking, the theories of economic growth fall into two major groups. In the first are those that deal with growth as the function of one or more variable factors. These theories generally seek to find some interacting relationship between factors and economic activities that may be responsible for inducing economic growth. They claim that economic growth can be achieved through stimulation of predetermined economic, social, and political activities.

In the second group are those theories that deal with economic growth as a going process. These theories suggest that a growing economy will most likely follow certain stages that can be easily distinguished and—if necessary—induced. Therefore, by inducing

---

[4] Rostow, *op. cit.*, pp. 103–4.

consecutively these stages of growth, an underdeveloped country can achieve the desired economic goal.

GROWTH THEORIES: MODEL APPROACH

Growth model theories generally select one or several factors responsible for economic backwardness or for a growth process. The major factors with the oldest tradition of recognition are land, labor, and capital. Other factors such as technology and propensity are later additions.

Theories built around labor consider population and labor the most significant causes for economic growth or backwardness. Two well-known names in this field are Ragnar Nurkse and W. Arthur Lewis. To them economic growth stems in one way or another from releasing unproductive workers from land and equipping them for industrial production.

Theories built around capital, on the other hand, consider capital formation the major cause of economic development. Only through capital is extensive and intensive use of workers possible. Capital can help increase the workers' productivity, thus bringing a higher standard of living and economic growth.

Mercantilism. Perhaps the first well established and well publicized ideas of growth belong to the mercantilist economists. To them, a nation's growth came through the accumulation of specie and a building up of the national treasury. Only through such an accumulation of wealth could a nation have grown politically and economically.

This belief led most mercantilist economists to advocate certain nationalistic policies—all designed to increase the nation's holdings of precious-metal stocks. These policies included stimulating exports to exceed imports, building up the merchant marine, and acquiring colonies. Many nations following these policies did indeed receive world-wide power and recognition—chief among them Spain, Portugal, and England. It is doubtful, however, that such mercantilistic policies were helpful in bringing better living conditions to the majority of the people who lived in those countries.

Classical Economists. The classical theory of economic growth was actually a reaction to that of the mercantilists. To the classical economists, the ultimate goal became the individual rather than the state. The classical theory of growth, in general, is an accumulation of many ideas which began with Adam Smith and was gradually developed and completed by his followers.

To Smith in particular, economic growth was the function of capital accumulation and the division of labor. Division of labor, when supplemented by capital, will induce higher productivity. According to this reasoning, the division of labor in turn will also become the function of capital formation. Capital formation, on the other hand, is the function of thrift and profits. Thrift depends on the rate of interest and profit on wages. Both wages and interest rates are flexible, to allow smooth operation of economic adjustments necessary to maintain full employment. Finally, all these are accomplished in an environment of *laissez faire* and free foreign trade.

Smith and other classical economists generally discounted the role of demand. This was mainly the result of their assumption, developed by J. B. Say, that supply creates its own demand; capital and division of labor thus remained the only two major factors in growth.

Thomas R. Malthus, however, introduced the first major limitation in the classical growth model. He reasoned that although a population increase may mean more productive workers, it also means more mouths to feed. Population tends to grow faster than the supply of food materials, and this will hinder economic growth. Malthus concluded that the population growth must—somehow —be halted if we are to achieve a continuous rate of economic growth.

David Ricardo introduced the second limiting factor. He believed that the supply of tillable land is limited. An increase in population will bring into production the marginal lands—requiring more capital and workers but yielding less. This will cause an increase in rent, which in turn will reduce profits and thus incentives. Ricardo did admit that an increase in the use of capital and more division of labor might offset the land's rate of diminishing return. He also advocated international specialization based on comparative advantage. This, he believed, would help all nations concerned to prosper more.

The classical growth model in general may be outlined in the following manner:

1. Economic growth is the function of capital accumulation and the division of labor. Through the application of more capital and further specialization of labor, the nation's level of production will increase, resulting in better living conditions for its citizens.

2. Division of labor is made possible by more and better application of machinery. This in turn depends on capital.

3. Capital comes from the nation's accumulated savings, the function of thrift and the rate of interest.

4. The process of capital formation is the function of profits. Profit, on the other hand, is the function of wage level, rent, and interest rate.

5. The level of wages is based on subsistence level, which in turn depends on the supply and price of food materials. Free foreign trade and import of foods can help reduce the wage level by increasing the real income.

6. The fluctuations in the rate of interest and flexibility of wages contribute to a smooth operation of the process of savings accumulation, its flow into capital, and adjustment in output–consumption ratio.

7. Increase in the level of production, caused by more use of capital and division of labor, will in itself create its own market, thus stimulating economic expansion. As economy grows, the higher standard of living will induce population growth, which will provide more members of the labor force, who will receive more wages and thus have more ability to consume.

8. In the classical growth model, all these things happen not through government intervention but with the help of the invisible hand in a free society. The entire process is furthermore helped by the development of money and credit.

There are, however, two major limiting factors in the classical growth model:

1. As population grows, there will be more mouths to feed. This, together with the fact that population tends to grow faster than the production of food, will put a limit to economic growth. Famines,

droughts, disease, wars, and intentional control may be an answer to this problem.

2. As population grows and the need for farm production increases, the supply of good and productive lands will be exhausted and a diminishing rate of return will come into play—it will cost more to produce the same amount of goods from inferior lands. This will increase rent, which reduces profits and discourages investment.

The classical model of growth can also be presented in a more dynamic manner, as in Figure 2.1. In this diagram the vertical axis

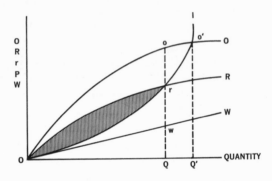

FIGURE 2.1. Static Classical Growth Model with Limiting Factors

represents monetary measures (rents, interests, profits, wages); the horizontal axis represents the output and income. The meanings of other letters used are:

W   total wages paid out to workers, which is the total labor multiplied by their real wages.

O   total output, which rises fast in the beginning; then the rate of growth slows down and eventually begins to decline due to the two limiting factors—population pressure and scarcity of good lands. The area between O and W represents the unpaid portion of laborers' production, that is, the surplus value.

R   The area between R (rent) and O indicates the total rent paid out in the society, which tends to rise with production as the rate of diminishing return sets in.

I The area between *I* (interest) and *W* represents the total interest paid out in the society, which also tends to rise as the society begins to use more capital.

The area between *W* and *O*, the surplus value, is shared among three factors—profit, interest, and rent.

The area between *o* and *r* enclosed between *I* and *R* illustrates profit—the major factor in economic growth. As production increases from *o* to the right, profit begins to expand at first, then both rent and interest begin to grow at the expense of profit. At production level *oQ*, the entire surplus value is absorbed by rent and interest, the minimum cost of capital. Capital growth at this point loses its most important stimulant—profit.

Several alternatives can be suggested to relieve this stagnation tendency, and their application is presented in Figure 2.2. Growth, being the function of profits, can be stimulated in any manner that can help increase the share of profits in the society. The share of profits in a society can be increased through either (1) lower wages, (2) lower interests, (3) lower rent, or (4) application of more machines and capital.

Lowering total wages paid out by increasing the area of surplus value (the area between *W* and *O*) will increase the surplus value area that profits must share with rents and interests. This can be

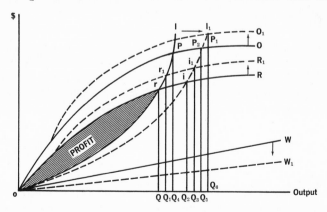

FIGURE 2.2. Classical Dynamic Growth Model

achieved by lower prices of food, the basis for the subsistance level upon which the real wage rests. An increase in the surplus value will increase profits, should rents and interests remain unchanged.

A reduction in total rents from R to R_1 will increase the share of profits from the surplus value. If rent is reduced from R to R_1 while interest payments (I) remain as they were, the total profit area will expand to cover the area or_1, (the area between the R_1 and I curves), and the output will rise from oQ (representing the previous profit level of or) to oQ_1. A reduction in the total interest payments from I to I_1 will also increase the total profits.

With such a reduction in interests, the total rent payments remaining unchanged, the total profit area will move from or (area between I and R) to oi, the area between I_1 and R. At this profit level the total output will stand at oQ_2.

However, should both rent and interest payments be reduced to R_1 and I_1 profits will expand to cover oi_1, the area between I_1 and R_1. At this profit level the total output will stand at oQ_3.

Expansion in profits is also possible if all lands are socialized and rents eliminated. In such a case the profit will cover oP, the area between I and O, with an output level of oQ_4. Should in this case the interest payments also drop to I_1, the profit will cover oP_2, the area between O and I_1.

The final alternative is growth through the use of machines and capital. In this case, output line O moves to O_1, increasing the surplus value area and naturally profits.

Post-Classics. During the period that followed Smith and Ricardo, most economic writers appeared less concerned with growth problems. They began emphasizing such questions as value and distribution. This, however, was probably a result of the fact that during this era growth had become a way of life—it was neither neglected nor forgotten; it was simply taken for granted.

However, as capitalism grew and with it the level of production, the market became scarce. The demand factor, conveniently brushed away by the classical economists, grew to become a vital factor. Many economists began to write on the possibility of economic stagnation and pointed out that investment could not grow indefinitely—it required some stimulant.

J. A. Schumpeter was probably the first economist to become concerned with economic growth since the early classical economists. To him innovation was a major stimulant for economic growth. Innovation, when successfully applied, leads to an increase in the entrepreneur's profits, which will in turn encourage investment and bring about economic growth.

Keynesian Model. The writings of John Maynard Keynes have undoubtedly become a source of inspiration to many economists concerned with economic growth. According to Keynes, economic equilibrium is achieved at a level at which aggregate demand $(C + I + G)$ equals aggregate supply (a production level that can be sold). Should the aggregate demand exceed the existing level of production, it will stimulate further investment through higher profit expectation. Any increase in investment or government spending will induce further income growth by the net increase in government spending time multiplier. The Keynesian model, however, operates only in the short run. Additional variables are necessary if it is to be employed in long-run development planning.

The Keynesian growth model can also be illustrated as in Figure 2.3.

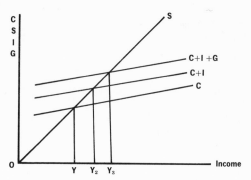

FIGURE 2.3. Keynesian Model

S   Aggregate supply
    C   Consumption function in respect to income increase
$C + I$ Aggregate demand (excluding government sector)
When $(C + I)$ equals aggregate supply, income will be OY_2.

Any increase in aggregate demand $(C + I)$, caused either by increase in investment or by government spending, will increase the national income (to Y_3) by the amount of increase in aggregate demand $(C + I)$ time multiplier. The reverse is also true.

The growth in the Keynesian model is, however, limited by the level of employment. An equilibrium level above full employment may induce inflationary pressure.

The Keynesian influence appears in several recent theories of economic development; examples can be noticed in the works of Nicholas Kaldor, Evsey Domar, and Roy F. Harrod.

According to Kaldor, for instance, growth comes when the rate of technological advance precedes and exceeds the capital investment. Such an increase in technological advance will help induce more capital investment by increasing the marginal productivity of capital.

Domar Model. Domar was primarily concerned with the rate of investment increase—the rate of increase in investment that can constantly keep the aggregate demand high enough to utilize the new capacities created, without creating inflation or deflation. If we assume total investment to exclude net investment, the economy will probably remain in stationary equilibrium; only net investment can bring economic growth. However, at one time or another net investment will occur and thus total investment will include a new portion—net investment. This increase in investment will naturally help increase the aggregate demand (see Figure 2.3). But, as the need for net investment is satisfied, the total investment, not including net investment, will drop once more. This drop in total investment will adversely affect aggregate demand and investment itself. Thus, to avoid economic contraction, investment must grow constantly.

Domar's mathematical model can be briefly illustrated in the following simplified manner.

Assuming a fixed level of output, this output will remain stationary as long as no additional net investment expenditure is added. An increase in the net investment expenditure does occur, especially when an increase in the total output is desired or anticipated. This, however, requires an additional increase in the next period's aggregate demand to justify the increase in net investment. So the main question is: How much annual increase in I is necessary to justify the net investment increase in the previous period? The equation begins with the change in output (Y) necessary to make use of net investment (I), that is:

$$\Delta Y = \alpha I$$

Here, α represents the marginal capital output ratio necessary to bring the change in output. In other words, it is monetary increase in output which is necessary to justify net I. On the other hand, the change in income is the function of change in investment multiplied by multiplier (m).

$$\Delta Y = \Delta I \times m$$

Now, by substituting the two sides of the equation to ΔY we will have

$$\Delta IM = \alpha I \quad \text{or} \quad \frac{\Delta I}{I} = \frac{\alpha}{m}$$

Accordingly, the required rate of growth in investment is directly proportional to α and inversely proportional to m.[5]

Harrod Model. Harrod's model is similar to that of Domar. In his theory, Harrod's major concern is to find a growth rate for output that is necessary to bring an induced investment (through accelerator) adequate to absorb that output. Total savings (S) at each period equal income (Y) times *APS* (α), or

$$S = Y \times \alpha$$

Using the accelerator (ϕ), on the other hand, induced investment (I_n) will be the function of the change in income time accelerator.

$$I_n = \Delta Y \times \phi$$

Now assuming an equilibrium where savings equal investment, we will have

$$S = I_n$$

or
$$\alpha \times Y = \Delta Y \times \phi$$
or
$$\alpha = \Delta Y / Y \times \phi$$

According to Harrod's theory, therefore, a natural rate of growth is achieved when the output can grow at a rate that can generate

---

[5] For a brilliant brief of Domar's Model Theory, see Franklin V. Walker, *Growth, Employment and the Price Level* (Englewood Cliffs, N. J., Prentice-Hall, Inc., 1963), pp. 293–94.

Table 2.1. Trial-and-Error Chart on Harrod's Model

Period	(Y) Output	$(\Delta Y \times 3)$ Induced I.	$(Y \times \frac{1}{4})$ Savings	$(Y - S = C)$ Consumption	$(C + I)$ Ag. demand	Ratio Ag.S.:Ag.D.		Result
t_0	440	0	110	330	330	440	330	Disequilibrium
t_1	460	60	115	345	405	460	405	Disequilibrium
t_2	480	120	120	360	480	480	480	Equilibrium
t_3	500	180	125	375	555	500	555	Disequilibrium

the necessary demand and maintain full employment. Finally, his tenet is that the process of capital formation is both "interacting and cumulative."[6] In other words, capital formation will bring an increase in income that will help increase capital formation.

Harrod's model can also be explained through trial-and-error analysis—as in Table 2.1. Let us assume accelerator (ϕ) to be 3 and the APS (α) to be equal to ¼. It is the purpose of the chart to show in which period the economy can generate enough demand capable of absorbing the entire output. At period t_0 the output is 440, and there is no induced investment. This output also provides income for the household, which is either saved or consumed. From this total income (or output) ¼ $\times$ 440 or 110, will be saved, and 330 will be allocated for consumption. At this period, therefore, the total demand generated $(C + I)$ amounts to 330, far less than is needed to absorb the entire output of 440. This points to disequilibrium and room for growth. Let us now move to period t_1, where the total output stands at 460. This level of output is capable of generating $\Delta Y \times 3$, or 60, induced investment and 460 $\times$ ¼, or 115, savings, leaving 345 for consumption. The aggregate demand $(C + I)$ of 405 in this period is still below the total output of 460, which again points to disequilibrium and future room for growth. At period t_2, however, the total output stands at 480, resulting in 120 induced investment, 120 savings, and leaving 360 for consumption. At this period, the level of output has finally generated enough demand $(C + I)$ to absorb the entire output. Equilibrium has now been reached. But let us assume that the total output (as in period t_3) stands at 500, resulting in 180 induced investment, 125 savings, and 375 consumption. At this level of output the aggregate demand becomes larger than the total output. We are again at a disequilibrium, though this time one of a different kind. Should we substitute the formula $(\Delta Y/Y)\phi = \alpha$ for the t_2 period, we will have

$$\frac{480 - 440}{480} \times 3 = \frac{1}{4} = \alpha$$

---

[6] C. P. Kindelberger, *Economic Development* (New York: McGraw-Hill Book Co., 1965), p. 83.

According to this illustration, the warranted rate of growth in output is $\frac{40}{480}$ or 8.3 per cent.

Other Theories. According to Albert Hirschman's theory, certain disturbances are necessary to start economic growth. The most typical of these disturbances are "inflation and balance of payment difficulties, on the one hand, and population pressure, on the other."[7]

Finally, some theories of economic development have concentrated mainly on finding and pointing out the existing problems in underdeveloped countries, in order to find ways to cope with such problems. Among these is the theory developed by Professor R. Nurkse.

According to Nurkse, most underdeveloped countries suffer from several basic problems:

1. Disguised unemployment or underemployment of a vast majority of the population—especially those on farm lands

2. The limited size of the market, caused by low income, low level of production, and poor transportation

3. Low inducement to invest due to limited market, low productivity, and problems of capital formation.

All these obstacles, by interacting on one another, create a situation known as the "vicious circle" of poverty. This in turn creates a chain reaction, which makes futile the efforts by most underdeveloped countries for progress. In Nurkse's words, "a country is poor because it is poor."[8] To start the process of economic development, the "vicious circle of poverty" must be broken.

MAJOR HISTORICAL STAGE THEORIES

These theories are generally descriptions of historical stages of what has happened in now-advanced countries on their path of development. The theories are often based on records showing what happened, but with no assurance that it would happen again —at least not in exactly the same manner and sequence. A general

---

[7] Albert O. Hirschman, *Strategy of Economic Development* (New Haven: Yale University Press, 1963), p. 156.

[8] R. Nurkse, "The Size of the Market and the Inducement to Invest." *Development and Society*, ed. D. E. Novak and R. Lekachman (New York: St. Martin's Press, 1964), p. 91.

study of these theories can nevertheless provide us invaluable ground for understanding and thus reasoning the growth process.

Most writers of the historical school have sought in some way to identify the periods of transition from one stage into another. Fredrick List was no exception. To List, economic growth in a society must, to an extent, be preceded by individual and political freedom. He divided a growing nation into the following consecutive stages:

1. The stage of savagery
2. The pastoral stage—mostly nomadic
3. The agricultural stage—advance nomads and farm settlements
4. Agricultural and manufacturing stage, where people begin to produce other needs of life
5. Agricultural, manufacturing, and commercial stage.

To List, stage 5 is the final stage. However, it has been proven that economic growth even varies considerably among nations that have advanced to List's final stage of growth.

Marx. Marx's theory on growth can be a controversial one. First, his is not a direct theory of growth, though its principal ideas can be read between the lines. Second, Marx can be classified either among those with model theories or those with stage theories.

To begin with, Marx strongly opposed the classical idea that supply creates its own demand. To him, the amount of surplus value taken from the worker creates a gap between people's ability to consume and the total level of production.

One might say that Marx treated growth both in the short-run and in the long-run time period. His short-run theory of growth can be explained in this way: At any time the value of products is determined on the basis of the social necessary labor required to produce it. But now and then a new firm may come up with some improvement in technology (somewhat similar to Schumpeter's theory of innovation). This firm will, of course, profit from this improvement in production—but not for long. Because of the intense competition in capitalism, other firms will follow suit. As a result, what was once an improved method now becomes an accepted method and a part of the average technology in calculating the social necessary labor.

In the long run, growth comes as a result of a major change—the change in the "mode of production." At any period of existence many necessary relations are created among the members of a society and all factors of production; all these relationships create the "mode of production." But the society always moves forward, while the "mode of production," protected by laws, customs, and traditions, tends to remain rigid and inflexible. There will come a time when the present "mode of production" can no longer satisfy the society's need. A mode which was a blessing once now becomes a burden. Marx's conclusion is simple: At this time the society has no alternative but to break this mode of production—in an evolutionary way if possible, through revolution if necessary. At this time a new "mode of production," more suitable to the developing society's need, will come into existence.

Discussion of the changes in the "mode of production" also brings up Marx's stage theory. As the result of changes in the "mode of production," our society has gone and will go through definite stages, leading to Marx's ultimate utopia. These are (1) the pre-capitalist stage, (2) the stage of capitalism and exploitation of labor, (3) the stage of imperialism, (4) the social revolution by the proletariat and socialism, and finally (5) full communism.

Balance of Payment Theory. Some economists have sought to explain a country's stages of economic growth in terms of changes in that country's net balance of payment. Much historical data points to the accuracy of this approach. According to Paul A. Samuelson,[9] a growing country in its process of economic development goes through the following stages, each with a different effect on its balance of payment: (1) young debtor, (2) matured debtor, (3) young creditor, and (4) matured creditor.

A young debtor is a country that has just begun its development efforts. This country tends to consume more than it can produce. It must therefore undertake borrowing to finance its ever-increasing consumption and to maintain its investment level.

A matured debtor is a country that has achieved a production level beyond its consumption. This country no longer needs to

[9] Paul A. Samuelson, *Economics, An Introductionary Analysis* (New York: McGraw-Hill Book Co., 1958), pp. 638, 639.

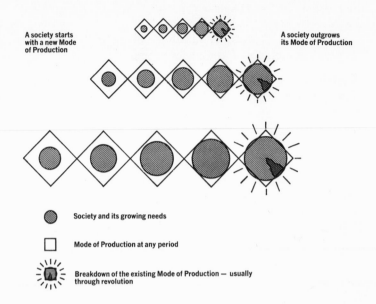

A society starts with a new Mode of Production

A society outgrows its Mode of Production

Society and its growing needs

Mode of Production at any period

Breakdown of the existing Mode of Production — usually through revolution

FIGURE 2.4. Long Run: Illustrative Description of Marx's Theory of Growth in a Society

borrow—and, in fact, by virtue of its export surplus will begin repayment of past debts.

A young creditor is a country that has paid off its debts but that, due to the existing export surplus, now begins exporting capital.

A matured creditor is a country whose ability to produce has fallen below its customary consumption level. In an attempt to maintain its traditional level of consumption, it begins liquidating past credits and investments abroad. This country once more will experience an increase in imports over exports.

Kindleberger[10] adds two more stages to the four listed on p. 40. First is the adult debtor, which falls between the young debtor and the matured debtor. This nation neither requires further borrowing nor has it started repayment. For a short time this nation

[10] Charles P. Kindleberger, *The Dollar Shortage* (London: Chapman and Hall Ltd., 1950), p. 75.

may experience a balanced payment. Second is the adult creditor, which falls between the young creditor and the matured creditor. This nation is identical to an adult debtor in balance of payment position, though for a completely opposite reason.

Rostow's Stage Theory.[11] One of the most celebrated stage theories of growth is that of W. W. Rostow. According to Rostow, a growing nation goes through six separate and distinct stages:

1. *The Traditional Society.* In a traditional society, food production absorbs about 75 per cent of the working force. The government is controlled by landlords or military personnel. The population in general seems to be ignorant of its own predicament—with little or no concept of social equality. All these factors put a ceiling beyond which these people cannot reach.

2. *Precondition for Take-off.* This stage usually starts with "gradual evolution of modern science and scientific attitude" and the widening of the market. Social overhead investment surges, agriculture experiences technological revolution, and import tends to increase. All these are met with increase in export of some natural resources and further efficient production and marketing methods. During this stage there are slow changes in tradition, people's attitudes, and organization.

3. *The Take-off.* At this stage the society witnesses a sustained "annual rate of growth of, at least, ten percent" through application of modern technology and "definite social, political and cultural victory"—victory by those seeking modernization over those who either cling to the traditional ways or look for other goals. Take-off does not necessarily start in all sectors of the economy. It may actually start in one or a few sectors better equipped for the leap forward.

4. *The Drive to Maturity.* At this time the society has successfully applied modern technology to "the bulk of its resources." Now the leading sectors have gathered momentum to displace the previous stage's leading industries. The society begins to show definite changes in the labor-force structure, in the ratio of farm and urban population, in the ratio of white- and blue-collar jobs and semi-skilled workers. The industries have grown in size and have become self-sufficient.

---

[11] For references to quotations, see Rostow, *op. cit.*, pp. 311–328.

5. *The Age of High Consumption.* During this age the economy becomes affluent. Economic development leads to an increase in security, welfare, and leisure.

6. *Beyond Consumption.* At this period, the society has become accustomed to leisure. There is a high rate of births and often increase in the marginal utility of new luxury goods at the expense of old goods.

APPLICATION OF GROWTH THEORIES IN THE MIDDLE EAST

Economic development cannot be taught or applied on a universal basis. No one theory can apply to all underdeveloped countries, nor is there a single procedure to start and achieve economic growth.

Most existing theories lack contact with the exact reality that exists in underdeveloped countries. They are too general and broad. They are generally based either on the past histories of developing nations or seek to analyze growth in now-advanced countries. The present underdeveloped countries in general, and the Middle East in particular, differ in background, location, attitude, social structure, and propensities from those countries upon which these theories are based; these theories usually deal with growth as a natural evolution of a society. For the Middle East as well as other latecomers, we must look for theories that seek to implement a systematic programming of economic growth.

Opinions have varied on whether being a latecomer in the field of economic development is to the advantage or disadvantage of present underdeveloped countries. Opinions advocating that being a latecomer is an advantage base their arguments on the following grounds:

1. A latecoming country can learn from the mistakes of others and can avoid repeating the same mistakes.

2. Achieving their present advanced technology has been very costly to the advanced nations, both socially and economically. The underdeveloped countries can easily copy most of their technological ideas.

3. Present underdeveloped countries also benefit from a much advanced economic science. They can improve their skill and know-how with less effort than was possible years ago.

4. Present underdeveloped countries can tap the capital resources of advanced nations. The international flow of grants and credits provides an invaluable source of capital for these countries.

5. Finally, the economic development in underdeveloped countries has been especially facilitated by improvements in transportation and communication. This has made economic and social integration more possible.

Some opinions, however, hold that the present underdeveloped countries actually have a more difficult time than the now-advanced countries in achieving their economic development. These opinions are usually based on the following arguments:

1. Because of the existence of advanced countries, economic development has become a political issue. This has created social and political unrest and instability that actually hinders progress.

2. Today, the developing countries are apt to find much stronger competition in their efforts to develop their manufacturing industries than was faced by Great Britain and the United States, a competition that comes from better and cheaper products manufactured in advanced countries.

3. There is always a danger that an underdeveloped country may try blindly to follow the footsteps of advanced countries with geographic, economic, and cultural differences. This can lead to misuse of resources, waste of effort, or even disaster and it can be exaggerated by the eagerness of the underdeveloped country to achieve speedy progress.

4. Finally, it can be argued that the present world situation has made economic development more challenging in many ways. Today, no frontier has remained undiscovered for colonization and use as a source of wealth for a growing country. Population pressure and political and ideological conflicts are other sources of limitation to the underdeveloped country's efforts for growth.

Not only do the general theories of growth often lack contact in the Middle East, but some of the recent theories designed especially for underdeveloped countries are also inapplicable. The Middle East's economic and social characteristics differ from those of other underdeveloped areas in the world. Application of any old or new theories in the Middle East would require so many alterations and rearrangements that often the content of the theory itself would be changed.

Growth theory for the Middle East must therefore be tailor-made. At least at this time, this is an almost impossible task, for the following reasons:

1. The area generally lacks adequate and dependable data upon which one might base a sound growth theory.

2. There is little or no knowledge about economic and social propensities in the area.

3. Economic development in the region is something new. There is no information on its process, nor is there a precedent for its application that can be used as a basis for a development theory.

4. The area in general, and each of the Middle Eastern countries in particular, have their own geographic, social, and economic settings and problems. This makes the application of a single theory very impractical.

Among most historical theories of growth, Rostow's stage theory is probably the most likely to apply in the Middle East. Of course, a certain degree of modification may be necessary. But, in applying this theory, we must keep in mind that the Middle East has gone no further than Rostow's second stage, the "Precondition for Take-off." There is no assurance that the trend will follow.

Generally speaking, since the late nineteenth century the Middle East has undergone four distinct historical stages (not, however, a completed set, and there will be other stages to follow).

1. *The Period of Submission.* This period was characterized by the existence of dominant colonial interests in the area. The governments were usually puppets of colonial nations and ruled with power and tyranny. The ruling class of landlords, sheiks, or army personnel were few and often corrupt.

The economy was primitive agrarian, and the few small or medium-size manufacturing industries were owned and operated by either the government or the ruling class. The development of major and basic manufacturing was often hindered by direct or indirect colonial intervention. The major basis for colonial interest in the area was, of course, extracting industries.

2. *The Period of Independence and Vacuum.* This period usually

began with discontinuation of direct or indirect colonial control in the area. In Iran, for instance, this period began with the rise of Riza Shah in 1925, who ended the Anglo-Russian Agreement of 1907 that had divided Iran's territory into two spheres of influence. In Iraq this period began in 1932, when the British Mandate was ended. This period started in 1922 for Egypt (with some reservations), in 1941 for Syria, in 1946 for Jordan, and in 1961 for Kuwait.

During this period, except for gaining political independence the governments changed little. The ruling class (except in Iran) remained unchanged, and usually sought to continue the traditional path. This period held a few blessings, however. Among these were the achievement of national unity and the gradual awakening of the society. Many students left for Western countries to receive higher education. Most of these students began the foundations of some improvements upon their return.

3. *The Social Revolution.* This period has been especially characterized by social unrest and discontent. Society has openly demanded political, social, and economic improvements. Now the question of economic development has become a political issue. Several Middle-Eastern governments have been overthrown through *coup d'etat* and/or revolution. This period began in 1958 for Iraq, when Kassim's revolutionary force overthrew and assassinated King Faisal II. In Egypt, this period began in 1952, when Nasser overthrew King Farouk.

This period, however, has not started with violence in all Middle Eastern countries. In several countries the existing ruling class has voluntarily launched radical political, social, and economic programs. The "White Revolution" and large-scale land reform by the Iranian monarch Mohammed Riza Shah Pahlavi is a good example. Evolutionary reform, in fact, is more likely to meet success in the Middle East than revolution is. This is because evolution is usually accompanied by some degree of the political and economic stability desperately needed in the area.

4. *The Period of Economic Planning.* It is difficult to separate this period clearly from the previous one. Many of the Middle Eastern countries are still in the third period; many others have begun both third and fourth periods at the same time.

Now economic objectives have become political objectives. No government survives long that has not promised or cannot deliver some degree of economic progress. In almost every Middle Eastern country, development programs are being launched, with or without foreign assistance. Some definite increase in the region's gross national product per capita and standard of living is noticeable. The agricultural sector shows definite improvement and new manufacturing industries are being established. The continuation of this path, however, is at one time or another either interrupted or terminated by political instability and revolutions.

In our treatment of the Middle Eastern economy we will unavoidably face certain questions in regard to the region's economic condition. These include such questions as: Are the Middle Eastern countries following a path toward economic growth, or are the stages mentioned nothing but some by-products of the world's economic and political changes? Can the Middle Eastern countries start a self-generating and self-sustaining growth, or is their present growth trend nothing but a result of foreign assistance and the region's oil production? Finally, can the Middle Eastern people accomplish their goal in a democratic environment or will they find it necessary to drift to socialism or political dictatorship?

These questions, as well as detailed theoretical and practical application of economic development programs in the Middle East, will be treated in the following chapters. The problems of economic development in the Middle East are treated in the following four chapters. Programs for the region's economic development are handled in chapters 7, 8 and 9. The final two chapters deal with the role of the United States in the economic development of the Middle East.

THE PLACE OF FOREIGN ASSISTANCE

The relation between economic theory and policy is one question that has been generally evaded by most economic theories. Economic theories have usually been applied to explain the possible relationship between causes and effects in model economies or to explain situations where statistical methods cannot be used, rather than to formulate a positive economic policy.

Of course, some specific studies concerning the relationship between economic theory and policy have been made in recent decades, and some useful conclusions have been reached.[12] But, despite these studies and the fact that recent developments in various fields of theory have clarified many economic problems, a considerable uncertainty still exists. This uncertainty especially applies to the extent that economic theories can become a practical ground for formulating economic policy. As the result of this uncertainty, the policy-makers have usually treated economic theory only as one of the many factors in guiding a nation's economic policies. The economic policy of a country is based, therefore, not only on theoretical views but on a combination of cultural, political, and economic forces as well.

The policy on foreign assistance, in particular, cannot as a nation's foreign economic policy be based on pure economic theory. Aside from economic factors, giving or receiving international aid often depends on social, political, and geographic considerations which economic theory alone does not touch. However, certain economic aspects of international aid, such as the needs and reasons for the direction of international flow of capital and technology and to some extent the possible economic results of such flows, may be explained through theoretical analysis.

The direction and the purpose of an international flow of capital and technology can probably best be explained by means of the relationship between economic growth and the position of a nation's balance of payments. That is, the net movements of international funds, aside from those caused by cyclical fluctuations, are the function of a nation's movement from one stage of economic growth to another.

The balance of payment growth theory has been already discussed. Accordingly, primitive countries which have not yet begun development efforts, matured debtors, and adult creditors (for a time) show equilibrium in their balance of international payment. The young debtors and matured creditors, though for a completely different reason, show a net deficit in their international balance of payments, while only matured debtors and young creditors may show a net surplus in their international balance of payments.

---

[12] See H. Tyszynski, "Economic Theory as a Guide to Policy, Some Suggestions For Reappraisal," *Economic Journal*, LXV, (June 1955), p. 195.

The process of economic development in the United States presents a good example of the cited historical changes. Not more than a century ago, the resources in this country were underdeveloped. It took a large and continuous inflow of goods and capital from Great Britain and other advanced European countries to develop its resources. Today, the whole picture has changed; the United States has become one of the most advanced countries in the world. As the result of a continuous export surplus, old debts have been paid off, and new credits have been extended.

In Great Britain, on the other hand, the story is different. During and after World War II, because of many factors, production fell below the consumption level. Old credits were liquidated and new borrowing had begun. Finally, many underdeveloped countries, primitive a century ago, have now begun their development efforts. These countries, in financing their economic development programs, have now become young debtors. We can assume, at least in theory, that these now-underdeveloped countries will sooner or later become matured debtors and young creditors, paying their past obligations to the now-advanced countries, who will by then have become matured creditors.

Consequently it can be concluded that underdeveloped countries should continue to borrow or help facilitate the inflow of international capital to maintain their level of investment until their own level of production can satisfy their internal demand. On the other hand, a country holding technological leadership and producing more than its internal demand "must export capital or die."[13] A cumulative rate of foreign lending by a young creditor country is necessary to facilitate its export surplus, and this lending must continue until the people's marginal propensity to consume moves upward to offset the surplus production.

The benefits from the flow of capital (in form of credits or grants) and technology from more developed to less developed countries are multilateral. This will help ease the process of economic transformation in both underdeveloped and advanced countries.

In advanced countries, such an outflow of capital and technology will help finance the export surplus, create outlets for excess savings over investment, and maintain a high level of employment and

---

[13] Kindleberger, *op. cit.*, p. 75.

economic activity. In underdeveloped countries such an inflow of capital and technology will help facilitate the process of economic development in the following ways: It will help provide the underdeveloped countries with the necessary know-how to plan economic programs; it will finance the necessary capital for economic growth without the need to reduce internal consumption; it will supply the underdeveloped countries with an ample supply of foreign exchange; and finally, it can help speed up the process of growth more than is possible through local capital, thus helping reduce political unrest caused by frustration and social unrest.

Chapter 3

PROBLEMS OF ECONOMIC
DEVELOPMENT: HISTORICAL SETTING

The present economic condition in the Middle East is not a short-run phenomenon. It is the result of the region's geographic location and long historical development. History, as explained by Ernest Jackh of Columbia University, "is also geography in motion."[1] The geographic factor in Middle Eastern history is especially significant, because no other region is so strategically located.

Economic progress in a region requires certain factors, such as political stability, peace, and security, that have long been missing in the Middle East. Economically and politically suppressed people who lack future security seldom think in terms of long-run planning. Their immediate concern usually does not go beyond their present-day needs, which are seldom productive or constructive. Such people often hesitate to put forth extra efforts or to invest part of their savings for the improvement of their productivity. This is because they have no assurance that such improvements will yield them benefits. This has been much of the story in the Middle East.

Political and religious wars are nothing new in the long history of the region. The geographic location of the Middle East has, furthermore, placed it in the path of many intercontinental conquests by Persians, Greeks, Romans, Mongolians, and Arabs. The conquest of the region by the nomadic Arabs under the flag of Islam undoubtedly holds a special position in the history of the area. For the Moslem religion, more so than any other major religion, was destined to become a controlling ethnic feature. It was designed to form a community which was to be a state as well as a church.

---

[1] E. Jackh, "Geographic Uniqueness," *Encyclopedia Americana*, (1956), XIX, p. 38e.

This political concept of Islam, leading to unlimited authority of caliphs,[2] and especially the lack of a unanimously accepted caliph, created too much attraction for that office to be left unclaimed. Soon after Mohammed died, a series of religious wars began among various Moslem groups or nations using religion as a scapegoat for achieving power or independence and thus violating the very principle of unity for which Mohammed had stood.

The conquest of Genghis Khan of Mongolia and his followers was also a major setback for the area, destroying most of its human, natural, capital, and cultural resources. Finally, an almost continuous struggle among small kings and large feudal families seeking glory and power effectively retarded the region's economic and social progress.

As the result of these internal and external disturbances, most of the area's wealth has been either destroyed or uneconomically distributed. The old social loyalty and obligations among the region's population have been weakened or destroyed, and instead social mistrust, fear, and irresponsibility have become dominant. The middle class has either disintegrated into the large, poverty-stricken majority of the population or has joined the upper class minority of landlords, merchants, or clergy. The outcome has been a highly discrepant society that is neither constructive nor progressive. The small minority, the ruling class, is too lazy to work and too satisfied to worry. The majority—illiterate, poverty-stricken, and disease-ridden—are in no position to improve their productivity or find incentive to do so.[3]

It is therefore evident that the roots of most present economic and social obstacles in the Middle East reach deep into the past. The sluggish rates of capital formation and technological improvement in the region are, in fact, only superficial problems. They can be easily solved if first a desirable cultural environment is created. "Development," in other words, as reported by the United Nations Conciliation Commission for Palestine, "will not achieve its true

---

[2] The principal head of religion, who at the same time is the head of state.

[3] This subject will be treated further in the following chapters. Also, for detailed discussion on the subject, see B. K. Madan, *Economic Problems of Under-developed Countries in Asia* (New Delhi, 1953), pp. 117–18, and W. O. Thweatt, "Economic Growth and Distribution in the Middle East," *The American Journal*, XVI, (January 1957), p. 122.

aim of eliminating human suffering and raising the living standards of the great mass of poverty-stricken people of the Middle East, if it is not accompanied by widespread social reform."[4] Thus, unless cultural and social ills in the Middle East are cured and a proper environment for progress is obtained, most economic programs designed and operated by the ruling class minority will become just another means for further exploitation and self-satisfaction.

THE INFLUENCE OF RELIGION

It is often true, in both underdeveloped and advanced nations, that religion does not encourage materialistic improvement. On the contrary, it may even stand in the way of materialistic push and intellectual integration. This is especially true in the Middle East, where religion has in many ways hindered economic and social progress. It has weakened the institution of government, limited social and economic progress by implementing certain inflexible rules, blocked the region's economic and social integration with other advanced areas, created regional controversy between Arabs and the Israeli government, and—finally—contributed to the region's social discrepancy.

From the death of Mohammed until a few centuries ago, almost all the Middle East was ruled by a caliph, who represented both state and church. The church, furthermore, directly ruled in Egypt and Turkey as late as the early 1900's, in Yemen till 1964, and still rules in Saudi Arabia. Indirectly, the church shows unsurpassable influence on the entire area's political decisions.

Moslem imams (high priests), claiming jurisdiction over the political decisions of most Middle Eastern countries, have long competed with and thus weakened the power of central governments. Examples are frequent of even powerful kings being forced to withdraw their decrees when opposed by the church. Church power can be demonstrated in the tobacco-concession case in Persia. In the mid-nineteenth century Nasser Eddin Shah (1848–1896), the powerful king of Persia, decreed a tobacco concession to a British subject. Several imams opposing this concession eventually

---

[4] United Nations Conciliation Commission for Palestine, *Final Report of the United Nations Economic Survey Mission for the Middle East,* Part I, The Final Report and Appendices (New York, 1949), p. 65.

condemned smoking. As a result almost the whole nation stopped smoking, including the members of the royal court. The concession had to be canceled.

Even today in most parts of the Middle East, governments fear and respect the influence of the clergy class who can, at any time, provoke the feelings of the majority for or against the central government or any of its members. In Iran, for example, in January 1963 Imam R. Khomaini protested against the Shah's land-reform program, which would undoubtedly hurt the large landowners. This created the worst riots since 1953 in the country, forcing the government to impose martial law and curfew.

Koran (the Mohammedan Scripture) rules are still the dominant civil code in most countries of the Middle East. The constitutions of most Middle Eastern countries require that all laws must conform to Islamic teachings. The Second Amendment to the Iranian Constitution, for instance, requires that at no time can the contents of a law contradict Islam rules. The decision on whether or not such contradiction exists shall rest on a group of at least five imams, who are also members of Congress. They are selected by the Congress from a list of twenty prepared by all church leaders. The decisions of this committee on religious acceptability of laws are final.[5] Hence, while certain Islamic rules in the region, such as prohibition of usury, permission for bigamy, restriction of the female's inheritance to one-half that of the male's, and the validity of the female's witness to one-half of that of males, do not agree with modern economic and social principles, new ideas are often opposed by religious groups.

It was Mohammed's conviction that Islam must stand for complete equality of human rights, regardless of race, color, or wealth. This teaching is repeatedly emphasized in the Koran, which states: "O Mankind! Lo! We have created you male and female, and have made you nations and tribes that ye may know one another. Lo! the noblest of you, in the sight of God is the best in conduct. Lo! God is knower, Aware."[6] The later teachings of religious leaders,

---

[5] *The Constitution and Penal and Military Laws* (Tehran: Taban Publishing), p. 13.

[6] *The Koran*, Sureh "The Private Apartments," Ayeh No. 13.

mixed with political and personal motives, however, became dog-
matic and prejudicial against the non-Mohammedan world. This
isolated the Middle East from economic, social, and cultural integration with Western non-Moslem countries.

Finally, although Islam basically frowns on class differentiation,
Mohammedan Imams have actually aggravated the region's class
differentiation by forming themselves into a strong minority which
stands second to no other group. This group of clergymen enjoys
every privilege of the other upper classes of the population. Some
of these privileges include participation in the country's management, owning large sections of private lands, managing Waqfs,[7]
and becoming engaged in business ventures. In fact, this is the only
class which can afford to be outspoken when even the landlords
cannot. This minority has joined forces with other minorities within
the ruling group. This group has, moreover, helped delay the region's
social and cultural integration by constantly teaching the poverty-
stricken majority of the virtues of patience and surrender.

FOREIGN INTERVENTION

During the past several centuries, while social and economic
progress in the Middle East was hampered by internal conflicts
and cultural deterioration, capitalism was blooming in the West.
At the same time Western colonial interests in the Middle East, as
in other parts of the world, began to develop. At first, the main colonial objective was to secure a source of material imports from the
East. With further industrialization in the West, however, colonial
interests shifted from securing imports to securing markets for
exports and exploiting resources in the colonies.

A student can easily find many documented cases of intervention
by foreign powers in the Middle East. Sir Winston Churchill, in
his celebrated book *The World Crisis*, refers to the Anglo-French
agreement of 1904:

> There were various clauses; but the essence of the compact was
> that the French desisted from opposition to British interests in

---

[7] Properties entrusted, usually to the church or a charity organization, to
be used for a particular charitable purpose.

Egypt, and Britain gave a general support to the French views about Morocco.[8]

Germany, of course, showed some dissatisfaction with this Anglo-French agreement, so some colonial rights were given to Germany in the Congo area. According to Churchill:

> The French government fully realized that the advantages they were gaining in Morocco justified Germany in seeking certain colonial compensations in the Congo area.[9]

Again speaking of the British role, he writes:

> I thought myself that the Germans had a certain grievance about the original Anglo-French agreement. We had received many conveniences in Egypt. France had gained great advantages in Morocco.[10]

In another book Churchill writes about the role of Great Britain in bringing a new monarch to Iraq and of the interests of Great Britain in that area:

> The Emir Feisal set out for Iraq in June 1921. At the same time I announced in the House of Commons that his candidature had the approval of the British Government. . . . In this way direct British administration in Iraq definitely ceased. It was replaced by an Arab government, acting indeed on British advice.[11]

Colonialism in the Middle East has undoubtedly played an important role in retarding the region's social and economic development. Colonial powers, in their efforts to maintain their interests in the Middle East, have exercised direct and indirect intervention in the region's affairs. They have influenced legislative and administrative offices. They have aggravated the region's political instability by distributing arms among tribes and by provoking the people and

---

[8] Winston S. Churchill, *The World Crisis* (New York: Charles Scribner's Sons, 1942), p. 12. Copyright © by Charles Scribner's Sons. Reprinted by permission.

[9] *Ibid.*, p. 28.

[10] *Ibid.*, p. 30.

[11] Winston S. Churchill, *The Aftermath* (New York: Charles Scribner's Sons, 1929), p. 492. Copyright © by Charles Scribner's Sons. Reprinted by permission.

clergymen against the central governments. On many occasions, they have resorted to direct economic and military sanctions.[12] For instance, in an interview with Mr. Henry Grady, the former United States Ambassador in Iran, this question was asked:

> We have heard that the British have exercised quite a good deal of political control in Iran over the past years. How do they do that?

and Mr. Grady replied:

> By developing influence. Of course, in Iran, with their ownership of the biggest industry there, their position economically is very strong. Any country owning an industry as big as The Anglo-Iranian Oil Company would in any case exercise influence, and they can take measures in Parliament to maintain that interest.[13]

To many Middle Eastern and some Western writers, colonial interventions in the Middle East have blocked not only much of the region's efforts for development, but also, at one time or another, hindered actions of other Western governments which might eventually have benefited the area. For example, during World War II, the Middle East Supply Center was organized by Allied Forces to ease some of the Middle East's economic difficulties. This was to

---

[12] See: C. M. Woodhouse, *British Foreign Policy Since the Second World War* (London: Hutchinson, 1961) (Economic interests of Great Britain in the Middle East).

Ittalaat Mahianeh (Tehran) Daymah 1329, p. 37. (Arms distribution among tribes by foreign elements.)

W. M. Shuster, *The Strangulation of Persia* (New York: The Century Co., 1912). (Military and economic sanctions.)

J. Kimche, *Seven Fallen Pillars, The Middle East 1945–52* (New York: Praeger, 1952), pp. 31–57. (Various types of foreign intervention.)

Arthur S. Millspaugh, *American in Persia* (Washington, D.C., Brookings Institution, 1946).

A. Daneshpour, *A Half Century of Economic Slavery* (Tehran, 1940), pp. 50–120.

Rep. Dr. Baghaei, Speech in 96th Iranian Congress; Hosain Makki, *The Black Book* (Tehran: Mohamad Ali Elmi Publishing, 1948).

Abolfazol Lesani, *Black Books or the Disaster of Iranian Life* (Tehran: Mehi Printing, 1949), pp. 360–65.

[13] Taken from a copyrighted interview in *U. S. News & World Report*, October 19, 1951, p. 13.

be accomplished by improving the region's capacity for production and by reducing its demand for imports. According to Martin W. Wilmington, however, this center "was doomed from the start" by the opposing forces within the Allied Nations. The opposition came especially from large business interests aroused by "their acute apprehension as to what such expansion would do to the market for Anglo-American exports in the area."[14]

Assuming the existence of colonial interests in the world in general, and in the Middle East in particular, a regional unity can, of course, provide a major threat to such interests in the area. Toward eliminating such a threat, such a colonial party will naturally seek to create a situation detrimental to regional unity and cooperation.

According to many Middle Eastern, South Asian, and African authorities, the colonial interests in these areas have done just that. For example, they point to the splitting of India and Pakistan in South Asia, the installation of Israel among Arab nations, the splitting of Syria and Lebanon, the existence of several small sheikdoms, the constant tribal uprisings in the Middle East, and the appearance of too many small countries in Africa. To these authorities it is obvious that, under the present circumstances, it will be years before any constructive regional unity can be accomplished. Of course, only a third party—the colonial power—can benefit from such a regional controversy.

Frequently, though, the evils of foreign colonialism have been exaggerated by the ruling class in the area. This has been to divert the attention of the long-suffering majority from internal ills by blaming others. In other words, the Western countries have more often than not served as a convenient scapegoat. Moreover, since the end of World War II, the Soviet Union, in her anti-West propaganda, has especially chosen this particular subject for special emphasis. She has charged that the "Western World is rich because the underdeveloped world is poor."[15] This Soviet approach, true or false, has gained considerable attention.

---

[14] Martin W. Wilmington, "The Middle East Center—A Reappraisal," *The Middle East Journal*, VI (Winter 1952), p. 156.

[15] Stephen Enke, *Economics for Development* (Englewood Cliffs, N. J.: Prentice-Hall, Inc., 1963), p. 5.

Chapter 4

PROBLEMS OF DEVELOPMENT:
SOCIAL AND ECONOMIC

The economic development or underdevelopment of the Middle East, as well as of other underdeveloped countries, is the function of many interacting factors. This can be illustrated as:

$$G = F\ (R_{ar}\ H_{lp.sf}\ M_{xi}\ C_{ne}\ T_{ar}\ G\ K)$$

That is, development or underdevelopment is the function of resources (R), human elements (H), market (M), capital (C), technology (T), regional cooperation (G), and constant disturbance factors including all exogenous factors (K). The human element includes labor and productivity (lp), and such other social factors (sf) as structure, education, health, attitude, and inventiveness. The market element includes external and internal (xi) as well as extensive and intensive factors. The capital element includes capital formation from internal voluntary and forced savings, and from external sources (ne). Finally, both resources and technology refer to past accumulation (a) or present rate of growth (r).

As much as the above factors can bring economic development into an area, their absence or lack of proper balance among them can result in economic backwardness. This is especially true in the Middle East. Aside from the historical setting, the region's economic problems stem from uneconomic social structure, lack of adequate and balanced resources, limited size of market, inadequate source of capital accumulation, poor technology, and lack of proper regional cooperation.

It is truly difficult to determine whether the economic backwardness in the Middle East is the result of its social problems or the social obstacles result from its economic backwardness. However, it is certain that neither can be studied without proper analysis of the other. It is equally difficult to classify many of the existing problems in the Middle East according to their origin. Limited market or inadequate incentives, for example, can be attributed to economic and social factors, among others. Major obstacles to the economic development of the Middle East are conservatively classified in Table 4.1. However, one may notice that even a careful classification of these problems leaves much room for debate.

Table 4.1.   Obstacles to Economic Development in the Middle East by Their Major Source of Origin

Social Factors	Economic Factors
1. Unbalanced social structure	1. Problems of capital formation
2. Social attitudes	2. Inadequate resources
3. Influence of tradition and religion	3. Unfavorable balance of payment and terms of trade
4. Political corruption and instability	4. Poorly organized financial institutions
5. Land problems	5. Problems of public finance
6. Rate of population growth	6. Economic insecurity and high risk of business
7. Strong family ties	7. Inadequate knowledge of their own economic structure

Social and Economic Factors	
1. Poverty	4. Limited size of market
2. Inadequate technical know-how	5. Low productivity
3. Lack of entrepreneurial ability	6. Low incentive for ventures
	7. Uneconomic saving and consumption habits

NATURAL RESOURCES

Except for petroleum in Iran, Iraq, Kuwait, and Saudi Arabia, and water in Iraq and in Egypt, the supply of most natural resources in the Middle East is limited and poorly distributed. Moreover, the full utilization of the existing resources has been handicapped by a shortage of capital, substandard technology, and the limited size of the market.

The natural resources in the Middle East and their distribution were examined in the first chapter. A short review at this point may, however, contribute to a better understanding of some of the existing developmental obstacles.

The Middle East, in general, lacks the adequate timberland and mines that enabled most advanced countries to become self-sufficient. Most of the existing mineral and natural resources in the region are of poor quality. Moreover, they are unevenly distributed and uneconomically utilized.

About 3.6 per cent of the world's forest land is in the Middle East, covering 10.9 per cent of the area. However, the entire forest area is located around the Mediterranean shore, extending to the northern section of Iran. Turkey, Iran, Jordan, and Iraq possess the majority of the area's forest land, amounting to 13.4, 11.7, 5.4, and 4 per cent of their total area respectively.

Except for oil, the existing supply of minerals in the Middle East is inadequate. Potash and phosphate are produced in Jordan for export. Iraq's mineral activities are unimportant.[1] In Iran, mining is of limited importance in the nation's economy.[2] Oil, of course, is the most important product of the Middle East, but its supply is concentrated in Iran, Iraq, Kuwait, and Saudi Arabia, as noted earlier.

Generally speaking, the Middle East enjoys a good supply of agricultural land. About 34 per cent of the region's total area— 4.3 acres per capita—is cultivable, as compared with 31 per cent of the total area or 3.7 acres per capita for the Free World. Arable land, however, is unevenly distributed in the Middle East. In Saudi Arabia, for example, 58 per cent of the area, 35.6 acres per capita, is usable. On the contrary, in the United Arab Republic only 3 per cent of the area, 0.2 acres per capita, is arable.[3] In Iran, about 40 million acres of land, 11 per cent of the total area, can be classified as cropland. About one-fourth of this land is in actual

---

[1] Department of State, *Economic Background Highlights, Iraq*, Revision No. 179 (Washington, D.C., November 1964), p. 4.

[2] Department of State, *Economic Background Highlights, Iran*, Revision No. 201 (Washington, D.C., March 1965), p. 2.

[3] Statistics and Reports Division, Agency for International Development, *Selected Economic Data for the Underdeveloped Countries* (Washington, D.C., June 1965), pp. 20–21.

cultivation in any year, the remainder lying fallow.[4] In Iraq, 26 per cent of the area, 4.1 acres per capita, and in Jordan, 13 per cent of the area, 1.6 acres per capita, is arable.

The supply of fresh water in most parts of the Middle East is both limited and poorly utilized.[5] Iraq and the United Arab Republic are the only two countries in the Middle East that enjoy an abundant supply of fresh water. Over 9 million acres have been irrigated in Iraq. However, "20–30 per cent of cultivable land has been abandoned in recent years as a result of salinization caused by irrigation without drainage."[6] The supply of water in Iran, though limited, may be adequate with proper conservation and irrigation. But about 48 per cent of all Iran's fresh water either flows out of the country or disappears in salty lakes and deserts without benefiting the soil. Jordan, Syria, and Israel are in desperate need of fresh water. Proper use of the Jordan and Yarmuk rivers can relieve this need in these countries, but such full utilization of these two rivers has so far been delayed by regional difficulties. Turkey, Afghanistan, and the countries of the Arabian Peninsula also suffer from a shortage of water.

HUMAN RESOURCES

In a democratic society, the full value of economic development will not be achieved unless it is accompanied by improvements in the living conditions of all: an increase in each person's share of goods and services.

Assuming a constant level of population, any increase in the supply of consumer goods in a country will result in a higher standard of living and is, therefore, a step toward progress. But in a real world where the population is continuously increasing,

---

[4] Department of State, *Economic Background Highlights, Iran*, Revision No. 201 (Washington, D.C., March 1965), p. 3.

[5] According to H. P. Hall (ed.), *The Evolution of Public Responsibility in the Middle East* (Washington, D.C.: The Middle East Institute, 1955), p. 74: "Water, which may be used as a source of power as well as for irrigation needs, is limited in comparison to the vast stretches of arid land which must remain unproductive without this life-spring. Moreover, the waste of available water supplies, erosion and salting of cultivable lands contribute to the increasing pressure of population." (Reprinted by permission.)

[6] Department of State, *Economic Background Highlights, Iraq*, Revision No. 179 (Washington, D.C., November 1964), p. 2.

merely a rise in a country's level of production may not be enough. So that each person may receive a larger portion of goods and services without reducing someone else's share, the total national product must increase faster than the population.

The task of maintaining a favorable ratio between the supply of consumer goods and population increase has often created a bottleneck in the economic development efforts of underdeveloped countries. The rate of population growth in the Middle East is among the highest in the Free World. For the region, in general, the rate of population growth amounts to about 2.5 per cent per year, compared with a 2.1 per cent increase in the Free World. Recent improvements in the region's level of health and income have accelerated the traditional high rate of population growth by lowering the death rate and increasing the birth rate.

Attempts at birth control are not in the best interests of the area for both economic and social reasons. Economically, most of the Middle Eastern countries suffer from inadequate population. This has to a great extent limited the success of their economic activities because of the limited size of the internal markets. A minimum population of from 20 million to 30 million people is necessary in an underdeveloped country seeking progress and industrialization. This minimum population is necessary to provide an internal market for its growing industries. This is especially true in areas similar to the Middle East where international markets are unavailable because of the competition from advanced industrial countries, and the hope for a regional market is hampered by the lack of cooperation.

In 1964 only three countries in the Middle East had a population of more than 20 million: Turkey with 30.8 million, the U.A.R. with 28.9 million, and Iran with 22.9 million. Other countries in the region definitely lacked the necessary population numbers to generate a self-sustaining economic growth. The population level in other Middle Eastern countries was:

Iraq	7.0 million	Lebanon	2.4 million
Jordan	1.9 million	Saudi Arabia	10.0 million
Israel	2.5 million	Syrian Arab Republic	5.9 million
Kuwait	0.4 million	Yemen	4.0 million
Afghanistan	14.0 million		

Despite the low level of population in most Middle Eastern countries, many of these countries were actually showing symptoms of population pressure. For example, population density during the same year was 475 persons per square mile in Lebanon, 310 per square mile in Israel, and 103 per square mile in Turkey.

From the social point of view, any attempt to control the population of the Middle East will meet violent opposition from both the church and the nationalists. Islam advocates marriage and children; nationalist extremists advocate the nation's superiority through larger population. Any plan for population control, if necessary, must be preceded by long-range programs of institutional and cultural adjustments. Accordingly, the only way out—at least in the short run—is to increase the region's level of production faster than the rate of population growth. However, aside from social barriers, any increase in the region's level of production is limited by the shortage of resources, low productivity, and regional conflicts.

THE SOCIAL STRUCTURE

History has left its most unfavorable mark on the social structure of the Middle East. Of all the existing problems in the area today, the social structure presents the greatest challenge to the region's economic development and has created an environment detrimental to most efforts for progress.

In a static frame of analysis, all existing obstacles are considered to be of equal importance. Viewed dynamically, social problems can be considered the most serious challenge. This is true because once social conditions are improved and the stagnant culture is changed, other problems can and will be more readily solved. Capital can be either generated or imported. Better technology can be adapted. Natural resources can be developed and more cooperatively shared.

In general, the social structure in the Middle East is extremely unbalanced. The majority of the population is controlled by a small minority exercising "great power both political and economic."[7]

The majority of the population in the Middle East has very little

---

[7] Department of State, *Economic Background Highlights, Iran*, Revision No. 201 (Washington, D.C., March 1965), p. 2.

wealth, no political power, and lives on a meager subsistence. Its members are poverty-stricken, illiterate, and in poor health. They neither know how to improve their position nor possess the means to do so. They have been promised better living conditions by many rulers on many occasions, but they have received nothing. They have been robbed, plundered, abused, cheated, and exploited in many ways and by many powers, both internal and external. All this has left a deep-rooted suspicion and mistrust in the people's hearts. They view most promises of help or attempts to improve their living conditions "with considerable and not unjustified suspicion."[8] The Persian Proverb, "a person bitten by a snake fears any black and white rope," clearly illustrates their position.

The problem of social imbalance in the Middle East has been especially aggravated in recent years by the development of better means of transportation and communication. During and since World War II, the poverty-stricken majority has finally come in contact with the way of living in more advanced countries. The people have compared their own living conditions with those of advanced nations and found many discrepancies. They blame Western colonialism and their own governments for the existing poverty. They want a better living, and they want it fast. This in turn has created social unrest and political instability, both of which are detrimental to the process of economic development.

On the side opposite the majority is the wealthy minority. This group, consisting of wealthy landlords, merchants, high military officers, and tribal chieftains, is in full control of the region's economic wealth and political power. Although governments constantly change hands in the Middle East, these are simply changes back and forth within the controlling group.

Recently, a small but influential class has appeared in the region's social structure—the middle-class reformist group. It consists of fairly well-educated groups of teachers, students, small merchants, professional men, low-ranking military officers, and (occasionally) clergymen. This class has directly and indirectly influenced certain evolutionary or revolutionary changes in the social, economic, and

---

[8] Ralph Linton, "Cultural and Personality Factors Affecting Economic Growth," *Development and Society*, ed. David E. Novak and Robert Lekachman (New York: St. Martin's Press, 1964), p. 193.

political structure of the region. On many occasions, it has actually aggravated the existing problems in the area by its lack of a common plan and by creating social unrest and political instability. Moreover, it has created a new environment which is not conducive to the inflow of international assistance. Being primarily nationalist, the group of intelligentsia holds no allegiance to either side of the international power bloc. This has created an atmosphere of resentment and mistrust on both sides. Socialists consider this new group of intellectuals a potential exploiting class and its popularity among the masses a threat to socialism in the area. The Western nations, on the other hand, consider the members of this group troublemakers who provide a threat to the world's balance of power and to their future interests in the region.

According to Ragnar Nurkse, the problems of progress in underdeveloped countries vary with the intensity of population pressure. The main problem in a densely populated area is that of disguised unemployment; the existence of too many family workers on a small piece of land has reduced marginal productivity to almost zero. These potentially productive human resources contribute little or nothing to the country's national production but consume a large portion of the farm output. On the other hand, the sparsely populated areas suffer from the lack of adequate human resources and from especially poor technology.

The Middle East suffers from both difficulties—not only from too many cultivators living on a plot of land but also from their poor production methods and technology. Professor Nurkse suggests that most of the disguised unemployment can be transferred into other fields of production without reducing the agricultural output. Whatever these new workers produce—regardless of the quality or quantity of the product—will be an addition to the total national output.

While this suggestion may be theoretically correct, its application in most underdeveloped countries in general, and in the Middle East in particular, has met with some difficulties. Attempts to shift the unemployed or underemployed rural population to industries and to improve their productivity has encountered strong opposition in the countries' congresses and among the influential minority, for two major reasons. First, the number of peasants on the land (or tribesmen in the tribe) has been associated with the landlord's (and tribal chieftain's) economic and political powers. Any attempt to remove some of these peasants from the land (or tribesmen away from their tribe) has been thus considered a direct threat to the landlord's prestige and power. Second, any attempt to release a portion of the population from the land is believed to require even further sacrifice on the part of the ruling class. Such programs of labor mobilization are believed to require large capital expenditures, not only to create jobs, build houses, and provide food for the new industrial workers, but also to increase the productivity of those remaining on the land. Health and educational programs must be launched to improve the cultivator's ability, and new techniques and tools must be introduced to increase his productivity. Most of all, a possible impairment of production incentives on the part of the remaining farmers who have been relieved of extra responsibilities must be prevented by providing them with more consumer goods.

All the measures mentioned require good government administration, voluntary sacrifice on the part of the ruling class, and capital investment. The congressmen in most Middle Eastern countries, loyal to the landlords, tribal chieftains, and rich merchants, have strongly opposed any legislation in land reform that may prove contrary to the minority's interest. Thus in most Middle Eastern countries, the national congress has become a device for controlling the minority's interests rather than protecting the rights of the majority. Indeed, during the past few years, some reform programs have appeared throughout the Middle East. However, a careful study reveals that none have been passed voluntarily in the national congresses. In some countries, such as Iraq and the U.A.R., these reforms have come as a by-product of social revolution. In other countries, such as Iran, these programs are pushed through by strong-willed reformers despite violent protests.

The unbalanced social structure of the Middle East has created an environment that is not conducive to a fast rate of economic development. The continuous regional, political, and institutional struggles in the area have created an atmosphere of mistrust and a lack of unity—not only among the poverty-stricken majority, but also among the ruling minority. This has further retarded economic development efforts in the region.

In a system whose stability is doubtful, even to its leaders, individualism and selfishness are natural outcomes. Individualism and profit-seeking, which in a well-developed society would create healthy competition, self-improvement, and entrepreneurship, have brought the opposite results in the Middle East. They have hindered the development of cooperation and coordination. Each person tries to get as much as he can and give as little as possible. "Let George do it" illustrates the way of life among most of the region's population. When anything is done, social interests are often sacrificed for personal benefits. Monumental projects are launched at the expense of practical ones.

As a result, in most Middle Eastern countries government has become a source of power and exploitation rather than a source of public service. Inefficiency in government administration and political instability have become prevalent. In ten years, 1942 to 1952, Egypt had seventeen governments; between 1949 and 1951 four military *coups* occurred. Iraq witnessed sixteen changes of government between 1941 and 1953 and eight military *coups* between 1936 and 1952. Since 1958 there have been two major *coups d'état* and several revolutions in this country, which has seen an average of two and a half changes of cabinet a year. Jordan had eight different governments between 1949 and 1953. In 1957, in less than one week, four cabinets were nominated by the King and failed. In the same year there were six cabinet changes, one military *coup*, martial law, and a three-month suspension of the congress. In 1963 Jordan saw four changes in cabinet, one attempted assassination of King Hussein, and one revolution. In Syria there have been fifteen revolutions within seventeen years. Iran and Turkey probably represent the most political stability in the region. The result in these two countries has been more concrete steps toward economic progress.

SOCIAL INVESTMENT

Just as successful cultivation of land needs a minimum preparation of the land itself, successful cultivation of economic growth in a country requires a minimum preparation of the country: improvements in the country's human and natural resources to prepare an environment for growth through a more efficient use of such resources. Improvements in human resources come through implementation of health and education programs. Improvements in the use of natural resources come through application of programs in irrigation, conservation, transportation, and communication.

The need for minimum social overhead capital expenditures for economic progress in underdeveloped countries has been unanimously emphasized by growth economists. Without such basic improvements in a country, a relatively higher capital outlet by the producers will become necessary to compensate for the lack of such facilities. Developments in roads and other means of transportation are necessary to mobilize resources, capital, and products. Improvements in the communications system are needed to bring better economic and social integration. Finally, education, industrial and agricultural training, housing and health programs will directly or indirectly increase the level of productivity and incentive. Private businesses cannot be expected to assume the responsibility for social overhead improvements, because such expenditures bring no direct feasible reward. But the absence of a minimum level of social overhead improvements will indeed hinder incentives for and abilities of private ventures. Because of the importance of social overhead investments to a country's economic development and because private parties cannot afford to undertake such capital expenditures, the improvement of social overhead capital has been generally considered a part of the government's functions.

In the Middle East, despite the desperate need for social overhead investments, the implementation of such programs has usually been blocked by the absence of long-run economic planning, inefficient government administration, and the lack of capital. The region's political instability in particular has left little or no room for social reforms and resource development. A government burdened by social and political controversies must spend most of its time and energy in defense of its own position. Such a government finds little or no time or energy to become engaged in long-run social investments which bring no immediate results. A new government generally opposed to the political views of its predecessor will also oppose its economic views, thus halting whatever projects had been undertaken by the former. All this has harmfully reduced the marginal productivity of capital in these countries.

PUBLIC ADMINISTRATION

The political structure of governments and public administration in most Middle Eastern countries has often proved detrimental to the region's process of economic development. The governments in the Middle East, regardless of type, are managed in an extremely centralized fashion. All major decisions are made in the capitol; all funds flow to the capitol; all expenses are appropriated from the capitol. This has proved harmful to the area's economic progress in three ways. First, the majority of decisions are made in the capitol by people who know little or nothing of the needs in other areas. Second, people living in faraway cities and provinces lack any form of political and economic independence. They can do nothing to improve their economic or political position. They soon lose interest and become indifferent to whatever goes on around them. Third, much of the money flowing into the capitol tends to remain there, thus building a large, exclusive capitol with monumental buildings and leaving most other parts of the country in a state of near ruin. There is moreover no administrative device to bring coordination among various government agencies.

Economic development in the Middle East has also been hampered by inefficient government administration. Civil positions possessing certain prestige seem to have attracted too many civil workers—more than necessary for the efficient management of the government. The result has been a system of extreme red-tape bureaucracy. Furthermore, while economic advancement in most Western countries has been a movement toward *laissez faire*, in the Middle East it is being pursued through government intervention. In many countries, this has added to the responsibility and burdens of the already inefficient government.

The political structures of governments in the Middle East vary, and with them vary their abilities to implement long-range plans. The republican form of government which brought democracy into many Western nations seems to have created an opposite effect in some of the Middle Eastern countries, where it has created a high office with much prestige in areas in which the meaning of democracy has not yet been well understood. The stakes are high and temptation is strong. Every group (especially the intellectuals) considers itself qualified and even destined for that office, and its members are not very discreet about how they might get it. All this has led to political (and thus economic) instability that has hindered the process of economic development and made improvements in public administration very difficult.

PRODUCTIVITY AND INCENTIVE

Productivity in the Middle East in both agriculture and industry is, with few exceptions, among the lowest in the world. The root of the problem, as in many other problems in the region, lies in the social structure. In a society where the majority are poor, illiterate, undernourished, and dominated by a small minority in full control of economic and political life, there is little or no force stimulating rise in productivity. The incentive to improve productivity is therefore very low among the Middle Eastern population. The majority of the people are in no position to improve their productivity and thus their living conditions. The wealthy minority, on the other hand, are more interested in maintaining their dominant position in society than in improving the living conditions of the people.

Inequality in the distribution of land in the Middle East has caused low agricultural productivity. This in turn has reduced the buying power of the rural population and the size of the market, and has weakened investment incentives. A peasant's or sharecropper's ability to produce is typically affected adversely by poverty and illness. Should his crop survive such unforeseen obstacles as drought and insects, the larger part of the product goes to the landlord, the landlord's agent, or the government. All this leaves the actual producer a share that is hardly adequate for even a low subsistence income. Thus he finds neither time nor incentive to improve his mind, body, or techniques. Land, seed, water, tools, livestock, and even human resources are often misused or wasted.

The low productivity of Middle Eastern agriculture has been further aggravated by the lack of incentive to increase production on the part of both the peasant and the landlord. The landlord,

satisfied with his share of income from the land, finds no reason
to risk extra capital to improve the technology and human resources
employed on his land. And even the landlord has very little faith
in the stability of the present system. He therefore tries to get from
the land as much as he can with the least possible contribution.
Moreover, any improvement in farm technology would also require
certain educational and training programs, which the landlord
either cannot afford or does not welcome, because any educational
development among the rural population is considered a direct
threat to the present system of land ownership and political rights.

Incentives for increasing production are even smaller on the part
of the peasants. In the first place, the sharecropper has very little
security of tenure in the same plot of land. He has no assurance
that he will be able to keep the land and receive the fruit of any
improvement he may bring about. Second, even when the cultivator is assured of retaining the same plot of land for years to come,
he still finds very little incentive to improve his methods of production, because the peasant does not receive the full benefit of
his efforts and any increase in production must be shared with the
landlord. A similar condition also prevails with regard to the nomadic
tribesmen.

Efforts to provide stimulating incentives for the cultivator by
giving him his own plot of land through land-reform and -distribu-
tion programs have not proved successful in most parts of the
Middle East because of some basic obstacles. To begin with, the
implementation of such programs has been slow both because of
the lack of interest on the part of the peasants who are to receive
land and lack of cooperation or even sabotage by the landlords.
Also, most of the region's peasants have no training for such independence. They know little or nothing of farm management, of
acquiring the necessary supplies, or of marketing their products.
Moreover, they know nothing of modern technology and lack both
the initiative to bring about such technological improvements and
the capital to finance them. Finally, under most land-distribution
programs, the farmers tend to lose their traditional security under
the land-tenure system. Independently, they have no reserve to
fall back on in time of need. They are likely to be wiped out and
migrate to other sectors at the first sign of hardship.

In recent years there has been considerable emphasis on industrialization throughout the Middle East. In most manufacturing industries in the region production methods are still primitive, equipment is limited, the knowledge of factory techniques is inadequate, and there is a drastic shortage of trained, skilled workers. In addition, the lack of comprehensive and practical labor laws, the absence of strong but nonpolitical labor unions, and low wages have adversely affected the workers' incentive. All this, together with general illiteracy and lack of training, has greatly reduced the factory worker's productivity.

Chapter 5

PROBLEMS OF DEVELOPMENT: CAPITAL FORMATION

The economic and social conditions in a country can be improved to a certain extent without heavy capital expenditure. Incentives to produce can be improved by better laws and land-reform programs, as well as by increasing the cultivator's share of farm production. Agricultural production can be increased by the use of better seeds and more efficient utilization of land, labor, and water. Improvement in agricultural efficiency, even in sparsely populated countries, will release some of the labor force for employment in industrial fields.

There is, however, a limit to a country's development without the use of capital. Improvements in social overhead investments such as transportation and communications, irrigation and hydroelectric-power installations, health and education programs, and the building of new industries are all necessary for basic economic growth. All these require heavy capital expenditure.

The formation of capital in the Middle East, though not the only necessary step for development, is an essential one. Whether in agriculture or industry, there is a direct relationship between the average capital investment per worker and the worker's level of productivity and income prospect. Institutional reforms in the Middle East are the most important step toward progress. But once a certain amount of institutional reform is achieved, the availability of capital for development projects becomes a decisive factor in the rate of development.

The rate of capital formation in the Middle East is very low. The low level of income and its unequal distribution have created a state of disequilibrium between savings available for investment and the potential demand for capital. The majority with an average propensity to consume equal to unity spend all they earn; the minority of the population that enjoy a surplus in income seldom offer savings for investment.

Growth in the Middle East, as in most underdeveloped areas of the world, is a gradual process. Before reaching for a level of economic development comparable to that in Western Europe and the United States of America, the underdeveloped country must at least bring its people's living conditions to an acceptable standard. From this point, growth becomes a more attainable goal. For a structured start toward economic growth in the Middle East, the growing working population must be usefully employed. A productive employment of this growing population, even in modest industries, requires an average capital expenditure of about $2500 per added worker or $1000 per added person. The annual population growth may be obtained by multiplying the number of population (P) by the rate of growth (g):

$$P \times g$$

The necessary annual capital expenditure can be obtained by multiplying the annual population growth by $1000:

$$Pg \times \$1000$$

Assuming a past accumulation of capital in the Middle East to have been sufficient, a minimum annual autonomous investment (I_a) is necessary to provide work for the growing number of workers. This can be shown as

$$I_a = Pg \times \$1000$$

In our equation, because the dollar amount is constant, the annual necessary autonomous investment becomes the function of the rate of population growth. The region's annual savings potentiality (s) can be obtained by multiplying its gross national product (O) by its average propensity to save (s):

$$S = O \times s$$

An equilibrium between the area's annual voluntary savings and the minimum yearly autonomous investment $(I_a = S)$ can assure

the Middle East of at least a source for financing a level of investment capable of maintaining a stable living standard.

This analysis has disregarded two other major forms of investment in the Middle East. First are these capital investments (I_c)
necessary to compensate for the region's capital deficiency because
of an inadequate rate of capital accumulation in the past. This purpose being met, the I_c need not be repeated. Second are investments
necessary for depreciation and maintenance of both past and current
investments (I_d). This investment, similar to I_a, must be repeated
annually. To finance and sustain an acceptable living standard from
internal voluntary savings in the Middle East, the following equation
may be necessary:

$$S = I_a + I_d + I_c$$

But, assuming that the Middle East can finance its (one-shot) past
capital deficiency through either internal sources or from external
capital, the following equation becomes a must if an acceptable
living standard is to be obtained and maintained:

$$S = I_a + I_d$$

That is, in order to start a self-sustaining process capable of building up the region's living conditions to an acceptable standard, the
Middle East must generate a minimum annual savings sufficient to
finance the needed annual autonomous investment. Of course, an
actual rate of economic growth in output per capita can be achieved
by increasing the investment side of the equation to a rate greater
than the rate of population growth.

A complete application of the above equation in the Middle East
is not practical for two obvious reasons. First, the exact calculation
of the region's capital deficiency (I_c) is not possible because of
inadequate data. Second, the calculation of the necessary annual
investment for depreciation is also limited because of the unknown
quantity of I_c. But a partial application of our equation is sufficient
to show that the region desperately lacks adequate internal savings
to generate economic growth.

With the Middle East's gross national product (O) of about
$29,290 million in 1963, and its average propensity to save (s) of

about 7.8 per cent,[1] the region's annual saving potentiality can be estimated by

$$S = Os$$

or $\qquad S = 29{,}290 \times 0.078 = \$2.28462$ billion

On the other hand, considering the area's total 1963[2] population of 119 million (P), and the region's annual rate of growth of 2.5 per cent (g), the amount of annual capital expenditure for autonomous investment (I_a) necessary productively to employ the growing population can be estimated by:

$$I_a = P \times g \times \$1000$$
$$I_a = 119{,}000{,}000 \times 0.025 \times \$1000 = \$2.975 \text{ billion}$$

Accordingly, the region's need for annual expenditures in autonomous investments exceeds its total savings potentiality by about $690,380,000. This can be shown as:

$$2.28462 < 2.975 \quad \text{or} \quad S < I_a$$

That is, there is an annual deficit of over $690 million in the Middle East's annual savings needed to meet the necessary autonomous investments. The severity of the deficiency in the region's voluntary savings will be increased when we add I_c and I_d to our equation.

The foregoing discussions show that the present level of voluntary savings in the Middle East is not sufficient to meet even the necessary autonomous investment needed to provide work for the increasing population, much less to start a steady economic growth. Other sources to finance growth exist in the area. Capital can be accumulated through forced savings, it can come from oil revenues, or it may be imported. But none of these sources is self-generating. They can, however, help generate future savings and assist their flow into investments by improving the level of national output, social structure, social attitude, and existing propensities to a desired level.

Placing the increased population on land also requires certain

---

[1] Estimated from Statistics and Reports Division, Agency for International Development, *Selected Economic Data for the Less Developed Countries*, (Washington, D.C., June 1965), p. 24.

[2] Estimated from 1964 figure.

capital expenditures. According to United Nations experts, agricultural production in the Middle East can be improved up to 25 per cent through institutional and legal reforms. Further development in the agricultural industry, either extensively or intensively, will require large capital expenditures for irrigation, afforestation, soil conservation, erosion control and reclamation, and the rural health and training program. Such expenditures, unless accompanied by balanced social improvements and better public administration, will result in no more than superficial monument buildings.

Despite the heavy demand for capital, the Middle East suffers not only from inadequate internal sources of capital, but also from obstacles that limit the region's ability to obtain capital from abroad.

INTERNAL CAPITAL

The general poverty and unbalanced distribution of income in the Middle East has been established. Consequently, the marginal propensity to consume among the majority of the population living very close to a bare level of subsistence is near unity; any increase in their level of income will generally be transformed into consumption. Moreover, the recent improvements in communications and contact with higher-income groups and Western ways of living have stimulated higher consumption among the lower-income majority by extending the range of their consumption habits. Henceforth, except for such measures as may be undertaken through government fiscal policies to create forced savings, the voluntary savings of the higher-income groups remain the only significant internal source of funds for capital formation.

The voluntary savings of the higher-income groups in the Middle East, small as they are, seldom flow into creative investments. The inefficiency of financial institutions to guide savings into investment, together with the traditional tendency of the wealthy minority toward luxurious living, have diverted most of their surplus income toward hoarding, entertainment, or foreign balances. This situation has been especially aggravated by the high risk of business ventures resulting from political and economic insecurity. The small savings that actually flow into investments are mostly diverted toward short-term mortgage loans or speculative commercial ventures.

The high rate of credit risk, together with a relatively large demand and lower supply of loanable funds, has resulted in an excessively high rate of interest. An annual interest rate of 50 or even 75 per cent on a one-year agricultural loan and 30 to 45 per cent interest on short-term (45 to 60 days) commercial loans is not uncommon. This has helped reduce the marginal efficiency of capital.

The high rate of interest, which under a normal environment stimulates savings, has very little effect on the volume of savings in the Middle East. Savings, at least under the present social and economic conditions, are interest-inelastic. The lower-income groups in the region, regardless of the rate of interest, have no surplus income to save. The higher-income groups are not motivated in their savings by the rate of interest. These savings are usually formed not for investment opportunities but because nothing else has yet been found to do with these surplus incomes.

The risks of business ventures in most parts of the Middle East are, furthermore, very high. The region's political instability (leading to the lack of stable economic policy), together with the absence of well-defined modern business laws, have limited the scope of any long-term, extensive investment undertakings. The profitability and even the principal of capital investments in most parts of the region are endangered by various forms of risk. These risks range from acute competition by foreign corporations or government-operated monopolies to inadequate physical security and weak and unstable governments. While one government may protect a certain industry, there is no assurance that the succeeding government will honor its predecessor's decision. In many cases the government may decide to enter, control, or monopolize a certain industry, thus competing with the existing private firms, limiting their scope of activity or even forcing them out of business.

Because of the high risk and uncertainty, a businessman planning a long-term investment venture often finds it very difficult to finance his venture, regardless of the quality or attractiveness of his plan. His chances to obtain all or a part of the necessary capital from financial institutions are limited by their capacity and restrictive policies. His chances of financing his venture by floating bonds and securities in internal markets are also limited by the lack of demand (at least for internal securities). The required capital must of necessity be supplied by the businessman or the promoter himself. In doing so, he accepts all the risks—ranging from theft, fire, or other unforeseen events to political and economic changes.

The high interest rate and risk have created a bottleneck in the process of capital formation in the Middle East. On the one hand, the lack of modern technology, the unbalanced social structure, and the limited size of markets have adversely affected the marginal efficiency of capital. On the other hand, a high rate of profit is necessary to justify the high risks and compensate for the high costs of investment.

Profits in an industry can be increased by either producing few products and selling them at a high price or by producing many and selling them at a lower margin of profit. Today, unless a product is of a rare kind, mass production and low profit margin have become essential factors for industrial development. In the Middle East, the possibility of industrial progress through producing few products at high prices is limited by the competition of cheaper and more attractive foreign products. The second possibility—mass production and lower profit margin—on the other hand, requires a reasonably large market, a high rate of capital formation, and a high productivity, all of which are absent in the Middle East. Mass production in the region is especially limited by the size of the market and slow rate of capital formation. Reduction in costs of production are, furthermore, limited by the high rate of interest and low productivity.

Ever since the industrial revolution in Western countries, size of market has been recognized as a major factor in industrial growth. Fortunately for the now developed countries, at the time of their industrialization the greater part of the world had not been yet developed and therefore offered no resistance or competition to the sale of their products. The Middle East today does not enjoy a similar advantage. While industrial development in the area is essential, among other things it is limited by the size of both external and internal markets. Externally Middle Eastern products meet on the world market those of well-established and highly productive competitors. Internally, the size of the market in the region is limited by extreme poverty, competition from foreign producers, lack of regional cooperation, and—in most countries—a small market.

An increase in the people's monetary income does not necessarily lead to an intensive expansion of the internal market. This is because any such increase in monetary income, unless accompanied by a proportionate rise in the production level of consumer goods, will merely create price inflation. In other words, the low rate of demand in the Middle East does not necessarily mean a deflationary gap. The region's economy suffers not from the lack of demand but from the low productive capacity. Applying Say's Law in the Middle East, we might conclude that any increase in the region's supply of goods will eventually create its own demand. According to the foregoing argument, while the capacity to produce in the Middle East cannot be raised unless it is accompanied by certain improvements in the size of the market, the capacity to buy and thus the size of the internal market is often the result of the capacity to produce.

In a country where the necessary capital is not being formed through voluntary savings, direct government participation has been suggested. In other words, the government must see that the necessary capital is formed and channeled into desirable fields through encouraging voluntary savings if possible, by forced savings and borrowing if necessary.

Direct government participation in capital formation in the Middle East is also limited by certain obstacles. The region's capital formation through government borrowing from the central banking system is especially limited by the area's extreme sensitivity to inflation. This is mostly the result of inelasticity of the supply of consumption goods. Inflation, if suppressed, will create a black market and reduce individual freedom; if not suppressed, it may lead to a breakdown of the financial system. Moreover, a country suffering from price inflation will become more attractive to foreign products and less attractive for the export of its own products. A free import policy will eventually drain the national reserve of gold and foreign exchange, while the introduction of controlled imports will require widespread government intervention in the economy. Besides, restricting imports into a country does not necessarily lead to an increase in savings. The released income, at least in the case of the

Middle East, is usually used to bid for the existing internal products and thus causes either further inflationary pressure or leads to an unbalanced growth.

It is not this book's intention to discount the role of some inflationary measures for the purpose of speeding economic development. A mild inflationary tendency in a growing economy is in fact desirable and necessary. Moderate inflation in a country can ease and speed up the process of economic transformation, especially by its effects on the profit margin and thus on incentive for entrepreneurship. Such an inflationary tendency, furthermore, tends to ease the problems of social and cultural adjustment.

In a country in which voluntary saving is not adequate to finance the necessary rate of capital formation, forced savings may be the answer. Creating capital through forced savings, however, is an extremely delicate matter. Forced savings as a form of confiscation affects industries, which it burdens. A miscalculation on the source upon which the burden of forced savings must fall can severely endanger incentives in essential industries.

In the present social and economic condition of the Middle East, certain fiscal measures may be necessary to stimulate private savings, generate forced savings, and encourage investments. Taxation, especially on land and income, not only results in more savings from those who can afford, but also contributes to a better distribution of income and wealth. But a full application of fiscal measures in the Middle East has been limited by several shortcomings. Among these obstacles are the inefficiency of government administration and the difficulty of collecting taxes. In fact, the inability of most Middle Eastern governments to impose direct taxes on the income and wealth of the upper class has led them to resort to indirect taxation. Thus, instead of reducing inequality of wealth, the tax system in most Middle Eastern countries has often aggravated that inequality. On the other hand, the level of income among the majority of the population is already so low that any attempt by the government to tax a part of their meager income may lead to social unrest and political instability. Finally, what forced savings the governments manage to accumulate are usually appropriated for military and police expenditures or for monumental projects.

Oil resources in some of the Middle Eastern countries provide an abundant source of capital. This source, if used wisely and cooperatively, can provide the entire area an ample supply of initial capital to bring about the environment necessary to start a self-generating process of development. But the useful employment of this source of capital in the Middle East also faces certain problems. In the first place, oil reserves are not distributed evenly among the Middle Eastern countries, and seldom are the proceeds from this source used cooperatively. This leaves some countries with a vast source of capital and some with none. Also, oil revenues cannot be considered a permanent source of capital. The supply of oil is limited, and its future demand is uncertain. It must be used now and only as a stepping stone for preparing the ground for future growth either before the supply is exhausted or the demand for oil is supplanted by that for other forms of fuel. This is not a far-fetched example. Similar situations occurred in many coal-producing regions. But in the Middle Eastern countries where oil is abundant, the revenue it produces is often used on nonconstructive programs and treated as if it were a permanent blessing.

EXTERNAL CAPITAL

The low volume of the domestic source of capital in the Middle East suggests another alternative—importing capital from abroad. In fact, the use of foreign resources for capital formation can be considered essential for a rapid rate of economic development. The capital inflow from abroad, if wisely encouraged and guided, can contribute to faster and smoother progress in the region.

The contribution of foreign capital to the process of economic development in the Middle East has been hindered by two kinds of obstacle. First are those which have helped reduce the flow of foreign capital into the region. Second are those that result from certain foreign investments in the region.

The recent attempts by some of the Middle Eastern countries to finance some of their capital needs from abroad have been burdened by the disappearance of the private long-term capital market in the traditional sense. The existence of many well-secured and popular securities in Western markets has presented a strong competition to the sale of Middle Eastern securities there and has limited the ability of many Middle Eastern countries' efforts to finance part of their capital needs through private foreign channels.

The inflow of direct foreign investments into the Middle East has also met several other obstacles, some old and some new. Among these are the threat of communism, nationalization movements, economic and political instabilities, and a weak legal framework for the region's economy. All these have discouraged foreign investors from undertaking major investment ventures in the region. Moreover, many of the Middle Eastern countries, suspicious of possible colonial influences believed to be associated with direct foreign investments, have virtually discouraged these forms of investment—either directly, by imposing certain legal limitations on foreign investments, or indirectly through unofficial practices. The major limiting factors on foreign investments in the Middle East may be summarized as follows:

1. Many Middle Eastern countries lack adequate and well-defined laws to encourage and protect foreign investments.

2. The existing laws are often inefficient and/or improperly administered.

3. The ambiguity of most of these laws leaves too much room for administrative rulings and interpretations. The lack of uniformity in interpretation of laws has increased the element of risk and insecurity for foreign investments.

4. The constant threat of confiscation because of nationalization or socialization and the lack of a uniform procedure for compensation has also exaggerated the risk element for investments in the area.

5. Aside from the above factors, the element of risk on foreign investments in the Middle East has been especially aggravated by the traditional bureaucratic supervision by the government and by economic and political instability in the area.

6. The definition of capital and profit is often too narrow.

7. The rights and inducements offered to foreign investors are often too limited or are conditional. For example, though in some Middle Eastern countries the repatriation of foreign capital and interests have been permitted, such repatriations are often conditional in regard to times and the amount that could be withdrawn each time.[3]

---

[3] For example, Law #156 of 1953 in Egypt and the Law for the Encouragement of Foreign Capital of 1955 in Jordan.

8. Foreign ownership of nonmoveable properties in most Middle Eastern countries is often limited or conditioned by law. This limitation is often extended to cover the area of operation or the line of business.[4]

9. The present laws often impose certain uneconomic conditions on foreign enterprises. These limitations often cover such areas as the number of foreign personnel, labor relations, utilization of local raw materials, and even sales activities.

10. Finally, in addition to all these difficulties, the Middle Eastern area often provides a poor background for large investment ventures. This is especially true because of the region's extreme poverty and very low social overhead investments such as the transportation or communications systems.

The profitability of direct foreign investments for the economic development of underdeveloped countries has been questioned by some economists. It is argued that aside from the traditional attachments of foreign colonial interests to such investments, they are usually channeled into extractive or export industries which contribute little or nothing toward balanced economic growth in the country. In Myrdal's words, "Such investments often merely establish enclaves which per se contribute little to the general development of the countries—they usually have a rather low employment effect—they count little in any realistic analysis of international integration."[5] To some other economists, among them Professor Nurkse, direct foreign investments in underdeveloped countries, attached to foreign colonial interests as they are, will still contribute toward economic progress in the country: "I am inclined to believe that even in the case of the so-called 'colonial' type of foreign investment . . . various direct as well as indirect benefits were likely to develop, contributing gradually . . . to the growth of the local economy."[6]

---

[4] For example, the law of 1947 in Egypt, the law of 1949 in India, and the law of 1952 in Jordan—all concerning foreign investments.

[5] Gunnar Myrdal, *An International Economy, Problems and Prospects* (New York: Harper & Row, Publishers, Inc., 1956), p. 107. Copyrighted © by Harper & Row, Publishers. Reprinted by permission.

[6] Ragnar Nurkse, *Problems of Capital Formation in Underdeveloped Countries,* (New York: Oxford University Press, 1953), p. 25. Reprinted by permission.

During the past two decades there has been a considerable increase in direct loans by the governments of advanced countries or by international agencies to the less developed nations. This has in many ways offset the disintegration of the international capital market and has facilitated the international movements of capital.

This method of capital transfer from the more developed to the less developed areas offers certain advantages to both the lending and the borrowing nations. From the creditor nation's point of view, a direct-loan negotiation by the borrowing government offers certain advantages over direct private-loan negotiations. A private investor, wishing to invest a portion of his savings in foreign countries, can now purchase securities floated by his own government, semigovernment, or international agencies for similar purposes. In so doing, the private investor can reduce his risks and supervision to the minimum level.

From the borrowing nation's point of view, financing economic development through direct loans offers a certain amount of freedom that could not have existed under direct foreign private investments. The underdeveloped country, by borrowing the needed capital within the limits specified in the loan contract, can design and manage its own development plans. The underdeveloped country can now coordinate all the existing plans into one master plan toward a balanced growth—more than could have been possible by many scattered foreign private investments. Moreover, the burden of paying interest or repaying the principal may help induce a pressure in the borrowing country for a better and more productive utilization of the borrowed funds.

The flow of international loans into the less developed countries is indeed not free from certain limitations. In the first place, such loans may be tied to some specific political and strategic conditions which often discourage the borrowing country. This is especially true in most Middle Eastern countries, which, as a result of past experiences, are often suspicious of any such conditions. They are usually careful not to enter into any agreement that may lead to a possible future intervention by foreign powers in the region. Also, the flow of international capital and technology into many Middle Eastern countries has been hampered on numerous occasions by reasons beyond their control. In more than a few cases, the obstacles to economic development in the Middle East have originated from without.[7]

The problems of inadequate capital and its improper use in most Middle Eastern countries have been especially aggravated by poor technology and inadequate know-how. Technology in most areas and in most industries is still primitive. But even when modern technology is employed, its efficient use is severely hampered by inadequate technicians and personnel training.

Research and innovation in most parts of the Middle East are also limited by existing social, political, and economic factors. Major research projects in the area are almost nonexistent. There is no major industry (except oil) willing or able to undertake a major research project. The governments are too involved with immediate political or basic economic matters to emphasize research projects that produce no immediate results. Moreover, the true value of research has not yet been recognized by Middle Eastern firms or government agencies because of inadequate education. Innovation in the Middle East, especially by the business sector, is strongly hampered by low incentives and the high risks of new ventures caused by the lack of economic and/or political stability and, thus, the lack of security.

While the existing problems of capital formation and technological development in the Middle East have undoubtedly limited the region's ability for economic development, these problems are often secondary to the existing social ills. The main problem in the process of economic development in the region lies not so much in lack of capital and technology as in the attitude of the people and the social structure. Progress in the Middle East must begin with institutional reforms and cultural improvement. Here in reality lies the most important obstacle to the region's progress, because any such movement for reform must be started and followed by a society which needs to be reformed itself. Thus any effort which may lead to the awakening of the people and an arousing of their interests, ambitions, and sense of cooperation is indeed the most basic step toward true progress.

Since the early 1950's there has been considerable development

---

[7] See discussion by Myrdal, *op. cit.*, pp. 334–36.

in various forms of technical aid by some advanced countries or international agencies in the Middle East. Among these are the United States Point Four and the United Nations Technical Assistance programs. These programs, by helping the people of underdeveloped countries to help themselves, have attacked the basic problems of backwardness at their source. They have especially helped most Middle Eastern countries in their efforts to fight such misfortunes as disease, lack of know-how, and low productivity. They have, furthermore, contributed toward social reform through rural development projects, education and health programs, and many social pilot projects. They have also helped speed up the process of development in the Middle East by giving technical and administrative guidance to the governments and to private concerns in planning and operating development programs.

Chapter 6

PROBLEMS OF DEVELOPMENT:
REGIONAL OBSTACLES

Many of the existing problems in the Middle East can be solved best through a cooperative approach among the neighboring countries. In a region in which resources are unevenly distributed and the size of most national markets is restricted by population scarcity, regional cooperation and joint attack on the problems is mandatory. Through regional unity the existing resources can be efficiently shared, markets can be widened, and development programs can be more effectively implemented by coordinated efforts. But, at least to this date, there have been many obstacles blocking the attainment of suitable regional cooperation.

Many nations of the Middle East, having recently obtained their political and economic freedom, are extremely jealous of their national sovereignty and independence. They are suspicious of any foreign influence, whether of faraway countries or their regional neighbors. Because of this, and also because of the historic struggles in the area, the doctrine of nationalism has become very popular in the Middle East. Nationalistic movements, together with deep-rooted social ills, have led to political conflicts and lack of cooperation within and among the Middle Eastern countries. Besides, either because the U.S.S.R. had long remained isolated from international affairs or because of the general ignorance among the majority of the population, the danger of communist colonialism has not yet been realized in most parts of the Middle East. In fact, the fear of one's neighbor often exceeds that of communism or any other form of imperialism. This situation has caused many of the Middle Eastern countries to "turn their thoughts and actions not toward the security of the whole region but to the security of one against the other."[1]

The development of nationalism among the Middle Eastern countries has limited regional cooperation, social and economic integration, and the full, efficient utilization of available resources. The economic and political welfare of the region as a whole or even of the concerned country has often been sacrificed because of nationalistic emotions.[2] The utilization of resources in most parts of the region has often been blocked by regional dispute and lack of cooperation.[3] Also, the operation of the principle of comparative advantage for industrial allocation in the region has been disregarded and even replaced by nationalistic laws, industrial protections, and import restrictions. Moreover, such regional incidents as the Arab-Israeli conflict and the Suez Canal incident or feuds for leadership have decidedly retarded the region's economic development.

THE ARAB-ISRAELI CONFLICT

On May 14, 1948, after a long period of Zionism and other organized efforts, the Israeli government proclaimed its independence. The new state, covering the western section of Palestine, was immediately recognized by the United States. Almost immediately after this proclamation, a state of warfare broke out between the new Israeli state and the Arab nations at several points. It took six months of effort and patient negotiation by the United Nations to stop the organized fighting, but the unorganized guerrilla warfare between Arab tribes and small Jewish partisan groups is yet to be stopped. In fact, at one time this regional conflict came close to starting major international warfare. This was in October 1956 when, despite

---

[1] Harry N. Hamud, *United States Policy in the Near East, South Asia and Africa, 1954* (Washington, D.C.: U.S. Government Printing Office, 1955), p. 932.

[2] An example is the case of the nationalization of the oil industry in Iran in 1950. This nationalization, at least at that particular time when the Iranian economy depended on oil revenues, proved an economic disaster for the country.

[3] An example is the case of limited utilization of water from the Yarmuk and Jordan rivers because of regional and border conflicts.

U.S. opposition, French and British forces invaded Egyptian territory in conjunction with Israeli forces. (Detailed discussion on this
subject will follow.)

Today, the Israeli state has not yet been recognized by any of
the Arab nations, nor has there been an effort on the part of Israel
to seek such recognition through a compromise. Arabs have especially refused to recognize the new Israeli state because it is foreign
and therefore a threat. On the other hand, the new Israeli state has
shown too fast a growth to be ignored by Arab governments. There
is a fear that the Arab population, noticing the economic and social
developments in Israel, will begin to wonder about their own government administrators. A report to President Dwight D. Eisenhower explained this side of the problem as follows:

> Israel is a danger to the Arab world—to its stagnation, to its
> human degradation, to the greed of its government classes. What
> the Arab governments fear is conquest—not by arms—but by
> example.[4]

The Israeli-Arab conflict has undoubtedly limited the rate of
economic development in the Middle East by creating continuous
social and political tensions, by burdening the already poor Arab
nations with a large number of refugees, by wasteful allocation
of resources for war purposes, and by limiting the efficient use of
certain shared resources.

THE PROBLEMS OF ARAB REFUGEES

By the end of 1953, about 874,928 Palestinian Arabs had taken
refuge in the surrounding Arab countries.[5] The problem of refugees
is of a kind that no one wishes to face, yet it has become a dilemma
for all. To Israel, they represent a constant threat. It was the United
Nations resolution which stated that an Arab may return to his
home or have restitution made to him.

Israel, though apparently accepting this resolution, cannot abide
by it for two reasons. First is the fact that Israel is short of living

---

[4] Nations Associates, *Security and the Middle East, The Problem and Its
Solution*. Proposals submitted to the President of the United States (Washington, D.C., April 1954), p. 135.

[5] *Ibid.*, p. 134.

room. As it is, the population density in that country is 310 persons per square mile as compared with 50 persons per square mile in the Middle East. Then, there is only 1.1 acre of agricultural land per capita in Israel, compared with 4.3 acres per capita for the Middle East. The return of Arab refugees will undoubtedly present a great burden to the economy of Israel. Second is the fear of what the placement of a large, unfriendly Arab minority in the country might do to its security. As a result, Israel has shown a minimum effort to comply with the United Nations resolution. According to Israel's former Ambassador Iban, about 48,500 Arabs have been successfully reinstated in Israel.[6] This, however, consists of a small fraction of the total number of Arab refugees. Israel has furthermore expressed willingness to compensate for refugees' properties provided that (1) the Arab world recognizes Israel's right to the Suez Canal, and (2) the Arab countries terminate their economic boycott of Israel. Neither of these conditions is, at least at this time, acceptable to the Arab world.

The absorbing of this large number of refugees has created a major problem to most Arab nations, some of which are already burdened by their own economic and social obstacles. This sudden increase in their population has aggravated the already acute problems of housing, health, unemployment, and shortage of resources. They consider Israel responsible. They have sought to help the refugees either out of pity or for political reasons. Besides, the filtering of these refugees into Arab nations has spread further rumors and general dislike of Israel, making any cooperative efforts between Arab governments and Israel impossible. The Arab governments, for one reason or another, have shown very little desire to compromise for peace. By 1957, about $300 million in aid had been given to the Arab refugees through UNWRA. Of this amount, 70 per cent was contributed by the United States and 24 per cent by Great Britain. The total contribution by the concerned Arab nations was 2.03 per cent by Egypt, 1.1 per cent by Syria, 0.8 per cent by Jordan, 0.6 per cent by Lebanon, 0.3 per cent by Iraq, and 0.2 per cent by Saudi Arabia.[7]

Undoubtedly, none have suffered as the Arab refugees them-

---

[6] Emil Lengyel, *The Changing Middle East* (New York: The John Day Co., 1960), pp. 338–39.

[7] *Ibid.*, pp. 337–38.

selves. They have lost their homes and most of their belongings. They have been crammed into small areas in which they can do nothing. About 214,000 refugees are settled on the Gaza Strip, a 25-by-4-mile piece of land, representing a population increase of about 221.3 per cent. More than 500,000 have gone to Jordan, representing 56.3 per cent of the population. They live in "misery, anxiety, and confusion." They are too proud to turn to Israel, and they have either been forsaken by other Arabs, who in one way or another limit their settlement, or have been used for political ends. They fear turning to the West because they remember that their plight was fabricated by Great Britain's actions in the United Nations and the United States' support.[8] So they often turn to the only alternative left—the Soviet Union or Red China, both of which have used this situation successfully for propaganda measures.

OBSTACLES TO THE EFFICIENT USE OF WATER SUPPLY

Perhaps one of the most significant issues in the Arab-Israeli conflict is the question of water. While the water supply in this area is adequate to meet the demand, its efficient utilization has thus far been blocked by the lack of mutual understanding and agreement. For Israel, tapping the existing sources of water, especially the Jordan and Yarmuk rivers, represents the only solution for bringing its southern plain into full production and relieving the country's dependence on food imports. Jordan, on the other hand, is desperate for water. With a cultivated area barely large enough to support its original population, it has had to absorb about a half-million Arab refugees. Syria and Lebanon, which are relatively arid and have no immediate need for water, have shown little willingness to accept a peaceful settlement. This is mostly because they fear that such a settlement might be interpreted as a *de facto* recognition of the Israeli government. Permission by Lebanon, for instance, to direct a part of the Litani River through a tunnel to the Jordan River would enable Israel to generate power on her side. Some of this power could be given to Lebanon in exchange for water, thus benefiting both countries. But this project, like several others, must await the distant compromise on both sides.

In 1949 Israel, in its first attempt to make use of the available

---

[8] *Ibid.*, pp. 336–38.

waters, planned to irrigate its dry section by canals channeling water from north and south. It also hoped to link this project to the Mediterranean–Dead Sea hydroelectric project. This attempt was opposed by the Arab nations. At the same time, King Abdullah of Jordan also came up with an irrigation project for the Wadi el-Arab. But this project, involving the Jordan and Yarmuk rivers, required Israeli permission. Israel showed willingness to consider negotiations. But due to opposition from the Arab League, Jordan suddenly withdrew from any involvement. In 1959, Israel declared a plan to bring water to its Negev Desert by pumping water from the Sea of Galilee. The Arab nations, in their vigorous attempt to halt this plan, threatened to dam up the source of the Jordan River.

After eighteen years of quarrel and guerrilla warfare between Israel and the neighboring Arab states, both sides are still as far from peace as they were when the argument started. There is, among other things, an ample supply of water in between the nations, which can benefit both sides. But neither party has been able to utilize this life-giving source or has been willing to allow the other side to do so. This has created a major obstacle to the economic development of at least a part of the Middle East.

Aside from the problem of Arab refugees and inefficient utilization of water, the existing Arab-Israeli conflict has hampered the regional efforts for economic development in several other ways. It has created a situation of constant warfare and insecurity that has proved detrimental for economic development. It has burdened the already tight budgets with a constant drain for war preparation. It has helped further regional frictions, not only between Israel and the Arabs, but also among the Arabs themselves, who have not always agreed on measures against Israel.[9] Finally, it has limited the scope of regional trade among Middle Eastern countries with each other and with other nations. For example, in January 1965,

---

[9] In 1965, President Bourguiba of Tunisia criticized Nasser's handling of the Arab-Israeli situation, calling for a more conservative treatment of the problem based on the 1947 United Nations Plan. This proposal met much Arab criticism. Beirut's *Al Maharrer* called him "Judas" and the U.A.R. assembly condemned and barred him from the United Arab Republic. See *The New York Times*, April 24, 1965, 1:8.

the Arab.nations strengthened their boycott against Israel.[10] Israel retaliated by requiring licenses from seven companies that had been involved in active trade with the United Arab Republic.

SUEZ CANAL INCIDENT

On July 26, 1956, the Suez Canal was nationalized by decree of Egyptian President Gamal Abdel Nasser. The nationalization of this internationally owned waterway created a bitter dispute among Egypt, France, and Great Britain. This led to a joint Anglo-French attack on Egyptian land on October 31, 1956, two days after the Egyptian Peninsula was attacked by Israeli forces. This attack was justified by both France and Great Britain, not as a measure against the nationalization of the Canal but as a step to end the war between Egypt and Israel.[11]

As the result of this attack on an Arabian land, general mobilization in all Arab states began and the third World War seemed very

---

[10] For example, the following is part of the blacklist, published by Jordan, of foreign firms which are to be avoided because of their trade relations with Israel:

1. Metropolis Brewery of New Jersey, Inc.
   1824 Lambert St., Trenton, New Jersey
2. Union Bag Comp. Paper Corp.
   Worth Building, 233 Broadway, New York 7, N. Y.
3. International Paper Co.
   220 East 42nd Street, New York 17, N. Y.
4. John A. Taylor and Sons, Ltd.
   7718 Gracechurch Street, London E.C. 3
5. Lanco S.P.R.L.
   30, rue Docteur Messman, Brussels 7, Belgium
6. Arcelik A.S.
   Sutluce Karaagac Caddese, No. 2–4, Halicioglu
   Istanbul, Turkey

See *The Economy of Jordan, Monthly Economic Magazine* (Amman: National Publishing), April 12, 1962.

[11] Existing records point to the fact that the underlying reason for the Great Britain–France joint attack on Egypt was in fact a protest against the Suez Canal nationalization. According to Great Britain's former Prime Minister, Sir Anthony Eden, he had told President Eisenhower on July 27, 1956, "that Great Britain was convinced the use of force was necessary against Egypt over Canal. . . ."

close for a while. Due to the determined efforts of the United Nations, the United States, and some other democratic nations, the
parties to the war finally accepted the United Nations' appeal for
a cease-fire. On November 17, 1956, an agreement was reached with
Egypt to admit the United Nations' forces on its land.

The economic, political, and social effects of this incident were
tremendous. Economically, it meant loss of life, property, and income, and the delay of some developmental projects. A short factual
account of the damages and immediate economic losses caused by
this incident may illustrate its significance as a regional problem.

On December 3, 1956, the British Admiralty charged that investi-
gations had shown that 49 vessels and bridges were destroyed in
the waterway, 11 of them in the main channel. The cost of clearing
the channel was estimated at $40 million.[12] According to Mohammed
Riad, the governor of Port Saïd, estimation of the immediate cost
of this "invasion" was about 3000 lives and £110 million in
property.[13]

The economic effects of the Suez Canal incident reached beyond
the direct costs to the parties in dispute. The indirect economic
burden of this incident was felt throughout the Middle East as well
as in many foreign nations, some of which had no direct involvement. On November 20, Syria canceled all her oil contracts with
British and French firms and banned all oil shipments to Europe.
The sabotage of Iraqi oil pipelines to the Mediterranean through
Syria prevented the delivery of more than 50,000 barrels of oil to
Western Europe. Lebanon, on November 5, put an embargo on
all oil exports. Saudi Arabia, on November 8, banned oil shipments
to Great Britain and France. As a result, the shortage of oil soon
became apparent in Europe. France was forced to ration fuel on
November 21, and Great Britain followed on December 17. Other
countries such as Sweden (on November 15), and Norway, Denmark, Italy, and Turkey (on November 16) found it necessary to
cut down their oil consumption by 5 to 20 per cent.

The Suez Canal incident was especially harmful to the process
of economic development in the Middle East. Despite the region's
need for capital and active human resources, many lives and prop-

---

[12] *Facts On File*, XVI (December 4, 1956), 402.

[13] *Ibid.* (November 21–27, 1956), 394.

erties were destroyed. The interruption in the Middle East's oil exports certainly delayed some of the economic programs financed from oil revenue. The halt in the canal transportation adversely affected not only the region's commerce but also the employment, and thus the income, of thousands of people who were engaged in services to the passing vessels. Finally, the total or partial mobilization in most Arab countries proved very expensive to their already burdened economies.

Aside from its adverse economic effects, the Suez Canal incident left deep social and political impressions in the Middle East. Socially, it intensified the already deep-rooted mistrust against so-called Western colonialism. It reassured most Middle Eastern people that their fear of foreign intervention was not unjustified. And it deepened the Arab fear and resentment against Israel, thus making the attainment of a peaceful Arab-Israeli settlement even more difficult.

Politically, the Suez Canal incident brought about precisely the situation most Western nations had hoped to avoid: Nasser emerged stronger than ever. His position became more secure and his popularity was increased. The power he had long dreamed about was finally handed to him by his enemies. Israel, faced with unfavorable opinion in the United Nations and the United States, was forced to pull back its forces from the Egyptian Peninsula and forget its dream of sharing in the Suez Canal management. Moreover, at least to most Arab nations, Israel was labeled not only a foreign element but also a potential aggressor and a threat that can always bring foreign intervention into the region. In about six months, the French government crumbled and gave way to Charles de Gaulle. France also soon lost its Arab-African colonies. In Great Britain, Anthony Eden retired from public office. The British position in the Middle East and North Africa became shakier than ever. The British-Jordanian Pact was terminated on November 27, 1956, by a unanimous vote in Jordan's House of Deputies. Altogether, there have been signs of the weakening of Western influence in favor of Soviet policy among several Arab nations. Even the United States, which disapproved of hostility and "had warned Great Britain and France repeatedly against the use of force,"[14] lost some popularity among

---

[14] *The New York Times*, January 27, 1960, A Report on President Eisenhower's News Conference.

the Arab nations because of the general feeling that the United States should have played an active role in defending Arab rights.

FEUD—ARABIAN STYLE

Perhaps the greatest obstacle to regional cooperation and unity in the Middle East is the social and political attitude of its people. Past experiences have left deep impressions on the region's culture. People have become cautious, individualistic, and very suspicious. The attitude of mutual cooperation, considered normal in most advanced nations, is usually absent in the Middle East—among its people and among its governments. The result has been a situation where each wants unity—but on its own terms. This has brought about constant feuds among the countries in the region and within each country.

The most significant among various feuds in the Middle East is the one that has developed among several Arab nations over Arab leadership. This feud in its recent version had its beginning with the start of the United Arab Republic. Egypt wants Arab unity, but with Nasser as its leader. Egypt's leadership has been challenged, at one time or another, by various groups and personalities throughout the Arab world. The greatest challenge to Egypt has come from Iraq, the Al Baath Party, and Bourguiba of Tunisia. The non-Arab countries in the Middle East have at times been forced to undertake some precautionary measures in defense of their own position. For example, there have been rumors that Iran, Turkey, Pakistan, and Afghanistan, in their effort to maintain a balance of power in the region, may form the "Arian Confederation."[15] The constant threat to the balance of power in the Middle East has created a situation of political and economic insecurity harmful to the region's cooperative efforts for progress.

On July 23, 1952, Gamal Abdel Nasser led an uprising in Egypt which forced the abdication of King Farouk and canceled the Constitution. Nasser, however, did not become the first president. But on April 18, 1954, when Mohammed Naguib sought to return

---

[15] *Ibid.*, September 28, 1958.

to the parliamentary system, he was removed and Nasser became president.

Soon afterward Nasser, who had accomplished the impossible in Egypt, began to win popularity and confidence among most Arabs, who had long looked for a capable leader. It seemed that whatever Nasser did and all the efforts by other nations to discredit him actually added to his prestige and popularity. A few months after Nasser became president, an agreement was reached (on July 27, 1954) with Great Britain to withdraw all its troops in twenty months. On June 13, 1956, British occupation of Egypt ended. On July 26 of the same year, Nasser nationalized the Suez Canal and somehow withstood the political storm that followed. In January 1957, Nasser and two other members of the Arab League—Syria and Saudi Arabia—signed a ten-year treaty with Jordan, in which they agreed to supply Jordan with money and arms to replace the deficit caused by the withdrawal of British subsidy. In 1958, despite many setbacks, the Aswan Dam project was launched and was to be completed in sixteen years. At this time Nasser was strong enough to follow his own policy of neutrality and of playing West against East.

From the start, Nasser's claim to Arab leadership did not remain unchallenged. The strongest challenge came from Nuri As Said, the prime minister of Iraq. Iraq, blessed by rich resources, has long been the center of culture and leadership in the Arab world. This competition between Iraq and Egypt became obvious around 1955 but did not necessarily end with the pro-Nasser revolution in that country. In April 1957, when Egypt, Syria, and Saudi Arabia failed to pay Jordan their agreed share of subsidy, a military *coup* by King Hussein of Jordan ended Egyptian-Syrian influence in that country. As the result of Hussein's anti-Nasser coup, riots and revolution by Nasser's followers began in Jordan. Iraq, using this opportunity, officially took sides with Jordan against the pro-Nasser and Syrian elements in that country. Saudi Arabia decided to pay its subsidy share of $14 million and joined sides with Iraq and Jordan.

On February 1, 1958, the United Arab Republic was formed. It consisted of two regions—Egypt as the Southern Region, and Syria as the Northern Region. Yemen was accepted as a federated member. During the same month Iraq and Jordan signed the Pact of

Unity forming the Arab Union. King Faisal II was elected Chief of the Union, and the military and foreign secretary posts were eliminated in Jordan. In March 1958, Saudi Arabia also joined the Arab Union. The two political fronts—the United Arab Republic and the Arab Union—began economic and political rivalry.

The Arab Union was soon terminated. On July 14, 1958, an apparently pro-Nasser revolution in Iraq was led by General Abdul Kassim. Kassim brought an end to the short-lived leadership of Iraq in the Arab Union. King Faisal II, his uncle, and Nuri As Said were assassinated. Iraq was declared a republic. Kassim announced that Iraq would follow the United Arab Republic policies but would also honor its international obligations. The new regime was immediately recognized by the United Arab Republic, followed by the Soviet Union. The United States, fearing Communist subversion, moved United States military forces into Lebanon, but finally recognized the new regime on August 2, 1958. After the Iraqi revolution, King Hussein declared himself leader of the Arab Union. But due to pressure from the United Arab Republic, he dissolved the Arab Union in August 1958 and re-established diplomatic relations with the United Arab Republic.

From the beginning Kassim did not show as much cooperation toward the United Arab Republic as was expected. He had ideas of his own, and none included Iraq's domination by Nasser. On October 7, 1958, an attempted coup against Kassim by his pro-Nasser deputy premier, Aref, failed. Subsequently Kassim began to drift away from the United Arab Republic. Fearing Nasser and agitated by the United States' military move following his revolution, Kassim began to favor Soviet policy. But soon, suspicious of the apparent increase of communism in Iraq, Kassim outlawed the Communist party. From that time on, Kassim's policies were never clear-cut. He had the vast resources of Iraq behind him but lacked an ally he could trust. He even brought to power the Baath party, and that later proved to be his major error. This period was characterized by constant violence and instability. Some of the major problems faced by Kassim were constant Communist subversive efforts, intervention by the United Arab Republic, riots and revolutions by nationalists or Nasser's followers, revolution in Kurdistan, pressures by both international blocs, and border difficulties with Iran and Turkey.

FIGURE 6.1. The Iraqi Parliament—a beautiful and modern building which has remained vacant for too many years.

Despite all his problems, Kassim was a popular figure among most Arabs. His claim to the newly independent Sheikdom of Kuwait (on the ground that the 1899 British Protection Treaty of that land was forged) made him the most favored personality in Iraq. Kassim also sought unity with Syria and Jordan (the Fertile Crescent). On September 29, 1961, a revolution by the Syrian nationalists and Army, who had resented that country's secondary role in the United Arab Republic, obtained Syria's independence. The revolution was inspired and indirectly supported by Kassim. The new Syrian regime was soon recognized by Turkey, Iran, and Jordan. It was recognized by the United States on September 29, 1961. Syria, Jordan, and Saudi Arabia, inspired by Kassim's indirect support, now formed an opposing front to Nasser. In the meantime Yemen, the federated member of the United Arab Republic, began to drift away.

For a short while the situation appeared gloomy for the Nasser side of the feud. But whether by coincidence, inspiration, or intrigue, things began to happen—almost all in favor of Nasser. On September 18, 1962, upon the death of Yemen's Imam Ahmad, army officers seized power in that country. On September 26 and 27, the rebel force declared the existing Imam deposed and proclaimed

Yemen a republic. Egypt used this opportunity to move troops into Yemen in support of the republican regime. Saudi Arabia moved to support the royalist tribes. Saudi Arabia and the United Arab Republic broke diplomatic ties in their skirmish over Yemen.

On February 8, 1963, a pro-Nasser coup d'état by army and air force (led by Abdel Salam Aref) ended Kassim's regime in Iraq. Kassim was executed the next day. On May 26, 1964, Gamal Abdel Nasser of the United Arab Republic and Abdel Salam Aref of Iraq signed an agreement in Cairo which may be considered the first step toward full Arab unity. This pact called for a joint presidential council to study means of unifying the two governments.

On March 8, 1963, a new revolution in Syria, probably inspired by the Iraqi revolution, brought to power a pro-Nasser government. Finally in April 1963, Egypt, Syria, and Iraq agreed to unite under the name of United Arab Republic, with Cairo as the capital and Nasser the first president. Iraq accepted Kuwait sovereignty. On February 10, 1964, a cease-fire agreement was reached in Kurdistan. On November 8, 1964, cease-fire came into force in Yemen. For the first time in many years peace seemed feasible in the Middle East. But experiences in 1965 and 1966 have proved that permanent peace and stability among the Arab nations is still a dream that cannot be achieved except by basic cultural reforms.

Nasser has never been able to find a clear path in his drive for Arab unity. His biggest setback has been his inability to cope with Israel in a manner his followers desire. Israel, which has so far served as a means of bringing the Arabs together, may eventually cease to serve this purpose. In fact, the subject of Israel has already started some disagreements—and even friction—among several Arab nations. For example, in January 1965, West Germany agreed to sent $80 million in arms to Israel. This was opposed vigorously by Nasser and his followers, who even threaten to recognize East Germany. Nasser's handling of the situation, however, was criticized by Tunisia's president, Habib Bourguiba, who was then severely reproached by Beirut's *Al Maharrer*.[16]

Another regional challenge to Nasser has come from the Baath party, which is a mixture of nationalism and Marxism. This party

---

[16] See footnote 9 on page 94.

started just before World War II and has attracted the intellectuals. All Baathists advocate Arab unity, but they are not in full agreement on how to achieve it. While some support Nasser, the majority believe that the center of Arab unity must be east of the Mediterranean. The party has shown tremendous power, especially in Iraq and Syria. Its influence in the Arab world was clearly illustrated in 1964 by the two consecutive revolutions of February 8 and March 8, in Iraq and Syria respectively.

The latest happening in the Arab feud was the February 23, 1966, coup d'état in Syria. This revolution, the country's fifteenth in the last seventeen years, is believed to have "obliterated" the pro-Nasser Baath regime in that country.[17] Although the new regime also calls itself Baathist, it has arrested all Baath leaders, including Michel Aflagh, one of the party's founders.

The problems of economic development in the Middle East discussed in the preceding four chapters do not function independently, nor can they be solved individually. All the existing economic obstacles in the region, by acting and reacting on one another, create many self-generating vicious circles which keep the Middle East in a constant state of backwardness.

This interrelationship of economic obstacles in the Middle East thus requires a simultaneous attack on all problems. Such an attack in turn requires a suitable atmosphere, ample capital, efficient use of resources, and know-how—all of which the region lacks. Economic development in the Middle East, moreover, must be started and operated by societies which in many respects have been considered incapable of carrying such a load. This is the most important obstacle to the economic development of the Middle East.

---

[17] See most United States newspapers' Associated Press reports on February 23, 24, and 25, 1966.

Chapter 7

PLANNING FOR ECONOMIC DEVELOPMENT: THE ROLE OF GOVERNMENT

Economic development is not a given condition, and there can be no definite standard for progress. A maximum level of economic development is in fact, unattainable because people's wants are unlimited. Progress in a nation must therefore be compared not with a selected universal standard, but with the country's previous standard of living in relation to its available means. A country is progressive when it shows a definite improvement in its basic variables as compared with previous years. In other words, any rise in a nation's productive capacity which exceeds the rate of population growth is a step toward development, even though the new level of productive capacity is still below the desired level.

The process of economic development, as has been explained, does exist in most parts of the Middle East. Agricultural and industrial productive capacities and the per capita national incomes in the region have shown definite improvements above the rate of the population growth. It is the purpose of this and the next two chapters to examine and evaluate the national and regional efforts for economic development and the results of such efforts in the Middle East. The accuracy of this analysis is necessarily limited by the need to classify development efforts under specific headings such as agricultural, industrial, or social projects. While such a classification of development plans is necessary to avoid a possibly complicated discussion, these efforts are inseparable and often affect more than one sector of the economy.

The economic and social backwardness of most underdeveloped countries has been related to the existence of a certain unfavorable cumulative process. This cumulative process in a society results from the interrelationship among social and economic factors whereby any disturbance on one factor is accentuated through reactions of the others.

A cumulative process initiated by unfavorable circumstances limits a country's ability to progress and may even retard the economy further, a process that has been called *the vicious circle*. But it should be borne in mind that a cumulative process works upward as well as downward. While most underdeveloped countries suffer from a downward spiral, the direction may be changed and the cumulative effects employed for faster progress. The main problem, however, remains in reversing this cumulative process.

While most economists agree that the existing vicious circles in underdeveloped countries must be broken and the course of the cumulative process changed, there is no unanimous agreement as to how this can be achieved. In many cases, the methods employed for breaking the vicious circles have proved more or less successful despite their differences. The method adopted by the U.S.S.R., for example, has been quite different from that employed in the United States. Japan, on the other hand, began its development in economic isolation. In contrast, most underdeveloped countries in the Free World today have begun their economic development through integration with other progressive nations.

The role and extent of government intervention necessary to break the vicious circles causing economic backwardness has also varied throughout the world. In the Soviet Union, economic development has been carried on under complete, dictatorial government intervention. In India (before independence), development programs were administered under the colonial power. In Japan (in the post-World War II era) economic progress took place as the result of the productive activities of many profit-seeking individuals, encouraged and regulated by government policy. In most Middle Eastern countries, development programs are designed and implemented by governments and are often aided by foreign technical and financial assistance.

A country's decision to follow any of the foregoing methods or a combination of these methods for the purpose of economic development is a matter of national policy. A national policy, in turn, is the result of the nation's historical development, social structure, and geographic location. But it must be kept in mind that an increase in government intervention, though it may hasten the process of economic development, will also limit the freedom of the individual in the society. Thus, a nation striving for rapid economic progress must first decide how much of its freedom can be replaced by government intervention. This decision is not an easy one. In many cases a government, though unpopular, may continue to rule despite its unpopularity. In some other cases, as in many Middle Eastern countries, the society may not be well enough developed to make a correct decision.

THE ROLE OF GOVERNMENT

To be successful, efforts for economic development must be preceded by certain social and economic preparations. The people of an underdeveloped country must first realize that their economy is underdeveloped. Then, striving for progress, they must be willing and able to make an extra effort and accept certain initial hardship.

The people's realization of their economic backwardness depends on their acquaintance with more advanced economies. A nation that is isolated can hardly find a comparative ground to measure its own condition. Economic integration can assist the process of economic development by breaking down cultural isolation and by bringing economic units and communities closer. Thus, the higher the degree of social and economic integration of the people of an underdeveloped country with the populace of more advanced areas, the stronger will be the motivation for development. Also, the stronger the people's desire for progress, the greater will be their willingness to cooperate for a common cause.

Social awakening and desire for development, however, do not by themselves mean progress. Development plans must be designed, resources must be efficiently utilized, capital must be formed and put into use, and above all, the socioeconomic structure and traditional handicaps must be reformed. In other words, dreams and hopes must be transformed into positive actions. Undertaking such activities depends, in turn, on the willingness and ability of people to accept responsibility.

Private institutions in most underdeveloped areas are not advanced enough to undertake the burdens of development efforts. It is often believed that the maximization of private profits "provides poor guidance for investment, particularly in less developed countries."[1] Thus, during the preliminary stages of economic growth and until private institutions in the country are capable of assuming their task, government must be the chief agency for implementing economic development programs.

THE BROAD OBJECTIVES OF THE GOVERNMENT'S ROLE

PUBLIC ADMINISTRATION AND LEGAL FRAMEWORK

The first important task of the government in an underdeveloped country is to correct and reform its own administrative organization. Corruption is, in this case, different from poor administration. A corrupt government, fearing for its own position, will not bring about any major social reform. Corrupt government personnel, seeking personal interest, abuse or misuse the funds allocated for development purposes. An honest but poorly administered government will accentuate the costs of progress by errors in planning, poor management, and duplication.

Recently, improvement of government administration has become an important part of development efforts in the Middle East. In most countries in the region, the educational requirement for public office has been raised and schools in public administration or similar fields have been established to train public servants. In almost every Middle Eastern country, new ministries have been founded and the functions of different departments have ben codified by new laws and regulations.[2]

---

[1] United Nations Economic Commission for Europe, *Economic Survey of Europe since the War* (Geneva, 1953), p. 179.

[2] For references see Ali Anwar, "The Recent Situation in the Middle East as seen by the Middle Easterns," *The Evolution of Public Responsibility in the Middle East,* a series of addresses presented at the Ninth Annual Conference on Middle Eastern Affairs by the Middle East Institute, March 4–5, 1955; ed. by Harvey P. Hall (Washington, D.C., 1955), pp. 11–19; *The Annual Report of the United States Operation Mission in Iran* (Tehran, June 1955), p. 22; Institute for Administrative Affairs, *Journal of Administrative Affairs,* Faculty of Law, University of Tehran, 1956, pp. 1–7; Ministry of Interior, *Iraq Today* (Baghdad, May 1953), pp. 60–61, 65–67.

An almost inevitable result of improvement in public administration is improvement in the legal framework of business and society. A good and capable government will bring about the suitable framework necessary for economic and social development. Thus a reform of public administration and an improvement in the capabilities of government officials may in themselves start a cumulative process of economic growth. The reform of public administration is neither the only solution nor an independent measure. Other development programs must be designed and implemented at the same time. In other words, economic progress in a nation requires a simultaneous attack on all problems.

RESEARCH

A simultaneous improvement of all economic factors in a nation does not necessarily bring a proportionate increase in national output. The process of increasing the national production in many combined and complex industries is actually not different from a similar process in a single industry. A mere increase in all factors of production by a certain percentage in a specific industry does not necessarily bring a proportionate increase in that industry's total production; this is a simple engineering fact. In order for the production capacity of an industry to rise a noticeable amount, certain changes—in production methods, combination of productive factors, and even managerial policy—are necessary. Similar to the situation in a single industry, a basic improvement in the country's economy as a whole also requires fundamental changes in economic, social, political, and legal institutions in the country. Such a drastic redesigning of the entire economic and social structure of a country requires large-scale research and planning. At least at the early stages of economic development, a greater concentration of efforts must be directed toward research into the country's assets and liabilities. The existing problems and handicaps must be recognized and thoroughly examined. The resources available to cope with such obstacles must be found and evaluated. Only with such complete knowledge can a country undertake a basic and lasting development process. Now development ends can be designed within the country's means and cures can be transformed into practical projects. The absence of such a study—or an inadequate one—can result in setting goals that cannot be achieved or planning programs that cannot be completed. This can result in a waste of available resources and in economic disorder.

Balance sheets of major advantages and handicaps for Iran, Iraq, and Jordan are presented in Tables 7.1, 7.2, and 7.3. These tables are neither comprehensive nor complete; however, similar tables, if fully completed and analyzed, may supply valuable guides for the Middle Eastern countries in their efforts for progress.

Table 7.1.   Iran: Balance Sheet of Major Advantages and Handicaps

Major Advantages or Available Resources	Major Handicaps
1. Oil; abundant source of capital	1. Inadequate arable land and water
2. A rather stable government	2. Low level of education (15–20%)
3. Existence of some mineral resources	3. Small market
4. Climate suitable	4. Land problems
5. Adequate forest lands	5. Minority influence exists
6. Good foreign relations and possible sources of foreign capital	6. Inefficient public administration
7. No burden of overpopulation	7. Very low level of income
	8. Low productivity in agriculture and industry
	9. Inadequately trained personnel and technicians

The private institutions in underdeveloped countries lack the capital and the ability for extensive research involvement, thus the necessary effort in research in these countries is believed to be one of the many responsibilities of the national government. Most Middle Eastern governments, realizing the importance of research but lacking the know-how for such projects, have either employed highly qualified foreign institutions to handle the task or have requested technical assistance from international organizations or friendly nations.

**Table 7.2.   Iraq: Balance Sheet of Major Advantages
and Handicaps**

Major Advantages or Available Resources	Major Handicaps
1. Oil; abundant source of capital	1. Extreme political and economic instability
2. Water supply abundant	2. Small market
3. Land very fertile	3. Minority influence exists
4. Climate very suitable	4. Low level of education
5. No burden of overpopulation	5. Inadequately trained personnel and technicians
6. Financial system well developed	6. Tribal problems (Kurds included)
	7. Involvement in regional problems
	8. Low productivity in agriculture and industry

**Table 7.3.   Jordan: Balance Sheet of Major Advantages
and Handicaps**

Major Advantages or Available Resources	Major Handicaps
1. Tourist attraction a good possible source of income	1. Poor soil and inadequate arable land
2. U.N. and U.S. aid	2. Inadequate water
	3. Constant border problems
	4. Lack of resources
	5. Refugee problems
	6. Small market
	7. Inadequate population
	8. Lack of financial resources
	9. Involvement in regional problems
	10. Persistent unfavorable balance of payment
	11. Low level of education

DEVELOPMENT POLICIES

Once the reasons for economic backwardness in an underdeveloped country are discovered, development programs must be designed and put into operation. Designing such projects is a very delicate matter. Every detail affecting the operation or results of such programs must be considered and examined before their execution. A slight error may often cause waste and failure. While such programs must be comprehensive enough to cover the whole economy and create a self-generating force toward progress, they must also be limited to the nation's available means and ability. The rate of population growth and the supply of natural resources in the country must be carefully considered. A policy of birth control, for instance, in underdeveloped countries such as Israel or Egypt which suffer from population pressure and a limited supply of resources will be a direct contribution toward faster progress. A rapid population increase in a country such as Iraq, which has a small population and a relatively abundant supply of resources, may actually contribute to its rate of development. Practicality and adaptability of the designed development programs is essential to their success. The vital task of designing such programs in most underdeveloped countries has also been resumed and supervised by the national governments.

Economic development planning also involves the determination of short- and long-term social and economic objectives. This is to establish a background for coordinated social, political, and economic efforts. Unless all development policies are geared into a well-organized plan seeking a well-defined objective, individual measures and uncoordinated steps will lead to waste and duplication. A central body or force is necessary to create such coordination among the various development efforts. In the absence of a natural or economic central force in most underdeveloped countries, this coordinating effort is also considered part of the national government's responsibilities.

To be an effective and self-generating force toward progress, planning for economic development must be comprehensive and balanced. Economic development in most underdeveloped areas does not necessarily follow Schumpeter's theory of economic growth.

Nurkse, questioning the applicability of Schumpeter's theory of innovation in underdeveloped countries, writes:

> Schumpeter's theory of economic development was intended to apply primarily to the rise and growth of Western capitalism. It is not necessarily applicable to the same way in other types of society.[3]

Development of one particular industry in an underdeveloped country, unless it is accompanied by a proportionate growth in other economic and social sectors, is not necessarily the beginning of an upswing in the economy. In many cases the lone developing industry fails to create its own demand. Besides, this industry, being burdened by various economic and social obstacles, may perish before benefiting the economy.

The increase in the supply of consumer goods in less developed countries is indeed necessary to meet the increasing demand. Meanwhile, to achieve a better standard of living and to stimulate incentives for further activities, there must also exist a simultaneous buildup of internal demand. Agriculture and manufacturing industries are in many respects complementary to each other's development. Development of agriculture in a country increases the supply of food and raw materials, releases extra workers from the land for industrial use, and deepens the internal market by raising the farmer's level of income. But simultaneous improvement in the manufacturing industry is also necessary to absorb the labor released from the land, consume the raw materials, and increase the supply of finished goods. These efforts are expected to draw a part of people's disposable income to provide incentives and reduce the danger of inflation. Communications and transportation in the country must also be developed at the same time to facilitate movement of labor and expand the size of the market, thereby increasing the profitability of investment ventures.

Despite the importance of balanced growth, social and economic sectors in underdeveloped countries seldom tend to grow in a balanced way. Some degree of guidance by a central body may be necessary. Guiding the economy toward a balanced growth, whether

---

[3] R. Nurkse, *Problems of Capital Formation in Underdeveloped Countries* (New York: Oxford University Press, 1953), p. 15.

by direct planning or through fiscal and commercial measures, is believed to be the most important responsibility of the central government.

CAPITAL FORMATION AND DIRECTION

Before attempting any major operation, the possible sources for financing development programs must be determined and examined. The nation's ability to sacrifice a part of its consumption to generate the necessary capital, the attractiveness of internal resources to foreign investors, and the possibilities of internal or external borrowing must all be examined and evaluated. Development programs in a nation should draw from such resources as bring the best results and require the least sacrifice. Financing economic development through a reduction in consumption in underdeveloped areas already suffering from a low level of consumption (as in much of the Middle East) is highly questionable. Such a reduction of consumption in these countries often results in serious economic and political disturbances.

Capital may be raised either from internal or external sources. Internally, capital formation can come from voluntary savings, forced savings, and/or the supply of such extractive industries as oil. External sources of capital include private and public foreign investment in the country, borrowing from foreign private or public institutions, foreign aid, and international agencies. Building up capital from internal voluntary savings requires an increase in the level of income and improvement in people's thrift. Building up capital through forced savings requires improvements in tax laws and public finance administration. Capital formation through both voluntary and forced savings, at least at the early stages of development, results in reduction in the already low level of consumption. Of course, with an abundant supply of an extractive industry such as oil, a country may successfully increase its supply of capital and meanwhile expand imports of consumer goods. But few countries in the world are blessed with an abundant supply of a resource capable of financing their growth, and fewer have been able to manage this income toward a basic economic growth efficiently. To raise capital from abroad, a nation must first resort to vast internal improvements in its legal sector and social and political attitudes. Laws should be passed to give protection to foreign investments and additional incentives must be provided to attract foreign capital. In recent years this has met with a growing obstacle—the nationalistic movements in most underdeveloped countries. An underdeveloped country hoping to obtain capital from abroad cannot afford extreme nationalism and—especially—hostility to the foreign supplier of capital.

Even when a suitable source of capital has been found, the efficient allocation of the available capital among various social and economic sectors is of significant importance for balanced growth. The lack of adequate social overhead investments in most underdeveloped countries has provided a bottleneck in these countries' growth. In an underdeveloped country where the social overhead investment (SOI) in transportation, communications, education, and so forth, is inadequate, capital expenditure on direct productive investments (DPI) will soon meet with the diminishing return. That is, a country's level of production cannot increase to its optimum level unless both the SOI and DPI receive proper attention.

Some international economists, including Hirschman and Kindleberger, have sought to explain the relationship between capital expenditures for direct productive investments and for social overhead investments through a simple input-output diagram, an approach presented in Figure 7.1. The horizontal axis represents social overhead investment expenditures (SOI), and the vertical axis represents direct productive investment expenditures (DPI). The line OY, drawn at a 45-degree angle to either horizontal or vertical axis, represents the country's path of balanced economic growth. The various combinations of SOI and DPI are represented by several levels of isoquants—I, II, III, and so on. In this diagram economic growth requires movement from isoquant I to subsequently higher isoquants II, III, and IV, representing production levels of $x + 1$, $x + 2$, and $x + 3$. By adding to its capital expenditures on SOI and DPI in equal amounts, a country will follow the path of growth OY in output from A to B, C, and D.

That is, OS capital expenditures on SOI and OP capital expenditures on DPI will result in a level of output equal to OA. By increasing capital expenditures OS to OS_1 and OP to OP_1 the level of output will rise to OB, and so on.

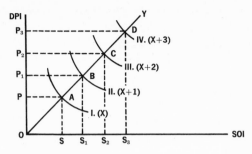

FIGURE 7.1. Balanced Growth Path in Relation to SOI and DPI Inputs

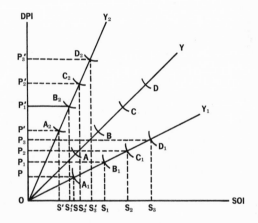

FIGURE 7.2. Unbalanced Growth Path in Relation to SOI and DPI Inputs

For one reason or another, a country may not decide to increase its capital expenditures on DPI and SOI in a similar proportion. An overemphasis on capital expenditure on SOI will direct output growth on a path similar to OY_1. In this case, as in Figure 7.2, there is a greater proportionate increase of capital expenditure on SOI from OS to OS_1 to OS_2 and to OS_3 than an increase in DPI from OP to OP_1 to OP_2 and to OP_3. As a result, output will grow from A_1 to B_1 to C_1 and to D_1. On the other hand, a country may tend to overemphasize capital expenditure on DPI and thus achieve its growth on path OY_2. In this case, there is a lesser proportionate increase in SOI from OS to OS_1 to OS_2 and to OS_3 than increase in DPI from OP'_1 to OP'_2 to OP'_3 and to OP'_4. The result will be an output growth from A_2 to B_2 to C_2 and to D_2.

There can, however, be no assurance that a country may either follow a balanced growth or constantly overemphasize on type of capital expenditure. Here, as in Figure 7.3, depending on the country's changing emphasis on the type of capital expenditure, output may grow from A to B'_1 or B'_2 and then back to C or from A to B_1 or B_2 and then to C. Of course, many other alternatives are also possible.

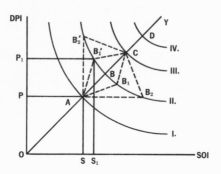

FIGURE 7.3. Zigzag Path of Economic Growth

At least in the Middle East, where the past SOI has been below the minimum requirement, an equal emphasis on DPI and SOI is not sufficient. Here, at least in the early stages of economic development, the isoquant, as in Figure 7.4, becomes kinked—increase in DPI cannot be substituted for the deficient SOI. Thus an increase in output requires a fixed combination of both inputs, with an emphasis on SOI. As a result (see Figure 7.4), in the early stages of development the growth path will slope to the right—an indication of an excessive need for SOI. After a certain minimum level of SOI is reached, the economy may follow a more balanced or other path of growth.

The allocation of resources for economic development in under-developed countries cannot be entrusted to private institutions. This is because such decision-making requires a comprehensive knowl-edge of all available resources and the ability to enforce the alloca-

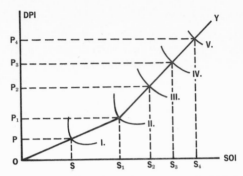

FIGURE 7.4. Growth Path in Countries with SOI Below
Minimum Requirement

tion policy. The governments of many underdeveloped countries
have undertaken the responsibility of allocating the available capital
and resources for economic development.

SOCIAL OVERHEAD CAPITAL EXPENDITURES

Among various types of capital expenditures necessary for economic development are certain types of investments which bring
no immediate reward. Their function is not to increase any particular material goods but to contribute to the process of economic
development in general. They tend to remove the cultural and
economic barriers in the country and thereby create a condition
favorable for better employment of productive capital and modern
technology. The major function of these capital expenditures, recently described as social overhead investments, is a dynamic one,
and their effect on the process of economic development is of a
long-run character.

Although social overhead capital expenditures are essential for
economic development, their public utility nature and the absence
of an immediate tangible reward has discouraged private investors
from undertaking such expenditures. Thus it has been generally
agreed that the responsibility for such expenditures must be assumed
by the government, which distributes the costs among various economic sectors.

Social overhead investments may be classified into the following two different but interrelated categories: investments for improvement of human resources, which may be called social investments; and investments made to improve general economic facilities, which may be referred to as public utilities. Also included here are capital expenditures that tend to improve a particular sector of the economy, through such improvements as irrigation or community development programs. These two types of social overhead investments will be discussed under sectors which they are designed to improve.

SOCIAL INVESTMENT

Economic development in a country is for the people, and its attainment must be desired and aided by the people. Unless the population of a country is psychologically inclined toward progress and physically capable of it, capital expenditures will only bring superficial improvements. In other words, there can be no self-generating economic progress unless the social and economic grounds are prepared.

In most underdeveloped countries this ground is not well prepared; in fact, it is often a cause for economic backwardness. Thus a country, in following a path to a successful growth, must incur certain necessary expenditures to improve its human resources. A group of United Nations experts, recognizing this fact, reported:

> In our opinion, most underdeveloped countries are in the situation that investment in people is likely to prove as productive in the purely material sense as any investment in material resources, and in many cases investment in people would lead to a greater increase of the flow of goods and services than would flow upon any comparable investment in material capital.[4]

Education and health improvements are of course of primary importance for progress. Education should bear the primary responsibility for breaking the socioeconomic inclinations that have been obstructing economic development. Improvements in health in a country, on the other hand, are also essential in order to raise the nation's productivity and ability. A man in poor health, regardless

---

[4] United Nations, *Measures for the Economic Development of Underdeveloped Countries.* A report by a group of experts appointed by the Secretary General of the United Nations (New York, 1951), p. 52.

FIGURE 7.5. A part of Iran's drive for economic development is the push for literacy—in this picture, some farm children receive free education.

of his skill or level of education, cannot be fully productive. Improvements in both health and education are therefore necessary to increase a people's productivity.

During the last two decades, educational and health programs have received considerable attention in most Middle Eastern countries. Sizable allocations have been made in Iran, Iraq, and Jordan for development programs for the improvement of human resources. The United States, under the Point Four Program, has also undertaken several health, education, and similar programs throughout the region.

Institutional reform and socioeconomic rehabilitation are also necessary prerequisites of economic progress. The traditional unbalanced social structure in underdeveloped countries has often counteracted development efforts. Social institutions must therefore be built up and new social habits formed. Moreover, public security must be improved to encourage investment ventures. Saving and investment habits must be changed to coordinate with other

FIGURE 7.6. Here we see tribal children receiving free education
in portable schools (tents) in Iran.

development efforts. Finally, the value judgment of the society must
be adjusted to include new factors. Social prestige, for example,
should cease to be a monopolistic privilege of landlords, military
officers, or politicians. It must also include smaller businessmen and
any other group that contributes to national production.

PUBLIC UTILITIES

Economic development in a country also requires certain social
overhead investments for material development. These investments,
while requiring heavy capital expenditures, are not productive by
themselves. Nevertheless, they are necessary to facilitate and encourage other investment ventures.

Transportation in an underdeveloped country must be improved
for the following reasons: (1) to expand the internal market for
agricultural and industrial products, (2) to facilitate the movement
of productive factors, and (3) to assist the internal and external
social and economic integration. Ports and airfields must be developed for similar reasons, as well as to facilitate the country's
external trade. Telephone, telegraph, and postal services must be
improved to ease economic and social integration and to contribute
to business expansion. Irrigation projects, especially in the Middle
East, are necessary to increase agricultural production. Other social
overhead investments in public utilities such as libraries and recrea-

tion facilities, by raising the standard of social welfare in the country, prepare the population for greater effort.

Considerable amounts have been allocated by the Iran, Iraq, and Jordan development programs for social overhead investments, especially in transportation and communication. In Iran, several projects of this sort have been completed or are in the process of completion. The Iranian railway system has been expanded and new roads have been built. In most cities, projects for paving streets have been started. Several modern airports have been built and port capacities have been enlarged. Electric-power plants have been installed in all large and medium-size cities. Postal, telephone, and telegraph services have been expanded. More than 35 per cent of Iran's second seven-year development plan or about $405 million has been allocated for the development of transportation and communications. Allocation of this fund money among various specific projects was as follows: about 45 per cent for highway improvement; about 23 per cent for railway improvement; about 6 per cent for the improvement of airdromes; about 13 per cent for the improvement of communications systems; and more than 2 per cent for mapping.[5] Iran's third seven-year development plan has allocated about 26 per cent or $649 million for the development of communications and transportation.

About 25.9 per cent of the Iraqi five-year development plan or about 79 million Iraqi dinars[6] was allocated for transportation and communications development. This amount was allocated among various specific projects as follows: 58.7 million Iraqi dinars for improvements in roads and bridges; 15 million Iraqi dinars for the development of the railway system; and 5 million Iraqi dinars for modernization of the airports. Iraq's new development program has allocated about 25 per cent or $384 million for the development of transportation and communications.

In Jordan, several projects for the improvement of communication and transportation facilities have been designed and some are under construction. The planned construction of a heavy road from the northern phosphate mines to the port of Aqaba is estimated to

---

[5] Bank Melli Iran, *Bulletin* (Tehran, May–June 1956), p. 193.

[6] Dinar equal to about $2.85.

require about a million Jordanian dinars.[7] Another road costing 4 million Jordanian dinars has been planned to connect the northern potash mines to the southwestern shores. The improvement in Port Aqaba has been estimated to require about a million dinars. Finally, 3 million Jordanian dinars have been estimated to be needed for the improvement of smaller roads throughout the country.[8] Jordan's newest seven-year development plan (1958–1963) allocated about 12 per cent of the total funds or 662,000 Jordanian dinars for development of the country's transportation. About 9 per cent of the total funds or 510,000 dinars was allocated for postal development.

THE NATIONAL DEVELOPMENT BOARD

The process of economic development is a long-run affair and therefore requires long-term plans. There is no short cut to progress. Development plans, to be successful, require time, patience, and continuous supervision.

The traditional political instability of the Middle East has created a major obstacle toward implementation of long-term economic planning. New governments seldom agree with the economic and political views of their predecessors. As a result economic policies, influenced by the numerous changes in government, have varied frequently, and a long-term economic or social project undertaken by one government is often endangered by the opposition of the new government.

The United Nations Economic Survey Mission for the Middle East, recognizing this fact, has pointed out the need for a central planning body in each of these countries. This central body was defined by the Survey Mission as "a national development board, fully contained within the sovereign jurisdiction of its governmental administration, charged with responsibility for planning balanced, over-all development, defining and recommending individual projects, and providing for their execution. . . ."[9] These development

---

[7] Jordan dinar equal to $2.85.

[8] Hamad Al-Farhan, *General Economic Planning in Jordan: Its Basis and Directions* (Amman: Chamber of Commerce and Industry, 1955), pp. 25–26.

[9] United Nations, Conciliation Commission for Palestine, *Final Report of the United Nations Economic Survey Mission for the Middle East*, Part I; The Final Report and Appendices (New York, December 1949), Recommendation No. 3.

boards, while operating under government jurisdiction, shall retain certain freedom and independence in long-run policies. It is hoped that once the board's major functions, responsibilities, and financial sources have been specified by the congress, they cannot be easily altered by new governments.

The duties of a development board are very broad. They include undertaking research, planning and executing development projects, and making recommendations to the national government concerning its economic policies. With economic and social conditions of the country in mind, a national development board must formulate an economic policy and prepare development programs suitable for that country. Economic development in a country, for instance, can be sought in either simple or cumulative ways. Simple development does not necessarily begin with vast capital expenditure or the introduction of new technology; it simply involves an increase in the efficiency of the existing processes, better coordination among various sectors, and less duplication. Cumulative expansion, on the other hand, involves an increase in the country's stock of capital, changes in relative factor ratios, and improvement in know-how and technology. A development board, among other things, decides on the degree to which simple and cumulative development programs are to be combined. It is also a part of a development board's responsibility to assist in the central government's progressive efforts, to negotiate with private, public, or international agencies to obtain financial and technical assistance, and to share in the management of this assistance. Finally, it should be remembered that the efforts of a development board are to supplement the development works of a country's regular governmental agencies and ministries, not to substitute for them.

World War II brought the nations of the Middle East closer to their Western allies and thereby facilitated their economic and social integration with more advanced areas. Consequently, the urge for better living, economic development, and international recognition soon spread over all the region. As the general movement for progress spread in the Middle East, the need for a permanent central planning board became apparent in many countries. Because of this need and in compliance with suggestions by many economic experts and survey missions, several central development boards were established.

IRAN's DEVELOPMENT PROGRAMS

Before 1949, most development programs in Iran, generally on a short-term basis, were undertaken directly by the central government. In 1946, a commission of fifty economists was organized to study and recommend a detailed plan for the nation's development. In 1948, the Over Seas Consultant Incorporated of New York was employed for a similar purpose. In August 1949, after a year filled with friction between this American firm and Iranian government representatives,[10] a comprehensive plan was designed and submitted. But the Iranian seven-year development plan, formulated by the 1946 commission, had been in operation since February 1949.

Iran's seven-year development plan, directed by the Plan Organization, called for an expenditure of 21 trillion rials,[11] or about $277.2 million over a seven-year period. This money was to be allocated among various fields, as shown in Table 7.4.

Table 7.4. Iran: First Seven-Year Development Plan
(in million U.S. dollars)

Public Sector Expenditure Allocation	Original Allocation	Per cent
Agriculture	69.3	25.0
Transportation	66.0	23.8
Industry and mining	39.6	14.3
Petroleum development	13.2	4.8
Communication	9.9	3.6
Social welfare	79.2	28.6
Total	277.2	100.0

Source: "Report of Plan Committee to Majlis," Khyam (Tehran, March 1955).

---

[10] See Alfred Michaelis, "Iran's Economic Structure," *Middle Eastern Affairs,* V (October 1954), p. 312.

[11] The *rial* is the monetary unit of Iran, which was equal to 3.07 United States cents at that time ($1 = 32.5 rials). Today one rial is equal to about 1.32 United States cents ($1 = 75.75 rials); all rial figures in this book are changed to dollars at this rate.

Programs under this plan were to be financed mostly from oil revenues. In case of a deficit, the government was permitted to borrow from the Iranian National Bank (Bank Melli Iran) up to 4.500 billion rials, and from the International Bank of Reconstruction and Development or from other foreign public and private agencies up to $250 million.[12]

The general objectives of this plan were defined as follows:

> Increasing the level of production and exports; providing the essential needs of the people within the country; developing agriculture and industry; exploring and exploiting mineral resources, particularly oil; developing means of transportation and communication; improving public health; and taking any measure for the purpose of raising the level of living and the level of education, improving public welfare, and lowering the cost of living.[13]

The nationalization of the oil industry in Iran and the subsequent drop in its revenue curtailed Plan Organization development activities. However, despite this major setback, some 130 projects were put into execution. According to United Nations experts, the Plan Organization, "though far from achieving its target, has made some headway in various fields."[14]

In September 1954, the Anglo-Iranian oil dispute was finally settled. Under the new negotiations between Iran and several international oil companies, Iran was to receive 50 per cent of net proceeds. Meanwhile, the United States resumed its aid to Iran. All this sharply raised Iran's sources of revenue and thus set the stage for a new comprehensive development plan.

In 1955, upon the termination of the first seven-year development plan, the second seven-year plan went into operation. It was the main objective of this plan to continue and complete the task undertaken by the first one. Article 1 of this plan defines its major purpose and scope as follows:

---

[12] United Nations Department of Economic and Social Affairs, *Economic Development in the Middle East, 1945–54* (New York, 1955), p. 87.

[13] Bank Melli Iran, *Bulletin* (Tehran, February–March 1949), p. 280.

[14] United Nations Department of Economic and Social Affairs, *Economic Development in the Middle East, 1945–54*, p. 87.

. . . The Government is duty bound, while executing programs already in process [the remaining credit balance of which amounted to 17,000 million rials on the first of Mehr 1334—September 24, 1955], in accordance with the Plan Law of 26 Behman 1327 [February 15, 1948] and the legal ruling of the Plan Committee of the Majlis [House of Deputies] of 23 Behman, 1333 [February 12, 1955] to execute the operation. Subject to Article 2, the total credit of which has been fixed at 52,800 million rials, from the date of the approval of this Law until the end of Shah-rivar 1341 [September 22, 1962]. The aggregate of operation already in process and operations, foreseen in this Law, constitute the Second Seven-Year Development Plan of Iran.[15]

According to Article 2 of the Second Plan Law, funds were to be allocated among various public sectors as shown in Table 7.5.

Table 7.5.   Iran: Second Seven-Year Development Plan
(in million U.S. dollars)

Public Sector Expenditure Allocation	Allocation of Funds	Per cent
Agriculture and irrigation	251	22
Transportation and communication	405	35
Industry and mines	90	8
Social improvements	156	13
Special regional programs	163	14
Administration, interest, etc.	97	8
Total	1,162	100

Source: Government of Iran, Plan Organization, *Review of the Second Seven-Year Plan Program of Iran* (Tehran, 1960), Table 4.

The source of funds for the second seven-year development plan was determined in Article 8 as follows:

Credit for development operation expenditures will be derived from oil revenues. . . . In order that the plan operation may not be curtailed the government is authorized to make up the shortage of the organization's requirements during the years 1334, 1335,

---

[15] Bank Melli Iran, *Bulletin* (Tehran, May–June 1956), p. 192.

and 1336 [1955/6, 1956/7, and 1957/8] up to an amount of $240 million by loans from domestic and foreign institutions. It is further authorized to make use of such credits as the need arises with the approval of the Joint Plan Committee of both Houses.[16]

A technical bureau, headed by an American and including nationals of four other countries, was set up to assist in the plan's over-all management. In addition to Iran's second seven-year development plan efforts, some $300 to $400 million was expended for public investment by nonplan government agencies during the same period. Altogether, Iran's second Plan Organization was successful in promoting an average annual rate of growth of about 5 per cent— about double the rate of the country's population growth.[17]

In September 1962, Iran's Council of Ministers passed the Third Plan Law, covering the period from September 23, 1962, to March 20, 1968. It is the goal of the third plan to bring an annual increase in the national income by 6 per cent or more, totaling about 35 to 40 per cent increase during the plan's lifetime.

Iran's third plan basically deviates from the methods used by the previous plans in two aspects. First, the new plan has placed equal emphasis on smaller projects and seeks to make use of experience gained from past ventures. Second is the deviation in the plan's *modus operandi.* In each of the two preceding plans, the Plan Organization received a specific portion of the oil revenue on the basis of which they formulated a series of independent plans and projects. In the meantime, ministries and other government agencies were free to formulate and execute similar programs from general budget revenues. In the new system, a comprehensive development program is to be formulated by the Plan Organization and allocated among various sectors. After an approval by the High Council, this plan is to be implemented by the appropriate ministries and agencies with the Plan Organization still exercising some general financial and technical supervision.

By early 1964 the total expenditures of the public sector in the third plan were estimated to be as shown in Table 7.6.

---

[16] *Ibid.*, p. 196.

[17] U.S. Department of State, *Development Program (Iran)*, Revision No. 195 (Washington, D.C., November 1964), p. 8.

**Table 7.6. Public Sector Expenditure Allocations and
Financing under Third (5½-Year) Plan**
(in million U.S. dollars)

Expenditures by Sector	Amount	Per cent
Agriculture and irrigation	600	22
Irrigation	(220)	(8)
Transportation and communication ...	667	25
Roads	(427)	(16)
Industry	292	11
Credit for private sector	(60)	(2)
Social (including local electric power)	1,007	38
Other	101	4
Total	2,667	100

Source: U.S. Department of State, *Development Program (Iran)*, Revision 195 (Washington, D.C., November 1965), p. 8. (Total includes nonprogram expenditures for administration and interest)

Table 7.7 shows the sources of funds for the expenditures in Table 7.6.

Table 7.7. Sources of Funds—Third Plan (by 1964)
(in million U.S. dollars)

Sources of Financing	Amount	Per cent
Oil revenue	1,760	66
Foreign loans	600	22
Central bank credit	213	8
Other	94	4
Total	2,667	100

Source: Same as Table 7.6.

THE IRAQI DEVELOPMENT BOARD

Prior to 1950, small-scale development projects amounting to only 35 million Iraqi dinars were carried on within the budget of the government. In 1950 the government of Iraq, striving for economic development and being stimulated by the increase in the nation's share of oil revenue, organized the Iraqi Development Board and designed a comprehensive plan for development. This plan required an estimated expenditure of 65.8 million dinars. Plans by the Development Board were furthermore supplemented by separate projects implemented by the newly established Ministry of Development.

In 1951, on request of the Iraqi government, the International Bank for Reconstruction and Development sent an economic survey mission to Iraq to study that country's potentialities for development. As a result, a comprehensive plan was designed and recommended. This new plan called for 168.5 million dinars' expenditure. Upon this recommendation, Iraq's six-year development plan was drafted by Law No. 23 of 1951 and its supplement, Law No. 6 of 1952. This plan required an estimated expenditure of 155,347,000 dinars, which were to be divided among various economic and social sectors as shown in Table 7.8.

Seventy per cent of Iraq's oil revenue was allocated to finance the country's development projects. The government was also permitted to cover any possible shortage in funds by borrowing from internal

Table 7.8. Iraq: Six-Year Development Plan, 1951/2–1956/7
(in Iraqi dinars)

Public Sector Expenditure Allocation	Amount	Per cent
Irrigation projects	53,374,000	34.2
Roads and bridges	26,766,000	17.2
Public buildings	18,018,000	11.6
Land rehabilitation, reforestation, animal and pasture developments, communications improvements, construction of airports and summer resorts	22,986,000	14.8
Industry and mining	31,050,000	19.9
Administration costs	3,153,000	2.2
Total	155,347,000	100.0

Source: Ministry of Interior, "The Economic Situation in Iraq," *Iraq Today. . . .* (Baghdad, May 1953), p. 80. (Percentages calculated from the original figures.)

and other external agencies. But, burdened by certain obstacles such as a shortage of technical personnel, skilled labor, materials, and time for the execution of some projects, the actual expenditures at the end of the plan period fell short of the original allocation.[18]

In 1955, Iraq's six-year development plan was superseded by a more extensive plan covering the years 1955–56 to 1959–60. The new plan called for an estimated expenditure of 304 million dinars, which were to be divided among various economic and social sectors as shown in Table 7.9.

Table 7.9.   Iraq: Five-Year Development Plan
(in Iraqi dinars)

Public Sector Expenditure Allocation	Amount	Per cent
Irrigation and drainage projects	111,250,000	36.7
Airports	5,000,000	1.6
Development of natural wealth	6,500,000	2.1
Educational institutions	8,150,000	2.6
Housing projects	8,750,000	2.9
Health establishments	10,750,000	3.6
Railways	15,500,000	5.0
Public buildings	18,650,000	6.2
Industrial & electrification projects ..	43,571,000	14.4
Roads and bridges	58,700,000	19.3
Other projects	17,178,000	5.6
Total	304,000,000	100.0

Source: Government of Iraq Development Board, *Development in Iraq* (Baghdad, 1955), p. 10.

As the result of the 1958 revolution in Iraq, the Development Board was dissolved and the six-year plan was discarded. A new Ministry of Planning was created. The Ministry designed a Provisional Economic Plan (PEP) which was to be effective January 1, 1960. In December 1961, however, the PEP was replaced by Kassim's Detailed Economic Plan (DEP) covering five years, 1961–

[18] Information obtained from U.S. Department of State, *Economic Highlights Background, Iraq*, Revision No. 179 (Washington, D.C., November 1964), p. 4.

62 to 1965–66. The DEP called for a total expenditure of $1,560 million, which was to be divided among various sectors as shown in Table 7.10. The proposed sources for financing this plan are shown in Table 7.11.

Table 7.10. Iraq: Detailed Economic Plan
(in million U.S. dollars)

Proposed Investment	Amount	Per cent
Industry and power	467	30
Building and housing	392	25
Transportation & communications	384	25
Agriculture & irrigation	317	20
Total	1,560	100

Source: U.S. Department of State, *Development Program (Iraq)*, Revision No. 187, (Washington, D.C., June 1964), p. 8.

Table 7.11. Iraq: Proposed Sources for Financing (DEP)
(in million U.S. dollars)

Proposed Source	Amount	Per cent
Oil revenue	885	56
Foreign loans	215	14
Public corporations	62	4
Other	398	26
Total	1,560	100

Source: Same as Table 7.10.

Kassim's Development Plan ran behind schedule and was revised and scaled down by the Baathist government to $980 million. The allocated programs for public investment and estimated private investments for 1963–64 is shown by sector in Table 7.12.

In 1963 the Baath Party was overthrown. The new regime has planned a completely new five-year development plan for the years 1965 to 1970. This new plan calls for 750–850 million dinars' expenditure, which is to be allocated among various sectors as follows:

Table 7.12. Iraq: Public and Private Investments, 1963–64
(in million U.S. dollars)

Investment Programs	Allocated Public Investment Program $ Million	Per cent	Estimated Private Investment $ Million	Per cent
Agriculture	30	16	3	2
Industry	39	22	3	2
Oil	—	—	29	21
Construction & development (ex. oil)	67	36	87	62
Transportation & communications	48	26	15	11
Other	—	—	3	2
Total	184	100	140	100

Source: Same as Table 7.10.

28 per cent for agriculture, 28 per cent for industrial development, 17 per cent for transportation and communication, 20 per cent for housing, and 7 per cent for electric power.[19]

JORDAN'S DEVELOPMENT PROGRAM

After several studies by British, American, and international agencies, the first comprehensive development plan in Jordan was drafted in 1953–54. This plan, covering the years 1953–54 to 1957–58, called for an estimated expenditure of $192.3 million. This amount was to be financed primarily from foreign aid. The most important long-run objectives of the plan were to find work for 60,000 unemployed persons in the country, to increase the exports and reduce the imports by threefold, and to increase the national per capita income by sixfold.[20] Allocation of the plan expenditures among various sectors is shown in Table 7.13.

The expected sources of funds for the above projects are shown in Table 7.14.

---

[19] *Statesman's Year Book* (1965–66), p. 1137.

[20] Hamad Al-Farhan, *General Economic Planning in Jordan: Its Basis and Direction* (Amman: Chamber of Commerce and Industry, 1955), p. 11.

Table 7.13. Jordan: Five-Year Development Plan
(in million U.S. dollars)

Expenditure Allocation by Sector	Amount	Per cent
Agriculture	69.1	35.9
Road construction	37.3	19.4
Education	31.1	16.2
Other	54.8	28.5
Total	192.3	100.0

Source: same as footnote 21.

Table 7.14. Expected Sources of Funds for Jordan's Five-Year Plan

Source	$ Million	Per cent
Jordan Development Board (mostly from Great Britain loans)	38.3	19.9
Jordan General Budget	53.5	27.8
Aid from the United States	42.7	22.2
U.N.R.R.A.	57.8	30.1
Total	192.3	100.0

Source: same as footnote 21.

The lack of adequate financial resources has been the most significant obstacle to the successful implementation of development programs in Jordan. The country's five-year development plan fell drastically short of its goals, especially because of inadequate funds. Internal sources for raising capital in Jordan are almost nonexistent. People are poor and resources are quite scarce. Thus, external sources of capital remain the only hope for financing the country's development plans. But even the successful application of foreign capital in the country has met a major bottleneck—insufficient natural resources to work on. In addition to this, the cost of foreign borrowing has created a drain on the country's already low foreign reserves. As of March 31, 1965, Jordan's external debts stood at 33,385,714 Jordanian dinars. Efforts to implement the recent devel-

opment plans will probably double this debt by 1970.[21] Because
of this difficulty the government of Jordan has not been able to
start and sustain systematic long-range plans for development. As
a result, since 1958 almost every major comprehensive plan for
development in Jordan has been either revised or set aside. Most
of the projects have been unsystematic, waiting for and following
the availability of funds.

In 1958 a comprehensive plan was designed calling for 5,656,000
dinars' expenditure. The concluding date for this plan was set for
March 31, 1963. This plan required expenditure allocations among
various sectors as follows:

> 519,000 dinars for postal development
> 1,000,000 dinars for the use of Yarmuk River
> 1,000,000 dinars for mineral development
> 200,000 dinars for development of water-wells
> 1,600,000 dinars for economics and industry
> 662,500 dinars for transportation
> 686,500 dinars for other purposes[22]

Early in 1962, Jordan acquired a 7.5-million dinar loan from Kuwait.
These funds were to be allocated for the development of the
following sectors:

> 4,000,000 dinars for the development of Yarmuk water
> 3,000,000 dinars for the development of phosphate mines
> 500,000 dinars for the development of water-wells[23]

During the same year, Jordan planned twelve projects in health,
irrigation, and water development.[24] These projects were to be
financed from U.S. aid and Jordan's budget.

In 1964, Jordan formulated a seven-year development plan covering 1964 to 1970. This plan calls for an expenditure of $250 million.
It is expected that 55 per cent of this amount will come from

---

[21] U.S. Department of State, *Economic Trend, Jordan* (Washington, D.C.,
July 1965), p. 28.

[22] Jordan Chamber of Commerce, *Economics of Jordan* (Amman: National
Publishing, 1962), pp. 65–66.

[23] F. Barakat, F. Kasab, M. Al Tijani, *Jordan Economy* (Amman: National
Publishing, 1962), p. 65.

[24] *Ibid.*, p. 67.

foreign private sectors. Private investments are to be directed toward projects in construction, mineral exploitation, manufacturing, and agriculture. Public expenditures are to emphasize improvements in: the Yarmuk River project, phosphate and potash mines, and industries.[25] Of course, the primary goal of Jordan's development efforts is "to promote economic independence by reducing domestic and foreign deficits."[26] The itemized goals of this plan have been defined by the Jordan's Plan Commission as follows:

1. The plan aims to bring 7.3 per cent annual growth in Jordan's GNP. This is about 3 per cent over the rate of the population growth. The total GNP is to rise from 138 million dinars in 1963 to 226 million dinars in 1970.

2. The plan seeks to reduce the balance of payment deficit from 41 million dinars in 1963 to 24 million in 1970. In doing so, a goal is set for a 195 per cent increase in the country's total exports in seven years.

3. The plan hopes to reduce Jordan's dependence on foreign assistance from 14 million dinars in 1963–64 to 6 million in 1970–71.

4. The plan expects to develop the tourist industry in the country from 30 per cent of all goods and services produced in 1963 to 38 per cent in 1970.

5. The plan wants to create jobs for many unemployed Jordanians and Arab refugees.

In 1965, Jordan was again revising its seven-year plan to bring better coordination between its needs and financial abilities. As it is, the successful application of any comprehensive development plan in Jordan depends on the country's ability to find a long-term source to finance its growth.

---

[25] See U.S. Department of State, *Economic Trend, Jordan* (Washington, D.C., July 1965), p. 5.

[26] *Ibid.*, p. 52.

Chapter 8

PLANNING FOR ECONOMIC DEVELOPMENT: AGRICULTURAL DEVELOPMENT POLICIES

Let us assume a person in a Midwestern state wishes to take a four-week vacation. He is not likely just to jump into his automobile and drive aimlessly for four weeks. It is more likely that for many days before the start of his vacation he has dreamed and thought about what he would like to do. He has probably decided upon a comprehensive vacation plan suited to his taste and based on his pocketbook. In compliance with this general plan he will have chosen the location for his dream vacation and decided on his mode of transportation. He will probably cash a check or borrow money to adequately cover the costs of his trip. He may have made a reservation for his lodging.

The above hypothesis does not deny the possibility that a man with no comprehensive plan may actually enjoy his vacation, but this enjoyment would probably be a coincidence. His lack of forethought can cause mishaps: he may run short of money; he may not find suitable lodging; his automobile may not be in shape for the trip. Accordingly, to a great extent, the success of a person's vacation can be assured by his foresight and advance planning—although this does not include arranging all the smallest details. While a comprehensive plan is necessary, day-to-day flexibility helps bring more satisfaction.

A similar process is often used in any undertaking, ranging from building a house to writing a book. A person planning a certain venture must ask himself such questions as: What is it I want to do? What are the existing obstacles? How can I best cope with these obstacles? What are the alternatives I can choose? What are my resources? Are there any new resources I might utilize?

A country planning long-range economic development programs is no exception to this principle. First of all it must decide on the goals it would like to achieve. Then it must find, classify, and evaluate the existing obstacles. Alternative measures to cope with existing problems and to start a self-generating process of economic growth should be determined. Finally, within the scope of its means and based on the country's historical background, geographic location, and social structure, a comprehensive long-range plan can be formulated. Meanwhile, priorities of programs and the general direction of the economy should be decided upon. Without such comprehensive planning, development efforts often lead to chaos and mass confusion. Economic planners must also keep in mind that as an economy leaps forward, certain economic and social variables such as demand elasticity, multiplier, and especially propensities tend to change; and as they change, so does their effect on the economy as a whole. As a result, long-range development plans must also contain a certain degree of flexibility to adjust to the changes in variables.

THE PLACE OF AGRICULTURE IN
DEVELOPMENT PROGRAMS

At least during the early stages of economic development in the Middle East, major emphasis should be placed on improving the agricultural sector. For a long time this postulate was questioned by most authorities in underdeveloped countries, as well as by some economists in advanced areas. Progress appeared to go hand-in-hand with industrialization. To many economists even today, dependence of a country on agricultural production is considered a sign of economic backwardness. Some economists, such as Colin Clark, have tried to show the existence of a certain correlation between people's occupations and their standard of living, with the tendency being that standards of living are lower in agricultural nations. Alfred Bonne is another economist who associates a higher standard of living in a country with industrialization. In Bonne's words:

> A higher per capita national income of the population always appears, together with an occupational structure in which a large percentage of the working population is engaged in manufacturing

and intermediary services—the so-called secondary and tertiary callings.[1]

References are made in Bonne's writings to several countries (such as India, China, Iraq, and even Egypt and Turkey) that suffer from a low level of national income because of their dependence on agriculture. Bonne concluded that without a shift in the vocational structure in favor of secondary and tertiary occupations in underdeveloped countries "no rise in standard of living among the mass of population is possible."[2] Several other economists, while accepting the need for agricultural development in underdeveloped countries, have argued that industrial and tertiary sectors must be developed at a faster rate than agriculture.

While industrialization can help raise a nation's standard of living, at least in the Middle East it must be of secondary concern. Industrial development in primary producing countries of the Middle East requires certain prerequisites based on agricultural development. Industrialization is the gravy, but agricultural development is the meat. Industrial development in the Middle Eastern countries can be obtained faster and easier if it is preceded by agricultural improvement.

It is true that in many primary producing countries, the disguised unemployed rural population may be profitably mobilized from agricultural to industrial sectors—but the agricultural productivity must first be increased. This is to compensate for the decline in the number of farmers and the increased demand for food and raw materials by the urban population and new industries. The supply of finished goods, especially in underdeveloped countries, does not always create its own market. Demand for these products must, therefore, be raised simultaneously with production. An underdeveloped country planning to expand its industries can expect little or no help from foreign markets. Their infant industries are too small, inefficient, and inexperienced to meet the competitive challenge of better and cheaper products abroad. On the other hand, an extensive improvement of the underdeveloped country's

---

[1] Alfred Bonne, *The Economic Development of the Middle East* (London: Routledge and Kegan Paul Ltd., 1945), p. 116. Reprinted by permission.

[2] *Ibid.*, p. 17.

internal market through a population increase is not feasible, at least in the short run. Intensive improvement of the internal market thus becomes of vital importance at the primary stages of industrialization. Perhaps the most important measure in improving the internal demand is through increases in farm production and in the farmers' income. Otherwise, any increase in internal production and in the workers' revenue will lead to agricultural price inflation and to deflation in industrial prices, neither of which is desirable in a developing country. The United Nations Economic Survey Mission in the Middle East, emphasizing the importance of agricultural development in the region, reported:

> Agriculture is the basic industry of all the Middle Eastern countries . . . two thirds of their population is rural . . . while most of the remainder are engaged in business dependent on or closely related to agriculture. In view of the most exclusive position which agriculture thus occupies in the economy of the region, it is obvious that the increased prosperity of the people and the ability to raise the standard of living must be achieved largely through the promotion of agriculture.[3]

PLANNING FOR AGRICULTURAL DEVELOPMENT

Planning for agricultural development in underdeveloped countries is not a simple task. It requires long-range programs, heavy capital expenditures, and institutional reforms. These efforts can be classified into three general categories: (1) capital expenditures, (2) institutional reforms, and (3) other protective measures.

Agricultural development in most underdeveloped countries requires heavy capital expenditures to increase the agricultural capacity for production through better utilization of resources. Large-scale irrigation projects are needed to bring the necessary water to farm lands. Other agricultural projects in land-erosion prevention, afforestation, and so on are necessary to improve soil and climate. General agricultural diseases must be fought and eradicated to protect the existing production and cultivators' inter-

---

[3] United Nations Conciliation Commission for Palestine, *Final Report of the UN Economic Survey Mission for the Middle East*. Part II: The Technical Supplement (New York, 28 December 1949), p. 2.

ests. All these programs require capital expenditures that are often too great for private cultivators. It is thus the responsibility of the central governments of underdeveloped countries to undertake such expenditures.

Agricultural development in a country does not always follow heavy capital expenditures. Institutional reforms, while essential for agricultural development, can also bring a certain degree of self-improvement. Legal reforms, in an attempt to increase and protect the cultivator's share of production and his right to land tenure, stimulate his incentives for further efforts and farm improvement. Legal penalties or tax levies on waste land may induce the landlord to improve his property. Finally, distributing agricultural lands among smaller farmers often helps prepare the ground for a self-sustaining development process in agriculture. This is usually achieved through stimulating the cultivator's interests and initiative as well as by creating healthy competition among smaller farmers in the field.

Distribution of land among smaller farmers, at least during the early stages, tends to reduce agricultural production because small cultivators generally lack the necessary capital to improve their farms and methods of production. Moreover, they often lack the needed experience in farm management, use of modern technology, and marketing. To be effective, therefore, land distribution and other agricultural development programs must be supplemented by certain other measures to prepare the background for self-generating progress. The following are among the most important supplementary measures necessary for basic agricultural development:

1. Small cultivators must be aided financially and technologically in order to begin and expand their production.

2. Better seeds and more suitable methods of cultivation must be introduced in order to improve the quality and quantity of farm production.

3. Extensive community development programs[4] are especially

---

[4] Community development programs, as defined in the FOA *Newsletter*, ". . . consist of the methods by the practice of which the manpower, ingenuity, and willing participation of village groups are mobilized and harnessed for self-help improvement undertakings. The automatic and greatly to be desired results are, or will be, the development of the confidence and competence of

needed to raise the ability of the rural population and to stimulate their participation in the process of agricultural development.

4. Rural vocational schools in various fields such as blacksmithing, dairying, poultry raising, fruit drying, beekeeping, livestock breeding, and farm management must be established to improve the cultivator's technical and physical ability.

5. The element of risk in farm production, caused by the traditional inelasticity in agricultural output with respect to price changes, must be reduced through certain price subsidization measures and crop diversification.

The agricultural sector in most Middle Eastern countries is in bad shape. It is owned, managed, and cultivated uneconomically. In many cases the word "abused" can be more suitably applied in this field than the label "underdeveloped."[5] Legal and structural improvements in the region's agricultural sector have often been opposed by the landlords or have been limited by the general poverty, poor health, and ignorance of the peasants.

The rapid population growth, low level of agricultural output per capita, and wasteful utilization of resources in the Middle East make agricultural development imperative. Meanwhile, the region's present agricultural condition, being hindered by institutional obstacles, cannot be left alone to be developed gradually or through private institutions. Therefore, while the inclination in the manufacturing industry tends toward *laissez faire*, the inclination in agriculture in underdeveloped countries is toward government intervention. Most Middle Eastern governments, recognizing this fact, have assumed active roles in agricultural development. In Iran, Iraq, and Jordan, for example, programs for agricultural development occupy the most important places in the general development programs.

Plans for agricultural development by the Middle Eastern govern-

---

the hundreds of thousands of villages and millions of villagers who constitute the rural masses in the economically and socially underdeveloped countries." FOA Community Development Division, Office of Public Service, Newsletters on Community Development in Technical Cooperation (Washington, D.C.: U.S. Government Printing Office, July 1954), No. 5.

[5] See discussion by Henry H. Byroade, *U.S. Foreign Policy in the Middle East*, U.S. Department of State Publication (Washington, D.C., 1953), p. 934.

ments have fallen into two broad categories. First are those intended to bring about physical reforms. These include such plans as irrigation and afforestation intended to raise the region's agricultural output through a better utilization of its available resources. These plans require heavy capital expenditures. Second are those plans which intend to bring about the necessary structural reforms. These plans seek to improve the cultivator's incentives and productivity through such measures as land reform or community development projects.

PLANNING FOR PHYSICAL IMPROVEMENTS

Much of the Middle East suffers either from inadequate water supply or uneven distribution of water. Large irrigation projects are necessary to cope with this difficulty. Even in such areas as Iraq and Egypt, where the water supply is adequate, the soil has often become saline and unproductive because of the lack of a flood-control system and the fast evaporation of flood waters. In such areas, projects for soil conservation, reclamation, and erosion control are essential. All these programs require heavy capital expenditures which the rural population cannot afford.

FIGURE 8.1. An irrigation project in Iraq that carries fresh, cool water to the dry and isolated parts of the desert.

Extensive agricultural projects, especially those concerned with irrigation, have received considerable attention in many Middle Eastern countries. By the end of 1954, the irrigation projects listed in Table 8.1 were under way by the Iranian government. In addition to these irrigation schemes, about 150,000 hectares of land were irrigated by drilling 2000 to 3000 deep wells.[6] From the 9.458 billion rials allocated for Iran's second seven-year development plan, 2.408 billion was for irrigation and dam construction and 1.000 billion for *qanat* and deep-well development. Afforestation and plant-pest control have also received considerable attention. Iran's second seven-year development plan allocated 1.098 billion rials for afforestation and 915 million for pest-control projects. In 1953, for instance, pest-control activities were extended to over a million hectares of land.[7] Iran's third plan has allocated $488 million for agricultural development. Today, of the country's total agricultural land, about two-fifths has been irrigated. With proper irrigation, the cultivable land in the country can be tripled.[8]

Table 8.1.   Iran: Irrigation Projects Completed or Under Way by End of 1954

Project	Irrigation Capacity (hectares)
Karum Dam & Karun-Zayandeh Rud Tunnel	50,000
Shahankareh Dam	15,000
Two dams between Kanegi & Zahak, Sistan for the use of Hilmand River water	45,000
Karkheh Project	80,000
Karej Dam Project	12,000–15,000
Two canals to make use of Aras Rud water	25,000
Golpayegan Project	5,000
Alvan Rud Project	4,000
Bampoor Project	1,500

Source: Seven-Year Plan Organization, *Monthly Bulletin of the Plan Organization,* No. 2 (Tehran, March 1954).

---

[6] Bank Melli Iran, *Bulletin* (Tehran, May–June 1956), pp. 3–10.

[7] U.N., *Economic Development In the Middle East, 1945–54,* p. 64.

[8] U.S. Department of State, *Summary of Basic Data, Iran,* Revision No. 211 (Washington, D.C., October 1965), p. 3.

In Iraq, irrigation projects have received greater attention than in most other countries in the Middle East. Between 1945 and 1953, the number of irrigation pumps was increased from 2757 with a total of 91,332 horsepower to 4339 with a total of 167,288 horsepower.[9] Iraq's six-year development plan allocated 335 million Iraqi dinars for the construction of ten dams expected to increase Iraq's crop area by 75 per cent and to raise the country's net annual agricultural income from 62 million dinars in 1945 to 222 million dinars in 1954.[10] "Give us thirty years," Nuri-Al-Said, then Iraq's hopeful Prime Minister commented, "and if nothing goes wrong, Iraq will have fifteen million to sixteen million acres under cultivation. That will be more than twice what Egypt has."[11] But many things did go wrong. By 1964, about 9 million acres were irrigated in Iraq. But in the meantime, 20 to 30 per cent of cultivable land was abandoned as a result of poor irrigation engineering.[12] Iraq's major irrigation projects, up to and including those of 1954, are shown in Table 8.2.

While in Jordan the shortage of water is felt more seriously than in most other parts of the Middle East, little has been accomplished toward basic improvement of the country's water shortage. Several irrigation programs have been designed and recommended by various economic missions and agencies in the country. But their implementation has usually been delayed by the lack of a cooperative agreement between Jordan and its neighbors for full utilization of the Yarmuk and Jordan rivers. Moreover, the successful conclusion of many projects has been hampered either by insufficient capital or by technological difficulties. Together with efforts for the realization of desperately needed irrigation projects, dry farming has also received considerable attention in Jordan. It has been estimated that dry farming in the country can be improved by 40 per cent within a 10-year period. This requires an estimated capital expenditure of 15 million Jordanian dinars. A mutual agreement based on the U.N.'s 1953 recommendation was reached between

[9] Ministry of Economy, *Statistical Abstract*, 1953 (Baghdad, 1954).

[10] U.N., *Economic Development in the Middle East, 1945–54*, p. 95.

[11] *The New York Times*, "New Garden of Eden" (January 9, 1956), 67:32.

[12] See U.S. Department of State, *Summary of Basic Data, Iraq*, Revision No. 179 (Washington, D.C., November 1964), p. 3.

Table 8.2. Iraq: Major Irrigation Projects, 1954

Project	Irrigation Capacity (hectares)
Hobbanich Scheme—use of Euphrates River	563,000
Mussayeb Canal—use of Euphrates River	48,000
Helleh Canal—use of Euphrates River	278,000
Tharthar Scheme—use of Tigris River; also a power station with 112,000 KW capacity	185,000-E
Dokan Dam on Lesser Zab River; also a power station with 170,000 KW capacity	320,000
Eski-Musel Dam	625,000
Bekhme Dam on Greater Zah River	600,000
Derhendi-Khan Project-Reservoir and Dam	309,000
Bani-Saad Barrage & Nahravan Irrigation Plans	223,000
Barrage Hawiji on Lesser Zab River	50,000
Dami-Kapu Dam on Adhim River	175,000

Source: U.N., *Economic Development in the Middle East, 1945–54*, pp. 113–16 and Government of Iraq, Development Board, *Development of Iraq*, pp. 13–23.

Jordan and Syria for the utilization of the Yarmuk and Jordan rivers. These schemes require an estimated expenditure of 30 million dinars and will irrigate about 500,000 dunam of land.[13] These projects alone are expected to raise the national income by 12 million dinars a year and to create jobs for about 30,000 workers. Some of the major agricultural development schemes recommended by the United Nations Economic Mission for Jordan are shown in Table 8.3.

At the present time, water development in Jordan is handled by three Jordanian agencies: (1) The East-Ghour Canal Authority, (2) The Central Water Authority, and (3) The Jordan River and Tributaries Regional Corporation.

1. The East-Ghour Canal Authority is in charge of a major irrigation scheme started in 1955. The scheme consists of five sub-projects revised in 1958 and to have been completed by 1963. In 1964 the first section of the scheme was completed and at present

---

[13] A dunam is equal to 50 square meters.

**Table 8.3.   Jordan's Major Agricultural Development Schemes
Recommended by the U.N. Economic Mission**

1. Yarmuk Canal Project: capable of irrigating 43,500 hectares of land in the Jordan Valley.
2. Jordan Canalization Scheme: for a storage dam 15 kilometers south of Basin.
3. Development of Wadi Zargan, with several dams, afforestation, terracing, housing projects.
4. Sahara Project: a project for dry farming, suitable for about 7000 persons and capable of irrigating 270,000 dunam of land.
5. Azraq Scheme: a minor irrigation for the utilization of several fountains and streams, capable of irrigating about 5520 dunam of land, and including 100,000 dunam of afforestation.
6. Jordan Valley Wadi Scheme: for better control and irrigation of Jordan's Eastern Wadi.
7. Zors Pump Irrigation Projects: capable of irrigating 4600 dunam.
8. Musa Bay Alami Scheme: to irrigate the eastern section of the country for Arab refugees.
9. Terracing Schemes: for planting 426,000 dunam of land with fruit trees around Nabuls, Remaleh and Adham.
10. Afforestation Project: calling for planting of 2 million seedlings in 20,000 dunam for afforestation, sowing seed in 25,000 dunam, and planting in 15,000 dunam in Arab Palestine.

Source: U.N. Conciliation Commission for Palestine, *Final Report of the UN Economic Survey Mission for the Middle East*, Part I, Technical Supplement (New York, 28 December 1949), pp. 76–80.

the authority is constructing the second section. The project is to provide irrigation to land lying between the Yarmuk and Zerka rivers. Thus far, a one-kilometer tunnel has been completed to divert water from the Yarmuk River. Another completed subproject is a 10-cubic-meter-flow-per-second canal extending 69 kilometers to the south with a distribution system covering an area of about 120,000 dunam of land.

2. The Central Water Authority was established in 1960 to exploit waters outside the EGCA. This authority has concentrated on ground-water development, research in hydrologic development,

geologic studies, mapping, well drilling, training, and village and city water-system development.

3. The Jordan River and Tributaries Regional Corporation handles water development as agreed by the Arab Summit Conference. Among other activities, the JRTRC has raised the sides of a 35-kilometer sector of the Ghour Canal to increase its capacity from 10 to 20 cubic meters per second. This corporation is also in charge of the Dam Al Mokhayebeh, which has a 200-million-cubic-meter water capacity, and Dam Al-Mogharer, which has a 350-million-cubic-meter water capacity.[14]

Structural reforms in agriculture have also received considerable attention in the Middle East. Legal reforms have been undertaken in most Middle Eastern countries to control land rents, increase the peasant's share of production, protect cultivators from the oppression of landlords, and prevent holdings of fragment lands.

PLANNING FOR SOCIAL AND STRUCTURAL IMPROVEMENTS

Perhaps one of the most important steps toward basic reform in agriculture is land reform programs. These programs have received considerable attention from agricultural economists and development economists during recent years. Land reform programs in this sense differ from agricultural improvements. They deal directly with the basic structure in the agricultural sector. The major objectives of land reform programs are:

1. To take the productive land away from large landowners and to reduce their power without immediate compensation.

2. To increase the tenant's security and incentive and to help increase his output through financial and technical assistance.

3. To guide and stimulate the compensation funds collected by the landlords toward productive industrial investments.

---

[14] See F. Kassab, F. Barakat, M. Al Tijani, *Economy of Jordan* (Amman: Jordan Chamber of Commerce), p. 36; *Seven-Year Economic Development Program, 1964–70*, Committee for Economic Development (Amman, October 1965), p. 203; U.S. Department of State, *Economic Trend, Jordan* (Washington, D.C., July 1965), pp. SA-20, SA-21.

4. To help release disguised unemployment from farm lands for productive use in industries.

5. To promote more equal distribution of income and help create a new middle class, which might bring a further balance in social structure.

Land reform programs are a long-run measure. To be successful, these programs require a host of complementary measures. There are good chances that in the initial steps of these programs output may actually drop. This is often because the new landowners lack capital and accumulated practical skill. Financial, technical, and legal aid to the new landowners is essential. Cooperative movements to a good extent can solve many of the financial and technological problems. Perhaps the gravest danger to a successful implementation of land reform programs is active criticism from the past landlords, who often point to the initial difficulties and temporary setbacks in land reform programs.

LAND REFORM IN IRAN

During the past two decades, Iran has led most Middle Eastern countries in its efforts to introduce basic land reform programs. Of the total land in Iran, 11 per cent is cultivable and is divided among 49,000 villages supporting about 75 per cent of the total population. Traditionally, the agricultural lands in Iran were divided into four major categories: crown land, public domain, endowed or waqf land, and private estates.

Crown lands were those owned by the late Reza Khan Pahlavi, the Iranian monarch. In 1941, these lands were given to the government to be used for charitable purposes. In 1949 they were mixed with public domain lands and were later transferred to the present monarch. In 1951, the Shah, Mohammed Reza Pahlavi, decreed their distribution among the cultivating farmers. These lands were priced at 80 per cent of assessed value of the land allotted and were to be distributed on the basis of 25 years' installment. The Emran Bank was created and took charge of the distribution of these lands. The bank also undertook the financing of farm improvements. The bank was also active in providing for technical assistance and forming cooperatives which were managed by the villages themselves. By 1962 more than 250,000 hectares, consisting of 517 villages, were distributed among 42,203 families. In January 1963, the administration of the remaining lands was turned over to the Land Reform Organization.

Public domain were those lands owned by the government and generally used for revenue purposes. The first effort to sell a portion of these lands was in 1931, when it was discovered that their costs exceeded their revenues. As of 1955, public domain lands were being distributed by the Public Domain Bonghah of the Department of Agriculture under the Law for the Distribution of Public Domain. By 1963, 173 villages had been sold to 8366 families under this law. In February 1963, a new decree placed these lands under the Land Reform Law. Since 1963, about 318 villages have been sold to 12,534 families.

About 15 per cent of the country's total cultivable lands were *endowed* or *waqf* lands. These lands may have been endowed either for personal and private use or for public and religious use. According to a 1963 decree, these lands were to be distributed among the cultivating peasants on a 99-year-lease basis.

More than 55 per cent of Iran's cultivable lands are *private holdings* of various sizes. The major emphasis of the country's land reform program has been directed toward the larger private and absentee landholders. The land reform programs of this nature in Iran began with the 1960 Land Reform Law and its 1962 amendment. This program is being implemented in three phases.

In phase one, major efforts were directed toward landlords who owned one or more villages. According to the 1960 Act, the ownership of each landlord was limited to 400 hectares of irrigated land and 800 hectares of dry land. The 1962 amendment revised the ceiling for land ownership to one village. Under this phase, about 12,875 villages have been distributed among 455,959 families.[15]

The second phase of this program is directed toward smaller land-owners. These landlords and their peasants are encouraged to rearrange their rent, sale, and distribution agreements in accordance with several progressive alternatives. The following consists of recent data on major steps in operation in the second phase of the program:

---

[15] Department of Statistics and Research, *Shah and People* (Tehran: Ministry of Information, 1965), p. 69.

1. Waqf (endowment) properties rented   7,322 units
2. Waqf (endowment) properties to be rented   737 units
3. Small landlords who have rented their land   118,053 units
4. Small landlords who have sold their land   2,096 persons
to farmers
5. Farmers who sold their cultivation rights   11,369 persons
to owner
6. Villages that have formed a cooperative   19,422 units[16]
corporation

The third phase of the program began in 1965 and seeks these major goals:

1. To increase agricultural output in order to provide food and raw material for new industries.

2. To raise the per capita income in the agricultural sector through self-help and cooperative efforts.

3. To stabilize farm prices.

Until the 1962 Land Reform Program, about 80 per cent of cultivable land had been owned by a few absentee landlords or the government and was farmed on a sharecropping basis.

According to this act, the government is responsible for the purchase and distribution of land among cultivators. The purchase value of these lands is based on the land's location, crops, and preceding year's tax payments. Landlords, who in one way or another paid a lesser tax, are able to receive less for their lands. The landlords are to be paid in ten equal installments. They receive cash for the first installment and nine payment orders with consecutive annual maturity. The term of payment has been adjusted from 10 to 15 years. The landlord receives 6 per cent interest on his outstanding loan. The peasants receiving land pay no interest on their debt. Should the farmer's earnings and payment fall below the sufficient amount to meet the annual payment to the landlord, the deficiency will be met by government grants.

The peasant, to receive a portion of land, must first accept membership in the local cooperative organization. He should also be a person without land, but directly involved in farm cultivation.

---

[16] *Ibid.*, p. 10.

Efforts are made to give a peasant the same plot of land he had previously farmed.

The Iranian Land Reform Organization began its operation on a small scale with only 20 members. In 1963, the organization had 1183 administrative and technical members and was actively involved in Tehran and several provinces.

In January 1963 (19 Daymah, 1341) the Shah, Mohammed Reza Pahlavi, announced his Six-Point Revolutionary Reform, known as the "White Revolution." The points of this reform are:

1. Abolishment of the landlord-peasantry system through legal and similar land reform programs.

2. Nationalization of forests throughout the country.

3. Selling government shares in factories to people and using the funds to support land reform programs.

4. Passing the necessary law to bring about profit-sharing devices for workers in manufacturing industries.

5. Reform in election laws.

6. Creating an Educational Corps to help facilitate implementation of the law of compulsory education.[17]

Because of some opposition, the Shah's six-point program for social reform was put to a nationwide referendum. There were 5,598,711 votes for and 4115 votes against the measure.[18]

LAND REFORM IN IRAQ

In Iraq, the Settlement Law of 1937 brought an end to the insecurity of landowners caused by the lack of title registration. Between 1937 and 1953, some 16,126,000 hectares of land, or about 68.4 per cent of the country's total land (except the desert areas), were registered. In 1951, a new policy of land reform was initiated by the promulgation of the government's Land Development Law Number 23. According to this law, about a million acres of government land were to be distributed among small farmers and other low-income groups such as industrial laborers, retired civil servants, and military personnel. Between 1951 and 1954, about 10,200 farmers were successfully settled on 510,000 hectares under the Dijaleh Project. Several other projects for the distribution of

---

[17] *Ibid.*, p. 4.
[18] *Ibid.*, p. 5.

1,125,000 hectares of land around Musel and 100,000 hectares around Baghdad and Basra were also undertaken at the same time. These lands were given to farmers on the basis of a 10-year trial period. After this period, if certain required improvement was accomplished, the farmer received a permanent title to the land. Finally, an Agrarian Reform Law in September 1958 limited land ownership to 1000 dunams (250 hectares) for flow-irrigated land and to 2000 dunams for rain-irrigated lands. Lands above ceiling were to be expropriated with compensation. The expropriated lands were distributed among cultivators in allotments of 30 to 60 dunams of irrigated lands, 60 to 120 dunams of rain-fed lands, or any combination of such lands. A cultivator receiving a plot of land was required to join the agricultural cooperative society in his area. He was assessed to pay in installments the compensation for the land, plus 3 per cent annual interest and 20 per cent of total administrative expenses. By 1961, about 4,381,441 dunams of land had been requisitioned from some 704 landlords and about 1,281,645 dunams of land distributed among 20,000 familes.[19]

The agrarian reform has nevertheless been slow in Iraq and has been repeatedly interrupted by political revolutions. To a great extent, the slowness in Iraq's agrarian reform can be attributed to lack of interest on the part of the peasants who are receiving land, as well as a lack of cooperation among landlords.[20]

LAND REFORM IN JORDAN

In Jordan, reforms in title registration and land taxation have been undertaken since 1928. Efforts have also been made to break down the system of periodic reallotment of land. Under the periodic reallotment system of Mushaa, each cultivator owned a certain number of shares of the cultivable land of the village. He received allotment of an area equivalent to the number of shares he held. The land thus held was cultivated by the farmer for a period not less than two and not more than nine years, depending on the customs of the village. At the end of the period, new reallotment

---

[19] U.N. Food and Agricultural Organization, *Progress in Land Reform*, Third Report (New York: Department of Economic and Social Affairs, 1962), p. 26.

[20] See discussion in U.S. Department of State, *Economic Background Highlights, Iraq*, Revision No. 195 (Washington, D.C., November 1964), p. 2.

was made. It was the primary aim of the Land Settlement Law to break down this system by permanent allotment of a parcel of land to each shareowner in relation to his number of shares. Jordan's seven-year development plan of 1964–1970 has turned over the land reform program to the East-Ghour Canal Authority. This plan has limited individual ownership of first-class irrigated land to a maximum of 200 dunams, but no less than 30 dunams. The East-Ghour Canal Authority has been authorized to purchase the land from large landholders and sell it to cultivators on a 10-year installment term. Meanwhile, cooperative movements have been encouraged to facilitate the transfer and successful use of the land. By March 1964 more than 30,969 persons had joined cooperative organizations.[21]

Land reform projects have also received attention in other Middle Eastern countries. In Egypt, the Land Reform Decree of 1952 limited land ownership by one person to 80 hectares. The new Syrian Constitution and Civil Code has provided that measures must be taken to encourage ownership of small and medium-size plots. In Turkey, more than 200,000 hectares of land were distributed among 42,000 families between 1945 and 1951. In 1952, 163,000 hectares were distributed among 38,849 families.

SUPPLEMENTARY MEASURES FOR AGRICULTURAL IMPROVEMENTS

Aside from land reform and other structural programs, most Middle Eastern countries have adopted measures to improve the ability, productivity, and incentives of small farmers. Financial and technical aids are being offered in various forms to small cultivators. In 1950, the capital of the Iranian Bank of Agriculture was raised from 300 million to 450 million rials to increase the bank's capacity for long-term loans at low interest rates. In Iraq, the functions of the Industrial and Agricultural Bank, established in 1936, were divided between two independent banks, the Industrial Bank and the Agricultural Bank, to improve their efficiency and scope of operation. Moreover, the capital of the Agricultural Bank was

---

[21] *Seven-Year Economic Development Program 1964–70* (Amman: Committee for Economic Development, October 1965), pp. 201, 202, 391.

raised and it now renders services similar to those offered by the Iranian Bank of Agriculture. In Jordan, the Agricultural Bank is, in fact, the most modern bank being operated on a national level. The functions of this bank, however, are not limited to the agricultural field.

Technical assistance in various forms is being supplied to most Middle Eastern cultivators. Several training schools have been set up throughout Iran and Iraq to train the rural population in various fields connected with agriculture. Experts are being sent to the fields to render technical advice and audio-visual demonstration services to rural populations. The United States Point Four Program and the Peace Corps especially have undertaken active roles in supplying technical service and advice to many Middle Eastern farmers. In October 1963 the Iranian Congress, inspired by the Shah's Six-Point Social Reform Program, passed the law to create the Educational Military Corps. Under this law, a portion of high school graduates eligible for military service are selected at random for the Educational Military Corps, and after some training they are sent to special centers in villages. The Iranian government has thus been able to make use of a portion of its military personnel to provide training and education for rural areas.

Community development programs have received particular attention in many Middle Eastern countries. In Iran, the establishment of village councils on regional and national levels was required by the decrees of August 14, 1952, and October 6, 1952, to assist the rural population in promoting the farmers' health and education. According to the latter decree, the landowner's share was reduced by 20 per cent, half of which was to go to the cultivator and the other half to the development and cooperative fund of the village. Of this latter amount, 70 per cent was to be spent for local improvements and the remaining 30 per cent for the betterment of larger cities. At the same time, several training schools were established in six provinces to improve the educational level of the rural population. Various types of pilot projects were undertaken in several parts of the country to arouse the cultivators' interest and incentives. See Figures 8.2, 8.3, and 8.4.

In Iraq, the responsibility for rural development has been given to a specially created ministry. Farmers' cooperatives have been

FIGURE 8.2. In Iran, under community development program based
on self-help and cooperation, some college student volunteers help
install a small but urgently needed irrigation pipe.

created throughout the country and various kinds of pilot projects
have been undertaken.

In Jordan, a community development institute was established
in conjunction with the United States Economic Mission in that
country. The primary aim of the Institute was to study and design
plans for rural development. The Ministry of Agriculture has expanded its scope of operation and services to people. Recently,
new programs in farm marketing news services and in agricultural
information have reached farmers for the first time. Rural development programs have received special attention under Jordan's
1964–1970 seven-year development program.

Briefly, the agricultural level of output has shown definite signs
of improvement in the Middle East during recent years. However,
due to the rate of population growth, the per capita increase in
farm output has been sluggish as compared with aggregate output.
The Index of Agricultural Output for the years 1959 to 1964 in
the region is shown in Table 8.4.

FIGURE 8.3. Under community development programs, Iranian farmers receive technical advice from college student volunteers who are directed by a group of experts. The pictures show two different, informal methods.

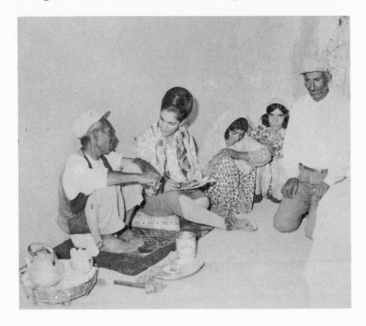

FIGURE 8.4. In Iran, under community development program, a farmer and his family receive advice and guidance from a community development worker.

Table 8.4. Index of Agricultural Production
1952–54 = 100

	1959		1961		1962		1963		1964	
	Total prod.	Prod. per capita	Total prod.	Prod. per capita	Total prod.	Prod. per capita	Total prod.	Prod. per capita	Total prod.	Prod. per capita
Middle East	122	105	125	103	134	108	138	109	140	107
Iran	126	110	131	108	130	105	141	111	124	95
Iraq	115	103	124	108	136	116	115	97	130	108
Jordan	72	61	147	118	88	68	92	69	199	145
Israel	193	154	218	165	143	175	241	167	268	180
Lebanon	101	87	118	97	128	102	136	105	140	105
Syria	90	71	109	80	172	122	152	104	160	106
Turkey	121	103	121	97	125	97	138	104	136	100
UAR	123	107	113	93	134	108	129	102	137	105
Afghanistan	114	101	113	97	119	99	117	96	121	98

Source: Statistics and Report Division, Agency for International Development, *Selected Economic Data for the Less Developed Countries* (June 1965), p. 20.

Chapter 9

PLANNING FOR ECONOMIC
DEVELOPMENT: OTHER POLICIES

According to the United Nations Economic Mission in the Middle East, industrialization must be treated as secondary to agricultural improvement efforts. This view does not disregard the importance of industrialization activities, but holds that industrial development in these areas must be dependent on and therefore preceded by agricultural development.

Industrial and agricultural development in underdeveloped countries complement each other's progress. Agricultural development supports industrial development by releasing the surplus rural population, by increasing the supply of food and raw materials, and by deepening the internal market for finished goods. Industrial development contributes to agricultural development by using the released labor force in more productive lines, by consuming the increased food products and raw materials, and by producing goods for rural consumption. Therefore, economic development in the Middle East should start with the agricultural sector, but industrialization also plays a decisive role in the success of development efforts.

INDUSTRIAL POLICY

Efforts for industrial development in a nation should be motivated by more than simply a desire for industrialization. Such policy should be based on the country's available resources, needs, and to some degree its comparative advantages. It is necessary to realize that true industrial development is not always achieved merely by heavy capital expenditures or even by superficial adoption of modern technology. Certain political, social, and cultural adjustments are also necessary.

The supply of such production factors as capital, technology, and human and natural resources varies from one country to another. For a successful industrialization program, the most suitable combination of these productive factors in the individual country must be found and utilized efficiently. A profitable combination of productive factors in one country may or may not be suitable for another country. A country's industrial policy must be tailor-made. It must be in harmony with and based on that country's characteristics. Industrialization in one country may begin in a completely different sector than it does in another country. In Sweden, for instance, industrial growth began with development in the lumber industry. In England, the industrial revolution started in coal and textile industries. The oil industry in several Middle Eastern countries seems to have started a similar drive for development.

Primary producing countries, such as the Middle Eastern countries, must conform to the following principles in planning industrial development:[1]

1. Those industries that utilize internal resources and raw materials must receive priority. Improvement in such industries will also contribute to the development of other economic sectors.

2. Expansion of industries requiring such scarce factors in the country as extensive capital, skilled workers, or raw materials must be avoided as much as possible.

3. The industrialization policy, at least during the early stages of economic development, must be directed to meet the increasing demand for consumer goods caused by heavy capital expenditure and a rise in agricultural income. Proper attention must therefore be given to the development of secondary industries in order to absorb a portion of the people's purchasing power. This is both to avoid an inflationary trend and to provide further incentives.

4. Industrial policy in an underdeveloped country must also be directed toward the country's self-sufficiency. This is to free the country from international fluctuations in price, demand, and supply, which are beyond the control of the national government and may interfere with that country's development process.

5. Production combinations suitable for most Middle Eastern

---

[1] The first three principles have also been suggested by the U.N. Conciliation Commission for Palestine, *Final Report of the UN Economic Survey Mission for the Middle East* (New York, December 1949), Part I, p. 63.

countries may in many aspects vary from those adopted by Western nations. As a result, no industrial devices should be taken over blindly from advanced nations unless they are modified to fit the exact economic and social condition of the using country. One must always remember that, as has already been pointed out, most economic theories developed by Western economists and based on Western economies do not necessarily correspond to the economic needs and situations of the Middle East. For example, the principle of comparative advantage, while it has assisted economic progress in Western countries, may on many occasions be profitably disregarded in the Middle East. A country like Jordan, suffering from acute unemployment problems, may actually gain by placing the idle workers in industries that show no comparative advantage but are easy to establish. The gain from such efforts lies primarily in reducing the volume of import and in lessening unemployment problems, not necessarily in increasing the over-all national production.

6. In designing plans for industrialization, considerable emphasis must be placed on using market forces, free competition, and private ingenuity. Private institutions, which are now unable to assume their expected functions in guiding the economy, must be developed so that they may eventually replace government functions.

Because of the shortage of entrepreneurial talent and the inefficiency of private leadership in most underdeveloped countries, their governments have found it necessary to assume responsibility and leadership in achieving industrial development. These governments have sought to induce industrialization directly by sponsoring certain industries and indirectly through financial, technological, legal, and political assistance. International economists, especially those advocating free international trade, have frequently questioned the wisdom of government protection of internal industries. Nurkse, for example, arguing against government protection of national industries, wrote: ". . . to put it bluntly, tariff protection, if it can help at all, can only help the strong—it cannot help the weak."[2] In other words, protective measures such as tariffs and quotas can do little to encourage capital formation in a country. The supply of capital

---

[2] R. Nurkse, *Problems of Capital Formation in Underdeveloped Countries* (New York: Oxford University Press, 1953), p. 106.

in most underdeveloped countries, because of the existing institutional obstacles, responds only slightly to such protective measures; and foreign capital is often engaged in fields that receive little or no benefit from government protection. On the other hand, Myrdal believes that the appeal to abolish industrial protective measures for the sake of international trade does have a "legitimate address,"[3] but only to industrially advanced countries.

Because industrialization in underdeveloped countries today faces certain unfavorable conditions that the presently advanced nations did not face, some degree of government protection is indeed justified. The Havana Conference on Trade and Employment, recognizing this fact and stimulated by efforts and recommendations by several Middle Eastern countries, "permits special government assistance, including measures against imports, if required for the establishment, development, and reconstruction of particular industries. . . ."[4]

Several Middle Eastern governments have assumed direct responsibility for improving national industries. In Iran, about 14.3 per cent of the first seven-year development funds, 16.1 per cent of the funds of the second plan, and 30 per cent of the third plan's funds were allocated for the development of industries and electric power.[5] Consumer industries, such as textile mills, sugar plants, cement plants, electric generators, and mining, have received special attention from the Plan Organization. The Industrial Bank has been expanded to provide financial assistance to the developing industries. Between 1957 and 1960 a total of $79,305,848 in loans was granted to larger industries and $1,755,390 to small industries. Of this amount, the textile industry received more than $24 million, sugar mills received more than $22 million, and the mining sector received more than $2 million.[6] Efforts are being made to increase the role

---

[3] G. Myrdal, *An International Economy; Problems and Prospects* (New York: Harper & Row, Publishers, Inc., 1956), p. 334.

[4] Article 13 of the Havana Charter of 1948.

[5] Iran Plan Organization, *Outline of the Third Plan* (Tehran, 1961), Table 4.1, p. 46.

[6] Department of Statistics and Research, Ministry of Information, *The Iranian Economy, Basic Changes* (Tehran, 1964), p. 9 (all rials have been changed to U.S. dollars at 75 rials to one dollar).

and contribution of the private sector in industrial development. Technical assistance has been provided to industries by the Plan Organization, cooperating with the United States Point Four Program in the country. The results of this aid have been very satisfactory.

During the last decade, industries have been established to produce products previously imported. New assembly lines have been installed to produce such consumer products as coolers, heaters, refrigerators, television sets, radio receivers, and motor vehicles. In the textile industry, for example, the number of spindles was increased from 200,000 in 1948 to 276,000 in 1954, and to 666,000 in 1962. Electric-power generation was increased from 550 million kwh in 1954 to 1500 million kwh in 1963. Sugar production was increased from 72,000 metric tons in 1953 to 177,000 metric tons in 1964. Cement production was increased from 53,000 metric tons in 1953 to about 750,000 metric tons in 1964.[7] Nationalization of the oil industry in 1951 was undoubtedly one of the most important events in Iran's industrial history. In 1954, an agreement was reached between the National Iranian Oil Company and a consortium of eight foreign companies. Under the terms of this agreement, the production of oil in Iran soon surpassed that produced by the Anglo-Iranian Oil Company. The greatest volume of oil production in Iran under the Anglo-Iranian oil agreement was 28.8 million metric tons in 1949. Iran produced 40.9 million metric tons of oil in 1958 and about 81 million metric tons in 1964.[8]

On March 2, 1959, the Iranian government, in cooperation with Western bankers, set up Iran's first Industrial Development Bank. This was a special effort to help spur internal and external private investment in the country. That same year, in an effort to meet minimum international standards, the Labor Act was passed. This law deals with such important measures as hours of work, holidays with pay, overtime, employment contracts, settlement of disputes, health, safety, and welfare. In 1960, a Worker's Social Insurance Law was passed. This legislation provides for a system of social

---

[7] Statistics and Reports Division, Agency for International Development, *Near East and South Asia Economic Growth* (Washington, D.C., September 1965), pp. 27–29.

[8] *Ibid.*, p. 28.

security benefits concerning, for example, accidents, sickness, retirement, death, maternity and other free medical attention.

In Iraq, the industrialization policy received considerable attention after World War II. According to the 1955 Law for the Encouragement of Industrial Undertakings, certain privileges were given to new and old industries through tax reductions, duty exemptions, and similar measures. A Minimum Wage Law was passed in 1955. Iraq's six-year development plan (1951/52–1956/57) set aside 19.9 per cent of its total funds for industrial and mining development. The five-year plan (1955/56–1959/60) allocated 14.4 per cent of its funds for a similar purpose. Kassim's Detailed Economic Plan (DEP) allocated 30 per cent of its total funds for industrial and power development. Iraq's Development Board and the Industrial Bank have supplied free technical assistance to private industries. Small industries especially have received attention and are being assisted by the Mortgage Bank (established in 1948) and the Loan Bank (established in 1951).

As the result of these efforts, definite improvement is noticeable in Iraq's level of industrial production. Cement production was increased from 177,000 metric tons in 1953 to a million metric tons in 1964. Sugar production was introduced, produced 1000 metric tons in 1960, and stood at 30,000 metric tons in 1962. The public consumption of electric power was increased from 342 million kwh in 1953 to 1063 million kwh in 1963.[9] The production of crude oil was increased from 28,186,000 metric tons in 1953 to 61,320,000 metric tons in 1964.

Iraq's DEP has allocated 166,800,000 Iraqi dinars for the country's industrial development. During recent years, many projects have either been started or completed in the country. The Karbala Canning Plant began production in 1962. A transistor-radio plant with an annual production capacity of 30,000 radios and 10,000 television sets was completed in 1963. In the same year a heater and cooking-stove plant was completed with an annual production capacity of 50,000 heaters and 100,000 cookstoves. Two industrial projects for artificial silk production and a cotton textile mill are expected to provide jobs for 1000 and 2000 workers respectively.

---

[9] *Ibid.*, pp. 27–29.

In 1964, a government dressmaking factory, which is expected to create jobs for 1000 workers, was completed. Under an agreement with the U.S.S.R., projects have begun in steel, electrical equipment, glassware, agricultural machinery, and cotton and woollen textiles.[10]

Generally speaking, Iraq's industrial policy is not yet clear. This can be attributed to the existing political instability in the country. In 1961, the Industrial Development Law exempted industrial equipment and raw materials from custom duties. It also exempted industries for 10 years from property taxes and from income tax, provided 90 per cent of an industry's nontechnical workers and 60 per cent of its capital is Iraqi.[11] In the meantime, the Industrial Bank provided easy financial credit to help industrial expansion. The Industrial Bank loaned out 569,000 Iraqi dinars in 1960, 968,000 in 1961, and 1,195,000 in 1962. The Industrial Development Law and the Industrial Bank's easy credit policy helped expand private capital expenditures in the industrial sector, probably for the 1964 kill. On July 14, 1964, the Iraqi government declared the nationalization of all banks, insurance companies, and 32 of the largest industrial and commercial concerns in the country. Among these nationalized industries were cement, asbestos, cigarette, spinning and weaving, steel, paper, leather tanning, and flour mills, as well as trading companies. Owners of the nationalized concerns were to be compensated by government bonds with 15-year maturity bearing 3 per cent interest.

In Jordan, industrial development has been limited by the lack of adequate internal resources and capital funds. The 1955 Law for Encouragement and Guidance of Industry has attempted to stimulate the flow of internal and external private capital into desirable industries through tax and duty exemption and by financial assistance. Other efforts to facilitate industrial development include Trade Union Law 35 of 1953 and Workman's Compensation Law 17 of 1955. Jordan's five-year development plan had allocated 6 million Jordanian dinars for industrial development. Because of financial inadequacy, most projects fell short of their goals. Two major industrial and agricultural projects are being considered under

---

[10] U.N. Department of Economic and Social Affairs, *Economic Development in the Middle East, 1961–1963* (New York, 1964), pp. 37–38.

[11] *Ibid.*, p. 38.

Jordan's recent seven-year development plan. The first is the Yarmuk Project, which also envisages the construction of two power plants. The second is an effort to exploit Dead Sea mineral resources. Other industrial projects that may receive priority in the near future are ceramics, fertilizers, pharmaceuticals, cardboard and paper, cotton and woollen textiles, food canning, and dairy products. Some industries have shown net growth during recent years in Jordan. Electric output was increased from 20 million kwh in 1958 to 40 million kwh in 1961. Cement production was increased from 114,000 metric tons in 1958 to 235,000 metric tons in 1962. Beer production was increased from 1000 hectoliters in 1958 to 7000 hectoliters in 1962. Cigarette production was increased from 737 tons in 1958 to 1020 tons in 1961.[12]

Development of mineral resources in most underdeveloped countries has proved to be one of the most important steps toward industrial and economic development, because such resources often attract foreign capital into the country and also because of the royalties collected for the exploitation of such resources. Examples of such utilization of resources for financing economic development are not hard to find. Oil revenues in Iran, Iraq, and Jordan—as well as in Venezuela—have served to finance the greater portion of those countries' development expenditures.

The government of Jordan, recognizing the importance of internal resources in financing economic development, has undertaken extensive exploration and resource development. The production of phosphates was increased from 164,000 metric tons in 1954 to 681,000 metric tons in 1962. On February 1, 1956, a 55-year oil concession was granted to an American company. In 1957, a similar concession was granted to a Guatemalan-Arab concern but was canceled in 1959. In 1963, Jordan produced 7048 metric tons of oil.

COMMERCIAL, FISCAL, AND FINANCIAL POLICY

Let us start our discussion with a simple example of the construction and operation of an automobile. An automobile is a combination of hundreds of individual parts that are made of different materials, look different, function differently, and are even made

---

[12] *Ibid.*, p. 39.

by different manufacturers. Further, a collection of all these parts does not necessarily create an automobile. These different parts must be skillfully put together and their functions coordinated and harmonized toward one purpose. Friction among the parts must be minimized by lubrication and their operation must be controlled by a central coordinator. For a completed automobile to function, it must be operated and guided by a capable driver through such devices as the ignition, steering wheel, and brakes. A small error by the driver could damage—or even completely destroy—the entire project.

Constructing and operating economic development programs in a country is, of course, more complicated than the process described above. While certain development projects must be designed and executed, their functions must also be coordinated toward the common objective. In many cases, the implementation of one or several projects may interfere with the operation of other programs; such contradictions must be eased without severely interfering with the nature of any program. For example, most underdeveloped countries require extensive social overhead capital expenditures. But such capital expenditures often lead to inflationary pressures that in many ways counteract the purpose of such expenditures. At this point, any measure to reduce the effects of inflation without interfering with social overhead capital expenditures is desirable.

Controlling and guiding various economic development activities toward a common objective is a highly difficult task. The ability to utilize measures for such control and guidance, moreover, is a power that can either help promote economic development or destroy a sector or the entire economy. This power must in consequence be entrusted to only the most capable hands and utilized with utmost caution and foresight.

The government's role in designing, directing, and coordinating various economic activities within a country has been recognized by most economists—to a limited extent by the classical followers and to a wider extent by modern economists. The ability of a government to make the right decision at the right time has often been a decisive factor in the speed and consistency of the development process. Any improvement in the government's ability to make the right decision will undoubtedly be an important contribution toward economic development itself. A government can guide and control various economic activities in a country either by passing public laws or by adopting fiscal measures and commercial policies.

FOREIGN TRADE

An underdeveloped country planning economic development, unless it isolates its economy from that of other parts of the world, will unavoidably show a growing rate of foreign trade and will have to face the problem of financing its rising imports. In the short run, imports may be financed from accumulated foreign exchange, gold reserves, foreign aid, or loans. In the long run, however, financing imports from such sources is neither possible nor desirable. This is because reserves of foreign exchange and gold are apt to be exhausted, and loans must be paid off. Consequently, unless a country is blessed with a heavy inflow of foreign capital or rich natural resources, attempts should be made to limit the imports to the most essential materials and to the nation's capacity for exportation. In other words, in the long run, imports must be financed from export revenues.

Improvement of the export position should receive considerable attention by underdeveloped countries shaping their industrial, agricultural, commercial, and fiscal policies. Once exports are raised, a corresponding increase in importation can be afforded. Such efforts by underdeveloped countries to promote export industries do not necessarily bring about a reduction in international trade; they may even contribute to the volume of international trade by supplying raw materials and semifinished goods needed by more advanced countries. Import restrictions by underdeveloped countries, while necessary to channel their foreign-exchange reserve into more suitable types of imports, do not necessarily mean import reduction, but rather a shift of emphasis from less to more essential imports. Table 9.1 shows that, despite the general increase in the volume of production in most underdeveloped (and developed) countries, the volume of both world exports and imports has increased considerably since 1938. Iran's industrialization objective has been declared as follows:

> The objective of industrialization in Iran is self-sufficiency . . . contrary to some belief, it is not the purpose of this self-sufficiency

Table 9.1. World Trade Volume by Sector
(in million U.S. dollars)

Area	Imports C.I.F.					Exports F.O.B.				
	1938	1948	1955	1960	1963	1938	1948	1955	1960	1963
World	25,400	63,600	98,400	134,900	161,100	23,500	57,400	93,600	127,800	153,500
Developed	17,900	41,200	64,900	88,900	110,200	15,200	36,700	60,600	85,400	103,400
Under-developed	5,800	18,600	24,300	30,000	32,000	5,900	17,100	23,700	27,300	31,500
Sterling	7,680	18,090	23,110	28,850	31,100	5,390	14,810	19,740	23,760	27,940
Free Trade(a)	6,290	12,880	17,520	22,690	26,050	4,150	9,560	13,760	18,220	21,760
Common Market(b)	5,130	10,650	19,840	29,590	40,340	4,360	6,680	18,920	29,730	37,550
Middle East	720	2,230	3,090	4,390	5,170	550	2,060	3,720	5,140	6,550

(a) United Kingdom, Denmark, Norway, Sweden, Austria, Portugal, Switzerland; (b) France, West Germany, Italy, Netherlands, Belgium.

Source: *U.N. Statistical Year Book, 1964* (New York: Department of Economic and Social Affairs, 1965), pp. 464–70.

to eliminate imports. No nation can today exist without foreign trade. . . . The purpose is to enable Iran to survive in times of international emergencies.[13]

The task of improving the balance of trade in underdeveloped countries is usually hindered either by the nature of their import–export situation or by their economic condition. The underdeveloped countries are generally producers and thus exporters of raw materials. Finished goods are their chief imports. While the international demand and price for raw materials are more flexible than their supply, the demand for finished goods by underdeveloped countries is less flexible than the supply of such commodities. In bad times, the price and volume of exports from underdeveloped countries fall faster than the price and volume of their imports. In good times, the supply of raw materials, being inelastic, cannot keep up with either the increasing demand by the advanced countries or the increasing volume of imports into underdeveloped countries. Furthermore, the shortage of raw materials often stimulates the industrialized nations to shift to synthetic materials. As a result and regardless of the economic condition, the balance of trade in underdeveloped countries often remains unfavorable. The traditional inflationary pressure in developing countries, moreover, tends to aggravate their unfavorable balance of trade by discouraging exports and encouraging imports. These unfavorable obstacles in underdeveloped countries can be removed or eased by certain structural reform in industries or through commercial and fiscal measures.

An underdeveloped country, striving to improve its balance of foreign trade, must undertake certain basic reforms in its industries. New industries must be established to produce consumer products to replace imports. Old export industries must be reformed and expanded, and new lines of export industries based on the country's comparative advantage must be developed. Efforts to promote export industries, however, should not become concentrated in one or a few lines. Differentiation in exports is essential to minimize the risks of international demand and price fluctuations. This is

---

[13] Department of Statistics and Research, Ministry of Information, *The Iranian Economy, Basic Changes* (Tehran, 1964), p. 15.

especially true in such countries as Iran and Iraq where the chief export is oil products. While today oil appears essential to the modern economy, it may not always remain so. Other forms of energy may sooner or later replace the use of petroleum—it has happened before and it can happen again. So, unless other export lines are developed in these countries, they may eventually face such obstacles as exhaustion of their oil reserves or a reduction in the world demand for petroleum. With this argument in mind, an official Iranian government publication declares: "Iran does not want to be only an agricultural nation, nor does it wish to specialize in oil. . . . The purpose is to preserve these industries and also diversify in other fields."[14]

Building new industries to reduce imports and to promote exports is only part of the industrialization task. These industries, at least in their early stages of growth, must be protected against more advanced foreign competitors, a result often achieved either through such commercial measures as custom duties and import restrictions or such fiscal policies as exchange control and tax exemption.

Promotion of export industries has not received adequate attention in most Middle Eastern countries. This lack of attention, at least in most oil-producing countries, can be attributed to the countries' lack of immediate need for such efforts. In fact, the proportion of oil exports to total exports in four major oil-producing countries in the Middle East has increased considerably in recent years. In Iran, the proportion of oil exportation to total exportation was increased from 53.7 per cent in 1938 to 93 per cent in 1964. In Iraq, the proportion of oil exportation to total exportation was increased from 57.4 per cent in 1951 to 90–95 per cent in 1964. Jordan, lacking such a rich resource, has encouraged its exports through export privileges, tax exemptions, and similar measures. But even in Jordan the greatest emphasis has been concentrated on developing two main resources —potash and phosphate.

In most Middle Eastern countries, import restrictions and promotion of the production of goods for importation substitutes have received wider attention than efforts to promote exports. Development of such consumption industries as sugar plants, tea-processing

---

[14] *Ibid.*, p. 15.

plants, textile mills, and soap factories has become the most important part of the industrialization policy in these countries. Various commercial and fiscal measures—such as exchange control, import restrictions and rationing, simple and multiple custom duties, and even barter agreements with other nations—are extensively utilized by the Middle Eastern countries.

FISCAL AND FINANCIAL POLICY

Improvements in a country's balance of trade makes little or no contribution toward capital formation and increases in the production level unless the additional income is somehow channeled into productive investment. This is because such an increase in people's disposable income caused by lower importation will have no constructive effect on the economy if the money remains idle (a condition termed *leakage*) or if it is used to bid on the existing stock of consumer goods, thus contributing to the forces of inflation. A fundamental reform in socioeconomic habits therefore remains the most important step for economic development. The task of guiding a nation's consumption and investment habits can be carried out partly through cultural and socioeconomic reforms and partly by fiscal measures.

Because changing a nation's cultural and social habits is a long-term task, and because human behavior can seldom be anticipated and often is not consistent with the growth process, fiscal policies remain a major short-run measure for the success of development programs. Through its fiscal policies, a government may seek to achieve one of these objectives:

1. *More equal distribution of income.* Private savings seldom flow into investment in underdeveloped countries. An effort to bring more equal distribution of income can thus help increase the level of consumption without hindering the rate of capital formation. An underdeveloped country can pursue this goal through such fiscal policies as progressive wealth and income taxation, social security, and old-age pensions.

2. *Reduce inflationary pressure.* Heavy capital expenditures on social overhead investments in an underdeveloped country often result in inflationary pressure. This is because such capital expenditures, while increasing the people's disposable income, do not bring

an immediate increase in the supply of consumer goods. Through various forms of direct and indirect taxation, the government of an underdeveloped country can reduce this inflationary pressure by absorbing the excess disposable income.

3. *Direct savings into needed investment.* One of the major obstacles in underdeveloped countries is that the existing private savings, scarce as they are, seldom flow into productive investments. Through fiscal measures such as tax exemption and subsidies, the government can channel available savings into the most desirable fields.

4. *Help reallocate disguised unemployment.* Several economists have suggested that to a great extent economic development can be achieved by diverting the disguised unemployment from farm to industrial sectors. This in itself can increase the level of production in the country because, while production and consumption of food materials remain unchanged, a large number of the people who were idle on farms now become productive in industries. There is one major problem involved, however. That is the question of how the excess farm production can be removed from the agricultural sector and transferred for use by the industrial population. Fiscal measures can both remove the excess production from farms and transfer these materials to the industrial sector.

5. *Maintain economic stability.* Aside from the inherent financial difficulties, most underdeveloped countries are strongly receptive to international financial and commercial crisis. An underdeveloped country can, through complementary financial and fiscal policy, maintain some degree of economic stability in the face of internal and external disturbances.

Until recently, the efficient administration of fiscal measures in most Middle Eastern countries was hindered by institutional resistance, lack of know-how, and inefficient public administration. Since the early 1950s, however, some basic reforms in fiscal administration and policy-making have appeared in most Middle Eastern countries. The United States Technical Administration Program and several international agencies have actively supplied technical assistance to the requesting countries. In Saudi Arabia, a sound and independent monetary system was established in 1952 with the aid of United States technical assistance. In Iraq, Egypt, Israel, Kuwait, Saudi Arabia, and Iran, new financial institutions were established and the older ones were improved. In public finance, income taxation has been in effect in all the Middle Eastern countries since 1938. Such taxes as those on lands, wealth, and income have also appeared as corrective measures in most parts of the Middle East. In Iran, for example, these improvements have been observed since the early 1950's:

1. A system of income taxation has been introduced.

2. Improvements are evident in budgetary administration.

3. Efforts are being made to improve the accounting system of the government's industrial and commercial enterprises.

4. Gradual improvements are evident in the accounting procedures of ministries.

5. A central banking system, in operation since March 22, 1961, is expected to improve the development of privately owned commercial banks.

6. A system of financial-stabilization programs has been in operation since 1959.

The monetary policy in a country affects the rate and smoothness of its economic progress. A mild inflationary trend often helps stimulate social and economic development. It increases the profit margin and thus encourages investment ventures. It facilitates the process of capital formation by increasing voluntary and forced savings potentials. It reduces the monetary value of imports necessary for development projects. And it reduces social resistance to institutional changes. A mild inflationary trend may, however, lead to two major problems: (1) it can harm the country's export industries by gradually raising the price level; (2) it may sooner or later get out of control and become runaway inflation. Runaway inflation can become an evil for the economy just as mild inflation can help bring a faster and smoother process of economic development.

Regardless of the cause of inflation, its effects on the economy and especially on export industries can be reduced through various fiscal and financial measures. Such measures, especially those which tend to curb the effects of inflation on export industries, have been widely utilized in the Middle East. Iraq and Jordan, for instance, following

the 1949 devaluation of the pound sterling, devaluated their monetary unit. In Iran, the value of the rial has fallen from $1=32.5
rials in 1950 to $1=44.5 rials in 1956, and very recently to $1=75.5
rials. These monetary devaluations have contributed to the reduction of the price of export materials in foreign countries.

REGIONAL PLANNING

Planning for economic development is not merely a national obligation; it is also a regional affair. Some development efforts must
start on a national level, but even these efforts can achieve better
results if they are accompanied by regional cooperation. Certain
other development measures can achieve better results if they are
designed and implemented on the regional rather than national
level.

The need for regional planning is especially important in the
Middle East. This is mainly because the economic, social, and
natural resources in the region are so unevenly distributed that
their optimum utilization can be achieved only through close regional cooperation. The United Nations Conciliation Commission
for Palestine, emphasizing this fact, reported:

> Each country of the Middle East will sooner or later learn that the
> resources of its neighbors have an important and frequently deter-
> mining influence upon the economic growth of each individual
> country.[15]

Regional cooperation is indeed a very important precondition for
well-balanced economic development in the Middle East. In almost
every economic, social, and political effort for progress one may
find evidence pointing to the extreme need for better regional cooperation. The following seven points are some of the major benefits
Middle Eastern countries can enjoy through regional efforts and
cooperation.

1. The economic development in Egypt, Syria, and especially
Jordan has undoubtedly been burdened by the inflow of Arab

---

[15] United Nations, Conciliation Commission for Palestine, *Final Report of
the United Nations Economic Survey Mission for the Middle East* (New York,
December 1949), Part I, p. viii.

refugees. But Iraq alone can absorb all of the Arab refugees. In this manner Iraq can not only contribute toward the economic well-being of its neighbors but can also use this additional source of population better to develop its own resources.

2. While Iran, Iraq, Kuwait, and Saudi Arabia enjoy large revenues from oil production, certain other countries (such as Jordan, Afghanistan, and Egypt) are handicapped by the lack of capital necessary to undertake their programs for development. A transfer of capital from the former to the latter countries can benefit both sides. Exploiting the surplus capital funds from the oil-producing countries will:

    a. assure their future prosperity

    b. control their internal inflationary pressure

    c. reduce a tendency for wasteful projects in the rich countries

    d. improve the potential market for export industries by raising the level of income in the region.

The borrowing country, on the other hand, will benefit from utilizing such capital to improve its economy.

3. In certain fields, some of the Middle Eastern countries have acquired skills that can be of great assistance to their neighbors trying to develop in similar fields. Exchange of such technical information can greatly assist the region's progress as a whole.

4. Social and economic activities, especially those dealing with interregional problems, require regional attack on the problems. For instance, programs for education, health improvement, disease eradication, communications and transportation improvement require close regional understanding, coordination, and cooperation.

5. Closely related to the argument above is the fact that industrial development in most Middle Eastern countries has been plagued by the countries' small populations and thus small market. In the meantime, throughout the region the supply of consumer goods is far below demand. Removal of trade barriers among the countries in the region will undoubtedly stimulate incentives for investment ventures by widening the market as well as help allocate industries on the basis of comparative advantage.

6. Better utilization of some natural resources in the Middle East definitely requires regional cooperation and understanding. A better utilization of the Jordan and the Yarmuk rivers depends on better

understanding and cooperation among Jordan, Syria, and Israel. A part of Shat-el-Arab, which wastefully flows into the Persian Gulf, can be diverted to give or sell water to wealthy Kuwait and its surrounding areas. Much of the natural gas in oil-producing countries is wastefully burned, but it could be used to produce energy for neighboring countries.

7. Regional security measures will be more effective against any form of foreign intervention than national measures.

Generally speaking, there has been little or no regional cooperation among underdeveloped countries. In the Middle East in particular, most efforts for regional understanding and cooperation have been severely hampered by national prejudice, lack of political stability and responsibility, and at times foreign colonial intervention. For many years Iraq, Jordan, Egypt, Palestine, and most countries in the Arabian Peninsula had a very close economic and political relationship with Great Britain. Syria was very close to France. Other more or less independent countries had very little chance to acquire any neighborly agreement with such colonized countries without becoming involved in negotiations with the colonial powers. This the independent nations of the Middle East were anxious to avoid. The independence of Israel, the problems of the Arab refugees, and especially the existing rivalry among a few Arab nations over Arab leadership have brought a new challenge for regional cooperation in the Middle East. Whenever the Middle Eastern nations can learn the true meaning of peaceful coexistence, when they can learn the meaning of unity for the sake of unity and not influence, and when they can reach a regional understanding of such caliber that common interests become superior to those of individuals, the economic and political progress in the region will have taken its first giant step.

THE ARAB LEAGUE

Despite the existing obstacles, attempts at regional cooperation have been made during the last two decades in the Middle East and some successful results have been achieved. The foundation of the Arab League is one of such attempts.

By 1943 most Arab countries (except Palestine) had more or less achieved their independence. For the first time they were able

freely to follow their longtime dream of Arab unity. In the fall of
1944 an Arab Conference met in Alexandria and formulated the
so-called Alexandria Protocol that drew the outline for an Arab
League. On March 22, 1945, the League was officially organized
at a meeting in Cairo. The original members were Egypt, Iraq, Saudi
Arabia, Lebanon, Jordan, and Yemen. Other Arab nations joining
the League were Libya (in March 1953), Sudan (January 1956),
Tunisia and Morocco (October 1958), Kuwait (July 1961), and
Algeria (August 1962). The Alexandria Protocol, recognizing that
complete unity or even an Arab federation was impossible, suggested unity through a league of sovereign states. The functions of
the League included mediation of any dispute that threatens the
peace of an area. There was also a plan for an all-Arab financial
organization to help develop the Arab states. The compact was
signed by Saudi Arabia, Jordan, Syria, and Yemen. In 1953, the establishment of an Arab Bank was proposed and accepted in the
Conference of Ministers of Finance and National Economy of the
Arab League to grant loans to governments or to development
agencies of member countries. In 1954, a plan for developing
Jordan's potash mines was introduced by the Arab League. A corporation was to be established for such a purpose, with Jordan
paying 750,000 Jordanian dinars in three years and with 3,650,000
Jordanian dinars of common stock to be sold in other Arab countries. Members of the Arab League guaranteed to cover other expenses and to exempt the corporation from taxes for a period of
10 years.

INDIVIDUAL CONFERENCES

Several conferences in social, economic, and political fields have
been held in the Middle East and suggestions for better regional
cooperation and policy-making have been submitted to participating
countries. Today, bilateral trade agreements exist among all countries in the Middle East; several multilateral trade and strategic
treaties also exist. In 1953, a trade agreement was consummated
between Syria and Jordan and a joint project was planned for the
utilization of the Yarmuk River. In 1956, the Arab League agreed
to help finance a company to be established in Jordan to exploit
potash from the Dead Sea. In January 1957, Egypt, Syria, and

Saudi Arabia signed a 10-year treaty with Jordan to supply that country with money and arms to replace the deficit caused by the withdrawal of British subsidy. In 1962 Saudi Arabia and Jordan signed an agreement on measures of cooperation in military, political, and economic fields. The same year Kuwait loaned Jordan 7.5 million Jordanian dinars (about $21,375,000).

The Baghdad Pact was undoubtedly the most important multilateral defense pact in the Middle East. It linked the Middle East with two major international defense organizations, NATO and SEATO. The Baghdad Pact, a mutual defense agreement, was signed on February 24, 1955, by Turkey, Iran, Iraq, Pakistan, and Great Britain. In April 1956 the United States became a member of the Economic Committee and Counter-Subversion Committee, in March 1957 a member of the Military Committee, and in May 1961 a member of the Scientific Council. The United States furthermore maintained observers at the Council meetings. A bilateral defense treaty was signed in Ankara on March 5, 1959, by the United States, Turkey, Iran, and Pakistan. On March 24, 1959, Iraq formally withdrew from the Baghdad Pact, and on August 21, 1959, the name was changed to Central Treaty Organization (CENTO).

THE ARAB COMMON MARKET

The longtime dream of unity in the Arab world has also led to the idea of creating a common market in the area. In the early 1950s an agreement was reached between Egypt, Jordan, Lebanon, and Saudi Arabia to reduce custom duties and to facilitate trade payments and the movement of capital among the participating countries. The full implementation of this agreement was delayed, however, by difficulties among the interested parties. In July 1957 a similar objective was pursued through an Agreement on Economic Unity by Jordan, Saudi Arabia, the United Arab Republic, Syria, Lebanon, Iraq, Kuwait, Yemen, Sudan, Libya and Western country (Morocco)—an agreement that was also discontinued because of difficulties in unification of such a vast area.

On April 13, 1964, an agreement to create an Arab Common Market was finally signed in Cairo by representatives of the United Arab Republic, Iraq, Jordan, Syria, and Kuwait. The plan went into operation January 1, 1965. Membership in the Arab Common Mar-

ket is open to all Arab League states; its basic objectives are to
provide for:

1. Freedom of movement for persons and capital
2. Freedom of movement for commodities within each country
and among the members
3. Freedom of stay for citizens of member countries in any other
member country
4. Freedom of movement of goods and transit as well as transportation equipment, and free access to seaport and airport facilities
5. The right of citizens of each member country to own property
and receive inheritance in another member country.

The Arab Common Market seeks achievement of these objectives
through the implementation of the following policies:

1. To create one commercial custom area within the territories
of member countries and to enforce similar regulations
2. To create similar import-export policies among members
3. To encourage similar transportation and transit policies among
members
4. To reach commercial agreements with other nations on a group
level
5. To bring coordination among members' agricultural and industrial policies, as well as efforts for economic development
6. To encourage cooperative efforts for social improvements
7. To coordinate taxes and duties among the member countries
8. To coordinate financial policies among its members
9. To unify statistical methods used by members
10. To undertake any other action necessary to obtain the first
two objectives.

The Arab Common Market has sought to abolish custom duties on
agricultural products and natural resources within five years by
reducing their tariff at an annual rate of 20 per cent. Toward a
similar objective in industry, the Arab Common Market members
have agreed to reduce custom duties on industrial products at an
annual rate of 10 per cent.

No doubt the Arab Common Market may help solve many of the
existing obstacles to the economic development of the Middle East.

But the success of this organization will have to depend on the ability of Arab countries to settle their differences and quarrels.

PROGRAM FOR ASIAN DEVELOPMENT BANK

In December 1963, at the request of ministers of 21 Asian nations, the United Nations Commission on Asia and the Far East began preparation of the Asian Development Bank. This bank is expected to function in ways similar to those of the Inter-American Development Bank, which began in October 1960, and the African Development Bank, which was organized in September 1964. In October 1964, a report of the *ad hoc* group of experts on the Asian Development Bank was sent to the member nations and to interested parties. A consultative committee was set up in March 1965. The members of this committee are Ceylon, India, Iran, Japan, Malaysia, Pakistan, Philippines, the Republic of Vietnam, and Thailand.

The Bank's major objectives are:

1. To attract new and additional capital to member countries
2. To provide loans for such programs as were not feasible up to now because of either the secondary nature of the program or inadequate capital
3. To encourage regional economic cooperation.

Other functions of the Bank include:

1. Loans for special projects
2. Loan to industries or sharing in local or regional investments
3. Loan to government agencies for public works
4. Loan or share in creating consortium to attract foreign capital, aid, and in implementation of development programs
5. Provide technical assistance in designing and implementing development programs
6. Bring regional economic cooperation and coordination to better implement economic development programs.

The Bank's capital is expected to reach the billion-dollar mark. This capital is to be gathered from membership, loans from other countries, financial markets, or international agencies as well as from grants-in-aid.

Chapter 10

PARTICIPATION OF THE UNITED STATES IN THE ECONOMIC DEVELOPMENT OF THE MIDDLE EAST

Assuming degree of economic growth as the basis for the flow of international capital and technology, the United States appears a logical source for the export of capital and technology to the rest of the world. This chapter therefore examines the development of United States aid in general and its application in the Middle East in particular, and makes an effort to evaluate the existing aid relationship between the United States and most Middle Eastern countries.

THE UNITED STATES AND FOREIGN AID

Present United States policy concerning international aid is rooted deep in the nation's historical background, as well as in more recent economic and political developments. Historically, the people of the United States have, since the foundation of the country, stood ready to extend a hand to other friendly countries in time of trouble —the result of certain cultural ties between the people of the United States with "old countries" as well as the development of a democratic and pioneer culture.

On May 8, 1812, foreign relief was given by the United States for the first time. Fifty-thousand dollars' worth of medicine and other relief materials was voted by the United States Congress to aid victims of a Venezuelan earthquake. In 1847, several vessels containing American relief shipments were sent to help the starving people of Ireland and Scotland. In 1871 several shiploads of relief materials from American people went to France and Germany to help relieve the famine there. On May 2, 1902, the United States Congress voted $200,000 to aid the victims of a volcanic eruption on the island of Martinique. In 1907, material relief was sent to the victims of an earthquake in Jamaica. In 1909, Congress appropriated $800,000 to help alleviate the suffering of earthquake victims in Messina, Italy.

All of the United States aid prior to World War I, and most of the aid during and immediately following World War I, was based on humanitarian objectives and was allocated for relief purposes. The emergence of the United States foreign aid policy as it now exists is the result of recent economic, political, and strategic developments.

DEVELOPMENT OF PRESENT UNITED STATES POSITION

For a long time after securing its political independence, the United States, as a result of its concern for internal problems, followed a policy of isolation, except for the handling of troubles that immediately threatened the security of the country. Two world wars, nevertheless, thrust the relatively new nation into the role of the world's leading political and economic power.

At the end of World War I, after having played a decisive role in terminating the European conflict, the United States came very close to playing a leading political role in the world. But the significance of the United States' position as a great power was not yet perceived. Senate ratification of United States membership in the League of Nations, for example, was lost by one vote. In many cases, the country not only failed to adopt policies suitable to its position as a creditor nation, but adopted commercial policies suitable for a debtor nation. It was during this period that the world saw a quick shift of economic and strategic power from Europe to North America.

The threat of World War II to the security and ideology of the United States and the events which followed proved to the American people that no country, especially one as strong and highly industrialized as the United States, can remain unaffected by international events. Such a country must participate in world affairs to protect its own economic and political interests, to help its friends in need, to resist aggressive forces, and to help prevent the possi-

bility of World War III. The destruction of Europe during World
War II and the existence of many Communist-subjected underdeveloped countries were direct hazards to both United States'
security and world peace. All these factors established the need
for a policy to aid the underdeveloped countries in their efforts
for economic development.

OBJECTIVES OF UNITED STATES FOREIGN AID POLICY

The foreign economic policy of the United States is determined
by three independent and sometimes contradictory factors: Domestic interests, international political and strategic considerations, and
humanitarian and/or universal idealism. The humanitarian idealism
is, however, often mixed with the other two factors and can hardly
be distinguished in the formulation of a long-run policy.

The United States has based much of its long-term foreign
economic policy on the belief that peace and prosperity are indi-
visible. In other words, it is the basic long-run objective of the
United States to gain world peace through prosperity. President
Truman reiterated in his 1949 inaugural address that foreign
assistance must contribute to "a world wide effort for the achievement of peace, plenty, and freedom." He went on to say that
"greater production is the key to prosperity and peace. . . ."[1]

World peace is believed to be more easily attainable if a certain
degree of international prosperity and equality exists. Meanwhile,
international equality and prosperity are reflections of more efficient
use of resources and greater international trade and cooperation.
Local and regional economic and political disturbances affect the
entire world. In the light of what has been discussed, one may
classify United States foreign aid objectives into three categories,
the primary purpose of which is world peace and prosperity:
(1) economic objectives that seek to improve world prosperity
and reduce inequality, (2) strategic and political objectives, which
strive to improve local, regional, and international security, and
(3) humanitarian objectives, which aim to uphold universal idealism
and reduce human suffering.

The long-run objectives of United States foreign aid policy, being

[1] President Truman's Inaugural Address, January 20, 1949, *U.S. Department
of State Bulletin* (January 30, 1949), p. 125.

based on certain factors deeply rooted in the institutional structure of the country, enjoy some degree of consistency. But the short-run objectives and thus the emphasis of the country's foreign aid programs have varied to meet changing needs and conditions. Such changes in the United States' short-run policy have nevertheless not altered the country's fundamental foreign economic policy.

Since the start of World War II, United States foreign aid policy has been classified into these four categories:

1. United States foreign aid policy during World War II (from July 1940 to June 1945).

2. United States foreign aid policy between the end of World War II and the beginning of the Korean War (from 1945 to 1950).

3. United States foreign aid policy during and immediately after the Korean War.

4. United States foreign aid policy since the mid-1950's.

Because World War II directly threatened American security and idealism, the immediate objectives of the United States aid policy were to help its democratic Allies fight the common enemy and to satisfy the immediate consumption needs of its Allies as well as those of occupied areas. This period was especially highlighted by such programs as the Lend-Lease Program, relief programs for occupied areas, and direct participation in the United Nations Relief and Rehabilitation Programs. During this period, $47,112,050,000 were given to Allies through Lend-Lease programs. The Defense Department alone contributed $807,260,000 under the civilian supplies programs. Voluntary aid by the Red Cross in this period amounted to $62,163,000. Meanwhile, $1,095,562,000 of credit under various programs was extended by several United States agencies to foreign countries.[2]

World War II left the world in poor condition. Almost all European industries were destroyed or shut down. World trade, except for one-way shipments of goods out of the United States, was at its lowest level. Millions of people were homeless, starving, and helpless. All of these conditions threatened world peace. It therefore became the primary postwar objective of United States foreign

[2] Figures from U.S. Department of Commerce, A Supplement to the Survey of Current Business, *Foreign Aid by the United States Government, 1940–1951,* (Washington, D.C.: Government Printing Office, 1952), pp. 85–96.

policy in general, and its foreign aid policy in particular, to attain a just and lasting world peace. In pursuing this aim, the United States emphasized such aid policies as the promotion of nondiscriminatory world trade and financial relations, help in the reconstruction of destroyed areas, and assistance to the unfortunate people of the world through various relief and rehabilitation programs. Some of the major programs during this period were the Interim Program, the Greek-Turkish Program, the China Aid Program, the European Recovery Program, the Korean Aid Program, and the Palestine Refugee Program. At the same time, the United States directly participated in many United Nations programs such as the Post-United Nations Relief and Rehabilitation Assistance (UNRRA), the United Nations International Children's Emergency Fund (UNICEF), and the International Refugee Organization. During the fiscal years 1946 through 1949, $9,842,802,000 in credits and $14,462,028,000 in grants were extended by the United States under various programs.

The occurrence of Korean hostilities and several other strategic incidents indicated that economic recovery programs could not by themselves attain the United States objective of world peace. To obtain this objective, economic aid programs would have to have been accompanied by certain military strength and the economic cooperation of the free world. Then, together with other international problems, communism appeared as a major threat to the free world's peace and security. The primary objective of U.S. foreign aid policy, therefore, became the counteraction of Soviet activities and the assurance of the internal and external security of friendly nations. Most of the United States aid during 1950–1951 (amounting to $9,138,110,000 in grants and $839,420,000 in credits) was thus allocated under Mutual Defense Assistance Programs. Recognizing that security in most underdeveloped areas is a direct result of social content and economic improvement, the Technical Cooperation Administration Programs (Point Four) were launched at that time.

By the end of the Korean hostilities and the abolishment of the immediate threat of a possible World War III, the short-run emphasis of United States foreign aid policy was shifted to bring basic structural development to the free world. This change of policy was mainly the result of the realization that any threat to world peace affecting all nations must be met by the cooperative efforts of all free, progressive, strong, and equal nations—not by one country and its satellites. Military and other strategic aid programs under Mutual Security Assistance Programs have remained unchanged. Together with these programs, the United States, through its Point Four, Food for Peace, and other similar programs or long-term development loans, has undertaken a positive attitude toward the development of friendly underdeveloped countries. A summary of United States foreign aid since the end of World War II is presented in Table 10.1.

THE COMPONENTS OF UNITED STATES FOREIGN AID

In fairness, any discussion of United States foreign aid must not be restricted to the recent financial and technical assistance abroad. It must also include the outflow of direct private investments and loans, the United States' commercial policies, and its international treaties and relations. But because this chapter is concerned mainly with direct United States participation in the economic development of the Middle East, and since other factors have generally been coordinated with this country's foreign aid policy, nondirect aid will not be treated in this book.

CREDITS AND GRANTS

Generally speaking, United States foreign aid in its recent form has been extended either through credits or grants. The U.S. Department of Commerce has defined credits as "loans or other agreements which give rise to specific obligations to repay over a period of years, usually with interest."[3] Grants were defined as "outright gifts for which no payment is expected, on which at most involves an obligation on the part of the receiver to assist the United States or other countries working toward our common objective."[4]

Credit may be extended to a foreign country either directly, through a United States government agency, or through international or private channels. In the latter case, these credits may

---

[3] U.S. Department of Commerce, *Foreign Aid by the United States Government, 1940–1951*, p. 2.

[4] *Ibid.*, p. 1.

Table 10.1. U.S. Foreign Grants (net obligation) and Loans (authorized) (fiscal year—in $1,000,000)

Year	Economic & Military	Economic Programs			Military Programs			Others
		Total	Grants	Loans	Total	Grants	Loans	
1946–65	116,090	81,443	49,191	32,252	34,647	32,354	556	1,738
1946–48	15,125	14,644	6,586	8,058	481	—	—	481
1949–52	22,383	19,541	16,082	3,458	2,842	2,517	—	324
1953–57	29,141	13,833	10,391	3,443	15,307	14,848	15	444
1958	5,341	2,936	1,727	1,210	2,404	2,325	39	41
1959	5,667	3,507	1,739	1,768	2,160	2,050	60	50
1960	5,143	3,298	1,958	1,340	1,845	1,697	21	127
1961	5,670	4,204	2,166	2,039	1,466	1,344	30	91
1962	6,441	4,915	2,267	2,647	1,527	1,427	21	79
1963	6,836	4,956	2,229	2,726	1,881	1,765	44	71
1964	6,237	4,714	2,043	2,670	1,523	1,415	83	26
1965	6,208	4,895	2,002	2,893	1,313	1,239	71	2

Source: Agency for International Development, *U.S. Overseas Loans and Grants and Assistance From International Organizations*, July 1, 1945–June 30, 1965 (Statistics and Report Division, Washington, D.C., March 18, 1966), p. 5.

be insured by a United States agency. Foreign grants have also been supplied through three different channels: U.S. government agencies, U.S. private individuals or agencies, and international agencies. As shown in Table 10.2, from the total $116.090 billion of United States aid since 1946, more than 71 per cent has been in grants.

MAJOR UNITED STATES FOREIGN AID PROGRAMS

All the United States foreign aid programs have either economic and/or military objectives. In some cases one may easily distinguish and classify these programs as having economic or military objectives. In other cases this recognition becomes difficult. Many military aid programs also seek economic ends and most decidedly affect the economic well-being of the aid-receiving countries. On the other hand, many economic programs may also seek military and strategic objectives. From the total of $116.090 billion in foreign aid given by the United States since 1946, $81.443 billion, or 70 per cent, has been classified economic aid (Table 10.1).

United States economic aid plans have been extended under numerous programs. Some of these plans, such as the Marshall Plan or Technical Cooperation Assistance, are very comprehensive and have included United States involvement in many countries over many years. But there are also certain specific programs, such as the Civilian Relief Program in Korea, the Philippine Rehabilitation Program, and Greek–Turkish Aid, which cover United States involvement in a certain area and at a certain time. Some of the major comprehensive American foreign aid programs are:

1. *The Lend-Lease Act of March 11, 1941.* The major purpose of this act was to win the war. This goal was sought by providing the Allied nations defense materials either by sale, lease, or gift.

2. *United Nations Relief and Rehabilitation Assistance and Post-UNRRA.* Through these two programs the United States contributed $3.442 billion.

3. *The Export-Import Bank of Washington.* The capital of this bank was increased and the bank became a major agency in providing loans to foreign countries. In December 1945, this bank provided a $3.75 billion loan to Great Britain.

4. *Interim Aid Program.* This agency was created on December

Table 10.2. Distribution of U.S. Aid: Grants and Credits
(in $1,000,000)

	1946–65	1946–48	1949–52	1953–57	1958–61	1962	1963	1964	1965
Total........	116,090	15,125	22,383	29,141	21,821	6,441	6,836	6,237	6,208
Credits	32,807	8,058	3,458	3,457	6,485	2,668	2,770	2,753	2,964
Grants	83,283	7,067	18,924	25,686	15,315	3,773	4,066	3,484	3,244

Source: Same as for Table 10.1.

17, 1947, to supplement the Post-UNRRA works. This program was justified by Congress as a "stop-communism" or "anti-Russian" measure.[5]

5. *The Economic Cooperation Act of 1948.* This program, better known as the Marshall Plan, was designed to bring economic recovery to Europe. This goal was sought through United States aid and cooperative efforts on the part of the European nations.

6. *Technical Cooperation Assistance Program.* This program, better known as the Point Four Program, began with the Act for International Development of September 1950. By providing the underdeveloped countries technical assistance this program seeks to help such countries help themselves in attaining their economic goals.

7. *Food for Peace Program.* This program started under Public Law 480, the Agricultural Trade Development and Assistance Act of July 10, 1954; the act provides for the sale of surplus agricultural goods for foreign currencies. This foreign currency is then given to the aid-receiving countries to use under one of the four titles of the act, as specified in the agreement.

8. *Peace Corps.* Since its beginning the United States has spent $246 million on this international aid program.

During the period between 1946 and 1965, the United States has made $1540 million capital subscription to four major international organizations, including $635 million to the International Bank of Reconstruction and Development, $550 million to the Inter-American Development Bank, $320 million to the International Development Association, and $35 million to the International Finance Corporation. During the same years, the United States extended more than $1.049 billion through various other international agencies.

DEVELOPMENT OF UNITED STATES AID
IN THE MIDDLE EAST

The reasons behind the United States' present interest in the Middle East lie not only in the recent shift of the world economic

---

[5] See *Hearing on Interim Aid*, House of Representatives, Committee on Foreign Affairs, 80th Congress, 1st session, November 1947, pp. 39–40.

and strategic leadership in favor of the United States, but also in the strategic and economic importance of the Middle East. It is therefore proper to include here a discussion of the development of the economic and strategic position of the Middle East in the free world, which has led to special interest on the part of the West concerning any development in the area.

FACTORS LEADING TO THE MIDDLE EAST'S PRESENT POSITION

The Middle East has often been referred to as the "center of creation," and the nations of the region have long played determining roles in world history. This influence is not only a result of the fact that the region has produced powerful empires and conquerors, but also because here have developed such civilizations as the Hellenic,[6] Byzantine, and Islamic, which have influenced world civilization in the past as well as the present.

Beginning with the eighth century the Middle Eastern nations, after a long period of political and cultural leadership in the world, were gradually driven into a state of semi-isolation that lasted for several centuries. This period of isolation was partly the result of regional events and partly caused by external developments. Internally, most of the Middle Eastern nations were, during this period, occupied with several religious and political wars, which were to destroy most of their wealth and communications systems and aggravate their social problems. Moreover, the development of religious prejudice against the non-Moslem world blocked the way for East–West commercial and social integration. Externally, most of the Western nations were also too much occupied with their own internal developments and political struggles to pay any attention to the Middle East. The discovery and substitution of the Cape Route for the traditional Silk Route (which crossed through the Middle East) was a major blow that furthered the region's isolation. During this period economic and social conditions in the Middle East began to deteriorate and consequently fell behind those of the Western civilization, which had then begun to develop. The outcome of these trends was the shift of political, economic, and cultural leadership from the Middle East to the West.

With the development of colonial power in Europe, the Middle

---

[6] Hellenism, though started in Greece, reached its peak in the Middle East, after it was introduced in the region by Alexander the Great and his followers.

East regained some of its lost importance. Now the untapped resources, the raw materials, and the potential markets of the region created a point of interest for Western imperialists. Soon afterward the strategic importance of the region as the crossroads of the three continents was recognized by the West. Competition began to develop among such great imperialist powers as Great Britain, France, and Russia to gain control in the area. In recognition of the strategic position of the Middle East, both Napoleon and Peter the Great repeatedly indicated that whoever controlled this region could rule the world.

By the end of the nineteenth century, the strategic position of the Middle East was especially improved by the discovery of oil in the region, the development of Germany as a great power seeking privileges in the area, and Great Britain's firm stand against Russian expansion in Iran. Meanwhile, because of improvements in communications and some degree of integration with the West, the people of the Middle East finally became aware that they were behind in development when compared with the West, and that they could not by themselves defeat the West's new machine of power. Seeking independence and progress, they increasingly endeavored to adopt means of power from the West. Such attempts at development by most Middle Eastern leaders at this time were limited by lack of know-how, lack of capital, and sometimes by direct or indirect sabotage by Western imperialists.

This new tension in the Middle East reached a climax during and after World War I, leading to the independence of several Middle Eastern countries. World War II completed what World War I had started. After 1945, several other Middle Eastern countries, such as Syria, Lebanon, Israel, and Pakistan, obtained their independence and the Western colonial interests in many parts of the region were reduced to their lowest level. The withdrawal of most Western colonial interest from the Middle East has, however, been offset by the development of interest by the two international powers, the United States of America and the Soviet Union.

ELEMENTS BEHIND THE MIDDLE EAST'S PRESENT POSITION

One of the principal outcomes of World War II was the shift in the world's economic and political leadership from Europe to the hands of one young country and one reorganized country. The former is the United States, which has based its fundamental policy on democracy and individual freedom; the latter is Soviet Russia, which follows Karl Marx's teachings of collective government. Almost all other nations of the world, either for political reasons or because of similarity in ideology, have followed these two nations by grouping into opposite blocs. This has created acute competition to draw into the two opposing orbits the few remaining so-called neutral nations.

In this cold war based on conflict of idealism, the Communists have successfully used the underdeveloped areas of the world for a breeding ground. In such areas, the revolutionary teachings and promises of Marxism have had special appeal among the dissatisfied people who seek a short cut to possible relief and happiness. Democracy, on the other hand, requires peace and prosperity for its strength and expansion. Consequently, just as the state of poverty and ignorance existing in certain parts of the world provides a breeding ground for communism, economic development in underdeveloped countries is a measure to halt Communist expansion.

Among the underdeveloped parts of the world, the Middle East especially holds an important strategic and economic position for the two opposing blocs. The strategic importance of the region rests mainly in its geographic location and in its supply of several important materials. Economically, the importance of the Middle East is likewise in its geographic location, its resources, and its markets.

DEVELOPMENT OF UNITED STATES INTEREST IN THE MIDDLE EAST

Although United States interest in the Middle East in its present form is a recent development, there is a long history of economic cooperation by American free enterprise in the region. The first official United States relation with the Middle East goes back as far as May 7, 1830, to that between the American Republic and the Ottoman Empire. The first American technical expert in the Middle East was Eli Smith, a missionary from North Ford, Connecticut, who in 1834 introduced the printing press to Syria. Ex-Confederate technicians, on the private level, also contributed their skills and knowledge to the development of the area after the end of the Civil War. American educational institutions, such as Robert College in Istanbul (1863), the American University at Beirut

(1866), Istanbul Women's College (1871), the American University at Cairo (1919), and others were established throughout the region to teach its people the modern skills of many fields. American experts, especially in finance, were hired by some Middle Eastern governments as advisers. Among these were W. Morgan Shuster, who was hired by Iran in 1911 as Treasurer General, and Dr. A. C. Millispaugh, who was also hired by Iran in 1921 as the Administrator General of Finance.

However, the original United States interests in the Middle East were fleeting ones. At the end of World War I, the United States returned to its policy of isolationism. But this isolation was not complete; the country began to feel that its oil resources were low and that new sources would have to be found and kept. The Middle East was the answer, and the United States pressed for access to this area and its oil. Fears were soon lessened, however, by subsequent discoveries of oil in the United States so that country's interest in the Middle East gradually began to wane.

The attitude of the United States toward the Middle East remained passive until the period immediately after World War II. During the war, United States interests mainly took the form of developing Saudi Arabian oil production and establishing a Persian Gulf–Iran route to Russia. In most other respects, the United States recognized that the Middle East belonged mainly to Great Britain and was happy enough to allow Great Britain to assume responsibility in the area. The United States merely backed British moves in the region, thinking that Great Britain's power and prestige were great enough to cope with any problems that might arise there. Despite the warnings of President Truman as to the weakness and instability of the Middle East as well as of its importance to the West, the United States failed to develop a tenable program for the region.

However, the occurrence of several crucial political events left the United States with no alternative other than to assume a more active role in the area. While the United States continued to believe that the British could control the Middle East, the Soviet Union was ready to challenge this control. In 1946 the U.S.S.R. refused to supervise the election in Greece and thus placed Turkey in a very serious position. A victory of the Communist minority in Greece would have caused repercussions in Turkey. This the United States could not accept. Tensions were further aggravated when the Soviets in 1946 also showed reluctance to remove their troops from Iran. In the absence of a counter British action, the United States took a firm stand in behalf of Iran and Turkey and gave the case full support in the Security Council of the United Nations. In 1947 Great Britain declared that it would and could no longer give support to Turkey or Greece, nor could it counter the Soviet Union in either of these countries. The withdrawal of British aid from Turkey left that country with a huge military expenditure which could soon have drained the country's entire strength. Recognizing the imperiled position of Turkey, the first major United States aid to that country was authorized under President Harry S. Truman. Thus began the United States aid program in the Middle East.

The British action in Palestine, the statement of its inability to cope with the Palestine situation, and its subsequent withdrawal more than ever involved the United States in the Middle East. With its limited international political experience, the United States now became involved in a thousand-year-old dispute—a situation that, regardless of results, could cause the United States to lose friends. Nevertheless, the U.S. involvement in the region's problems was now complete, and a long-run economic and political policy had to be formulated.

In September 1951 Greece and Turkey were given full membership in NATO. On November 24, 1951, despite opposition by Egypt and accusations by the Soviet bloc, the Middle East Command was organized. Together with the Baghdad Pact (now CENTO), this command linked the defense of the Middle East to the Collective Defense Treaty of Southeast Asia through Pakistan, and to the North Atlantic Treaty Organization through Turkey. Thus a strong defensive bloc was created against southward Soviet expansion. Moreover, various forms of military assistance have been given to the Middle Eastern countries to insure their independence, bring about political stability, and make more effective economic development efforts.

Chapter 11

REVIEW OF UNITED STATES AID
PROGRAMS IN THE MIDDLE EAST

During the post-World War II period it became clear that world peace and prosperity could be preserved only by the cooperative efforts of free, politically stable, and economically prosperous nations. Consequently, because the problems in the Middle East were decidedly structural and could not have been solved by military assistance alone, the United States committed itself to a vast program of economic and social development in that area.

Credits for economic development and budgetary relief have been extended to many Middle Eastern countries by the Export-Import Bank of Washington, D.C., and by several other United States agencies. Economic and technical aid, as well as emergency and financial relief assistance, have been supplied on numerous occasions to several of the Middle Eastern nations. Under the agreement of September 22, 1953, with Iran, relief supplies and packages were sent to that country. Emergency relief was given to Jordan under the Emergency Wheat Aid Agreement of October 14, 1943, and under the Relief Supplies Agreement of June 29, 1954. Afghanistan received relief aid under the Emergency Wheat Aid Agreement of January 8, 1953. Egypt received relief aid under the Relief Supplies and Equipment Agreement of October 30, 1954.

Many agreements have also been reached between the United States government and various Middle Eastern nations for economic development assistance. For example, development assistance has been given to Jordan under the Economic Assistance Agreement of December 20, 1951. Lebanon has received development aid under the Special Economic Assistance Agreements of June 11 and 18, 1954, and under the Development Agreement of June 23, 1956.

Under agreements for the supply of surplus agricultural commodities (PL 480) negotiated with several Middle Eastern countries, two forms of economic support have been given. One is the use of such agricultural commodities as have helped these nations cope with their consumer goods shortage. The other is the use of funds derived from the sale of these commodities in free markets; these funds have been utilized to finance the needed development projects or public works. Through 1965, Iran had received $112.8 million under this agreement. Other Middle Eastern countries receiving similar assistance during the same period were Iraq, $25.1 million; Jordan, $76.8 million; Israel, $320.8 million; Syria, $63.2 million; Turkey, $419.0 million; and the United Arab Republic, $850.7 million.[1]

Technical assistance has also been offered to most Middle Eastern nations under the Point Four Program. Iran was the first nation in the world to request technical aid under this program. As a result, a comprehensive agreement for technical cooperation assistance, the Memorandum of Understanding, was reached between Iran and the United States government on October 19, 1950. Saudi Arabia signed a similar agreement on January 17, 1951. Agreements were reached between the United States and Afghanistan on February 7, 1951; with Jordan on February 27, 1951; with Iraq on April 10, 1951; with Egypt on May 5, 1951; with Lebanon on May 29, 1951; and with Turkey on August 6, 1951.

COMPONENTS OF UNITED STATES AID IN THE MIDDLE EAST

The United States direct aid programs[2] in the Middle East, regardless of their nature, are generally applied in the form of either credits and/or grants. Through credits the United States has provided the Middle Eastern countries with financial assistance to

---

[1] Source same as Table 10.1; pp. 12–22.

[2] Aid programs that include direct transfer of goods, services, and funds from the United States to the Middle East, as contrasted with other U.S. economic aid through efforts for U.S.–Middle East trade development, encouragement of U.S. private investment in the Middle East, etc.

enable them to cope with their immediate financial difficulties and to undertake certain economic and social projects. This type of aid is, of course, subject to repayment of the principal, and generally some interest. Through grants-in-aid the United States has provided financial and technical assistance to the Middle Eastern countries which were unable to finance their development commitments through future obligation. A United States grants-in-aid program in a Middle Eastern country may, however, be transferred into a credit account upon the ability of the aid-receiving country to undertake future obligations and upon a mutual agreement between that country and the United States. United States aid programs by grants and credits in the Middle East since 1946 are shown in Table 11.1.

UNITED STATES CREDITS

Generally speaking, the United States has extended credit to those Middle Eastern countries that possess some potential sources of revenue but need immediate funds to develop their resources and carry on their development projects, meet their urgent administrative expenses, finance their essential imports, and/or strengthen their military and political positions. Consequently, from a total of $473.6 million in economic aid to Jordan since 1946, only $5.7 million has been in credit (see Table 11.9), primarily because Jordan lacks any potential source of future repayment of capital and interest. Iraq and Iran, on the other hand, possess rich resources that can provide repayment of any future obligation. As a result, between 1946 and 1965 Iraq received $52.6 million in economic aid, of which $23.3 million was through credit (Table 11.8), and Iran received $837.3 million in economic aid of which $391.8 million was in credit (Table 11.7). Altogether, during the years 1946 through 1965, the United States authorized $9.7747 billion in aid to the Middle Eastern countries. Of this amount, $3.1855 billion was in credits and $6.5892 billion was in grants (see Table 11.1).

United States credits to the Middle Eastern countries may be put into the following three categories: (1) credits for economic development; (2) credits resulting from the sale of United States overseas surpluses or U.S. merchant ships; (3) credits extended for military objectives. Depending on the nature and objectives, United

**Table 11.1.   Cumulative United States Aid in the Middle East,
by Components, 1946–65**
(in $1,000,000)

	Total Aid	Credits	Grants
Middle East	9,774.7	3,185.5	6,589.2
Afghanistan	307.1	64.7	242.4
Iran	1,549.5	391.8	1,157.7
Iraq	99.0	23.3	75.7
Jordan	510.6	5.7	504.9
Israel	1,073.4	705.1	368.3
Lebanon	88.4	9.5	78.9
Saudi Arabia	136.1	75.5	60.6
Syria	83.0	49.3	33.8
Turkey	4,755.2	1,020.6	3,734.8
U.A.R.	1,080.9	821.7	259.3
Yemen	39.1	———	39.1
Central Treaty Org.	52.4	18.3	34.1

Source: Personal calculation from data in: Agency for International
Development, *U.S. Overseas Loans and Grants* . . . , pp. 7–25.

States credits in the Middle East have been extended through various United States departments or agencies. The major U.S. credit
agencies are the Export-Import Bank of Washington, D.C., the
Agency for International Development (AID),[3] the Office of the
Foreign Liquidation Commission (OFLC) of the State Department,
and the Central Service Administration (CSA).

The greater portion of the United States credits in the Middle
East, as shown in Table 11.4, are extended as project loans for
economic development. Between 1946 and 1965, from $3.559 billion
in military aid to the Middle East, only $84 million was in credit,
$27.6 million to Israel and $56.4 million to Saudi Arabia (Table
11.4). Some of the major United States development loans to Iran
and Jordan since 1958 are shown in Table 11.2.

---

[3] These credits were previously extended through the International Cooperation Administration (ICA), the Mutual Security Agency (MSA), and
the Foreign Operation Administration (FOA).

Table 11.2. U.S. Development Loans, by Project, 1958–65
(in $1,000)

	Year	Authorized	Signed	Expended
Iran Project		139,212	139,212	118,898
Economic Development	1958	45,912	45,912	45,912
Highway Construction	1959	63,200	63,200	63,200
Industrial & Mining Dev. Bank .	1959	5,200	5,200	2,620
Highway Construction	1962	6,000	6,000	4,979
Bandar Abbas Port	1963	15,000	15,000	1,660
Master Electrification Plan	1963	2,400	2,400	527
Service for Nat'l Airline Co.	1964	1,500	1,500	—
Jordan Project		4,107	2,467	2,467
Phosphate Mines Expansion	1959	1,269	1,269	1,269
Electric Power	1959	1,198	1,198	1,198
Damiya Junction–N. Shouna Rd. Reconstruction	1965	1,640	—	—

Source: AID Operations Report, FY 1965, pp. 35–36.

Other United States development loans in the Middle East since 1958 are:

1. Lebanon: two project loans; $5.37 million authorized, $4.892 million expended.

2. Syria: four project loans; $18.16 million authorized, $3.215 million expended.

3. Turkey: twenty-four project loans; $330.449 million authorized, $173.483 million expended.

4. U.A.R.: seven project loans; $65.7 million authorized, $39.587 million expended.

The United States has also contributed indirectly to the flow of credits into the Middle East through its financial and administrative influence in the International Bank of Reconstruction and Development. Since the establishment of this bank through April 1956 alone, this agency extended a $12.8-million loan to Iraq, $27 million to Lebanon, and $59.6 million to Turkey. The United States government has also encouraged the outflow of American private investment and credit abroad through direct investment guarantees. As of 1965, the United States investment guarantees in the Middle East, by the type of guarantee, were as shown in Table 11.3.

Table 11.3. United States Investment Guarantees, by Type, 1965

	Convertibility	Expropriation	War, Revolution & Insurrection	Extended Risk
Afghanistan .	Yes	Yes	Yes	No
Cyprus	Yes	Yes	Yes	Yes
Iran	Yes	Yes	No	No
Israel	Yes	Yes	Yes	Yes
Jordan	Yes	Yes	Yes	Yes
Turkey	Yes	Yes	Yes	Yes
U.A.R.	Yes	Yes	Yes	Yes

Source: President's Annual Report to Congress, *The Foreign Assistance Program* (Washington, D.C.: Government Printing Office, 1965), pp. 61–62.

UNITED STATES GRANTS-IN-AID

It has been the principal objective of the United States grants-in-aid programs in the Middle East to maintain a certain degree of economic, social, and political stability, and to promote a self-generating force for progress. Both of these are believed to be necessary for the peace and prosperity of the free world. Through its various types of grants-in-aid programs, the United States has provided Middle Eastern countries with desperately needed capital and/or technical resources to help them in their efforts for progress. The priority of an aid program to a Middle Eastern country is based on the following considerations:

1. The strategic importance and the geographic location of the aid-requesting country
2. The urgency of such an aid program in the requesting country
3. The probable impact of such an aid program on the mutual security of the free world
4. The ability (or inability) of the requesting country to finance the needed project through other sources.

5. The general attitude of the requesting country toward the United States and its ideology.

According to the above considerations, Turkey and Iran, because of their strategic location and because of their favorable attitude, have received the largest share of United States grants-in-aid in the Middle East. About 56 per cent of the United States grants-in-aid in the Middle East have gone to Turkey. Iran has received over 17.5 per cent of all United States grants-in-aid in the area. During the years between 1946 and 1965, a total of $6.5892 billion in grants-in-aid was extended to the Middle Eastern countries. Of this amount, $3.1142 billion was for economic development and $3.475 billion was for military purposes (see Table 11.4).

THE NATURE OF UNITED STATES AID PROGRAMS

The short-run objectives—and thus the nature of United States aid programs in the Middle East—have varied according to the time and place to correspond to the strategic and economic needs of different localities. Generally speaking, the nature of U.S. aid programs in the Middle East may be grouped into three different but interrelated categories:

1. *Military assistance*, which aims to strengthen the defensive position of the region and to bring about some degree of political stability.

2. *Emergency and relief programs*, which seek to help remove economic, social, and political pressures that might lead to possible crisis, and also to prevent overutilization of resources.

3. *Economic programs*, which tend to assist the people of the Middle East in their efforts for economic, social, and political progress.

MILITARY ASSISTANCE

The United States has contributed to the political and military strength of the Middle East through various direct and indirect efforts. Direct efforts include both technical and financial assistance. The indirect efforts involve activities such as those that have helped the region's defense unity and have fostered political stability in the area. The economic value of United States military aid in the

Middle East, however, lies in the benefits the population may receive from the added military expenditures as well as from the added political security. Both of these help generate an environment that will lead to higher income and business expansion.

United States military assistance in the Middle East has not been extended on equal terms, but according to the aid-receiving country's strategic value for the defense of the region and of the free world. Consequently, as shown in Table 11.4, the bulk of these aid programs has been concentrated in Turkey and Iran. These two countries hold a special geographic and strategic position in the area. From the $3559 million in United States military aid extended to the Middle East between 1946 and 1965, more than 74 per cent has gone to Turkey and more than 20 per cent to Iran.

More than 97 per cent of United States military assistance in the Middle East has been provided under grants-in-aid programs. This may be based on the following arguments:

1. Most Middle Eastern governments have rightly been reluctant to allocate their limited resources to expand military strength at the expense of economic development. They have not failed to recognize the importance of their own defensive strength, but they have learned from past experience that military strength without a basic social and economic reform often leads to dictatorship, oppression, and even foreign influence. This the Middle Eastern people gravely fear.

2. Today, the building of an effective defensive strength requires such heavy capital expenditure that none of the Middle Eastern countries can afford to do it. Additional assistance is therefore necessary to build the area's defensive power to a minimum standard.

3. The defensive strength of the Middle East benefits not only the region itself, but also the entire free world. Accordingly, because the Middle East cannot provide for an effective defense, it is the responsibility of all members of the free world to do so.

The starting point of United States military aid programs in the Middle East may be said to be November 7, 1941, when Turkey was declared eligible for Lend-Lease aid. This eligibility was later extended to Egypt (on November 11, 1941), Iran (March 10, 1942),

Iraq (May 1, 1942), and Saudi Arabia (February 18, 1943). During the period between 1946 and 1965, $3.559 billion in military aid was extended to the Middle East under various programs (see Table 11.4).

UNITED STATES EMERGENCY AID PROGRAMS

The government and the people of the United States, on many occasions and under various programs, have come to the aid of the Middle Eastern people in time of trouble. The basic motive behind relief and contributions such as those given through CARE, HOPE, and the Red Cross by the people of the United States is humanitarian. But the primary objective of emergency and relief aid programs by the United States government is to assure economic, social, and political stability in the region, thus preventing any possible crisis that could endanger the security of the free world. United States emergency relief programs in the Middle East, in general, fall into three major categories: (1) Relief Assistance to Arab Refugees, (2) Emergency Aid to Iran, and (3) other urgent relief programs for such unforeseen events as famine and flood.

Relief Assistance to Arab Refugees. The greater portion of United States aid for Arab refugees has been extended through such programs as the United Nations Relief and Work Agency for Palestine Refugees (UNRWA) and the United Nations Children's Emergency Fund (UNICEF). The UNRWA was organized in December 1948, following the Arab-Israeli truce agreement. By early 1956, this agency had provided relief for 835,986 registered refugees and shelters for about 335,000 refugees who were unable to find homes of their own. As of mid-1965, the United States had contributed $288.5 million to world-wide programs through this agency. UNICEF especially has concentrated its efforts on providing aid for the children among the Arab refugees in the form of supplies, equipment, and medical care. During the same years, the United States extended $58.5 million for emergency relief and economic development (Title II of PL 480) and $17.5 million to voluntary relief agencies in Jordan (Title III of PL 480).

United States Emergency Aid to Iran. In August 1953 the government of Iran was faced with an economic catastrophe, the result

Table 11.4. Cumulative United States Aid in the Middle East, by Nature, 1946–65
(in $1,000,000)

	Total	Economic Aids			Military Aids		
		Total	Credit	Grant	Total	Credit	Grant
Middle East	9,774.7	6,215.7	3,101.5	3,114.2	3,559.0	84.0	3,475.0
Afghanistan	307.1	304.0	64.7	239.3	3.1	—	3.1
Iran	1,549.5	837.3	391.8	445.5	712.2	—	712.2
Iraq	99.0	52.6	23.3	29.3	46.4	—	46.4
Jordan	510.0	473.6	5.7	467.9	37.0	—	37.0
Israel	1,073.4	1,045.8	667.5	368.3	27.6	27.6	—
Lebanon	88.4	79.7	9.5	70.2	8.7	—	8.7
Saudi Arabia	136.1	47.4	19.1	28.3	88.7	56.4	32.3
Syria	83.0	83.0	49.3	33.8	*	—	*
Turkey	4,755.2	2,119.9	1,020.6	1,099.5	2,635.3	—	2,635.3
UAR	1,080.9	1,080.9	821.7	259.3	*	—	*
Yemen	39.1	39.1	—	39.1	*	—	*
CENTO	52.4	52.4	18.3	34.1	—	—	—

* Less than $50,000.
Source: Same as for Table 10.1, but with personal calculations made.

of the nationalization of the oil industry. To cope with its immediate expenditures, to preserve the level of public employment, and to meet administrative obligations, the Iranian government further "ruined the country's economy by deficit financing; borrowing without backing; issuing notes without security; in a period of non-revenue."[4] Meanwhile, a satisfactory settlement of the oil dispute was not yet in sight. This grave economic and political crisis in Iran had thus "jeopardized the stability of the entire Near East Area."[5]

On August 19, 1953, upon a request from General Zahedi, Iran's new prime minister, and to help maintain economic and political stability in that country, $45 million was authorized by President Eisenhower to enable the Iranian government to meet the costs of essential operations. During the period from August 1953 through 1956, a total of $106 million in grants and $42 million in credits was made available by the United States government for budgetary assistance to Iran.

United States Emergency Aid to Iran proved essential for that country's economic and political stability. Among other things, this emergency aid saved the finances of the government and of the National Bank (Bank Melli) by stabilizing the value of the rial, providing the needed exchange for essential imports, and contributing to the country's level of employment and economy by financing forty-eight projects in public works. The dollars granted by the United States were made available to Iranian importers and to government agencies through the USOM/Iran. Importers paid in rials for this foreign exchange and these rials were deposited to the credit of the Iranian government for its immediate administrative and other necessary expenditures. After the necessary expenses were met, the extra rials were set aside for public works in the following proportions: 20 per cent for developing provincial cities, 20 per cent for highway improvements, 10 per cent for railroads, 10 per cent for education, and the remaining 40 per cent for other mutually agreed-upon programs.

---

[4] ICA, *In Time of Trouble*, J. B. Hollisters, Director (Washington, D.C.: ICA Office of Public Reports, 1955), p. 11.

[5] *Report to The President* by FOA, January 1953 to June 1955, p. 12.

Other Relief Programs. In addition to budgetary aid to Iran and relief assistance to Arab refugees, the United States, during the postwar period, stood ready to extend a helping hand to Middle Eastern countries struck by famine, flood, or other unforeseen troubles. These emergency programs have on many occasions brought relief to the people of the region and contributed to their economic and political stability.

Jordan was the first Middle Eastern country to request and receive relief aid from the United States. On December 18, 1951, according to a United States–Jordan agreement, 9650 long tons of wheat were shipped to Jordan to help that government cope with a serious food shortage in the country. This shipment, costing $1.4 million, was financed by the MSA as a part of the technical and economic assistance to Jordan. The wheat was sold through private channels, and the revenue was used by the government for its development projects in agriculture, health, education, water resources, and small-scale industries. Several other emergency assistances have been given to Middle Eastern countries on a similar basis. For example, the 1953 famine in Jordan brought another 10,000 tons of wheat under emergency aid into that country. In 1954, 25 tons of garden seed were shipped to Iraq to alleviate the shortage of food and vegetables washed away by the Tigris-Euphrates Basin flood. Iran received emergency aid for budgetary relief in 1953 and to meet exchange shortages in 1954. On April 7, 1952, emergency assistance was extended by the United States to more than a thousand Iranian students in America who, because of the dollar shortage, could not receive funds from home. This program was extended in September 1952 to cover the period ending August 1953. Through Titles II and III of the Agricultural Trade Development and Assistance Act alone, the United States had extended $240.3 million and $489.1 million respectively, as of mid-1965. The United States has, furthermore, under supporting assistance, extended such aid as budgetary support, relief, and rehabilitation to several Middle Eastern countries. During the 1964–1965 period, this assistance amounted to $6,964,000 in Afghanistan, $406,000 in Iran, $67,000,000 in Jordan, $113,000 in Saudi Arabia, $34,942,000 in Turkey, $10,104 in Yemen, and $5,692,000 to CENTO.[6]

---

[6] AID *Operations Report,* 1965, p. 52.

UNITED STATES ECONOMIC ASSISTANCE

Aside from defense support programs which also affect the Middle Eastern economy, United States economic development assistance in the region is generally extended under the following four inter-related and supplementary categories:

1. Development loans
2. Technical Cooperation Assistance
3. Supporting assistance
4. Food for Peace (PL 480) Program

The primary objective of United States economic assistance in the Middle East, as well as in other parts of the world, is to help the aid-receiving countries achieve a self-supporting growth as much as possible. Usually most United States economic assistance in an aid-receiving country is discontinued as soon as the country can resume its self-support. It is primarily for this reason that in 1965 no new commitments were made by the Agency for International Development (AID) in Greece or Iraq. Other countries that received no AID commitment for 1965 were Southern Rhodesia and Nationalist China. These countries, however, will still be eligible for long-term loans from the Export-Import Bank, sales of U.S. surplus food under PL 480, and cultural exchange programs. Other important objectives of the United States economic assistance programs are:

1. Improving the aid-receiving country's balance-of-payment condition
2. Eliminating food shortage and difficulties
3. Helping develop private-enterprise systems.

The United States economic assistance programs in the Middle East are usually financed from:

1. Funds directly appropriated for a specific program
2. Funds transferred from military appropriation for economic use
3. Funds accumulated from the sale of United States–granted materials to the Middle Eastern countries.

In each case, a special account is created to segregate such funds from local accounts in order to minimize the possibility of their waste and improper use. A relative distribution of United States economic assistance since 1949 by major category is shown in Table 11.5.

Economic Development Assistance. It is necessary to keep in mind that, regardless of type, all United States economic or noneconomic assistance programs are interrelated. One cannot isolate the effect of one particular program on the region or a country's economic position. In fact, the effectiveness of one program may strongly depend on the successful application of another.

Table 11.5. Cumulative United States Aid in World and in
Middle East and South Asia, 1949–65
(in $1,000)

	Commitments	Expenditures
Total: World	40,030,192	36,238,205
Development loans	6,653,714	3,772,255
Technical cooperation/development grants[1a]	2,531,039	2,375,497
Defense support/supporting assistance[1b]	27,145,917	26,544,218
Other, including international organizations	3,699,522	3,546,263
Total: Middle East & South Asia	9,103,365	7,557,929
Development loans	3,994,285	2,567,992
Technical cooperation/development grants	657,552	640,508
Defense support/supporting assistance	4,198,640	4,115,743
Other, including international organizations	252,888	233,686

1a. T.C. through 1961, D.G. thereafter. *1b.* D.S. through 1961, S.A. thereafter.
Source: AID *Operations Report, 1965*, pp. 50–51.

Military assistance programs in most developing countries are essential to provide the countries with some degree of political and economic stability. Lack of political stability and professional and personal security often creates an environment not conducive to economic progress.

Economic development loans are necessary to provide developing countries financial aid to build the needed capital, provide an exchange for importing development materials, and help implement the key economic and social projects. Without such assistance, economic development in most underdeveloped countries will be a long and painful process.

Political stability and capital, though essential to a country's economic development, are not sufficient. A third factor is necessary to aid these two factors toward the country's economic development. Many underdeveloped countries in the world possess adequate resources to finance their development, and some have enjoyed long-term political stability. But they all lack the technical know-how to make use of their resources. In fact, a marked degree of economic development in a country can be achieved by improvements in health, education, public administration and transportation, for example. Technical Cooperation Assistance by the United States has provided many underdeveloped countries just such an opportunity.

Finally, one cannot neglect the role and importance of emergency and contingency assistance in the economic development of the Middle East, as well as in other underdeveloped countries. Such assistance, by alleviating economic and social crisis, has made possible the continuation of other social, political, and economic projects.

In 1965, development loans constituted 87 per cent of all funds committed by AID in the Middle East and South Asia region. Most of these loans have been extended as project loans. That is, to become eligible for such a loan, the underdeveloped country must present a well-defined project, one that should meet certain standards necessary to generate economic growth. Loans may be extended, for example, to build power plants, irrigation systems, and transportation facilities; to help increase productivity in key sectors; and to raise funds for development banks. Terms of a loan depend on the aid-requesting country's repayment capability, foreign-exchange position, and the nature of the project. During 1964 and 1965, Iraq received no development loan and Jordan received only $393,000. This was due to Iraq's lack of financial need and Jordan's inability to repay. Iran received a $4,043,000 development loan during 1964 and 1965. Turkey and the UAR received $168,071,000 and $31,718,000 respectively for the same two years.

In 1958, about 50 per cent of the total ICA programs in the

Middle East fell into the category of supporting assistance. In 1965, only 5 per cent of the total AID programs were for support assistance. This was, in a way, the result of an economic development trend in the region that has reduced the Middle Eastern countries' dependence on this aid category. United States supporting assistance has been offered for the following programs:

1. Relief and rehabilitation
2. Maintenance of minimal government services
3. Provision for essential commodities
4. Operations to maintain peace
5. Public works projects
6. Budget supports
7. Emergency disaster relief

During 1964 and 1965, United States supporting assistance to the Middle East was:[7]

Afghanistan	$ 6,964,000
Iran	$ 406,000
Jordan	$67,000,000
Saudi Arabia	$ 113,000
Turkey	$34,942,000
Yemen	$10,104,000
CENTO	$ 5,672,000

Technical Cooperation Assistance. United States Technical Cooperation Asssistance in the Middle East in its recent form originated with President Truman's Inaugural Address in 1949. In this address, the President asked for a "bold new program" for making the benefits of the United States' "scientific advances and industrial progress available for the improvement and growth of the underdeveloped areas."[8] Consequently, a new category of foreign assistance known as Technical Cooperation Assistance or the Point Four Program was born. The principal objectives of the Point Four Programs in the Middle East, as well as in other underdeveloped areas of the world, have been described by the lawmakers as follows:

---

[7] Personal calculation from data in AID *Operations Report,* 1965, p. 52.

[8] *Department of State Bulletin,* January 30, 1949, p. 125.

> To aid the efforts of the people of economically underdeveloped areas to develop their resources and improve their working conditions by encouraging the exchange of technical knowledge and skills and the flow of investment capital to countries which provide conditions under which such technical assistance and capital can effectively and constructively contribute to raising standards of living, creating new sources of wealth, increasing productivity and exchanging purchasing power.[9]

The United States Point Four Program (Technical Cooperation Assistance) has been especially formulated to aid the economically and socially underdeveloped countries, such as those of the Middle East, South Asia, Africa, and to some extent Latin America. The economic value of United States Technical Cooperation Assistance in the Middle East lies not merely in its financial contributions but especially in its attempt to inject new life and modern technology into the stagnant and old-fashioned economy of the region. For, more than any other type of United States economic assistance in the area, Technical Cooperation Assistance is directed to eliminating the sources of the existing problems and structural defects. It seeks to cure the causes of backwardness rather than the symptoms.

While the long-term objective of the United States Point Four Program is to help the underdeveloped countries achieve self-generating processes of growth, the intermediate objectives of this program can be classified into two interrelated categories: (1) programs that seek to improve the region's human resources and (2) programs to help the Middle Eastern governments in their efforts for progress.

The task of social reform in a socially underdeveloped country, as in the case of the Middle Eastern countries, consists of three complementary steps. The first step involves the task of awakening the mentally isolated, stagnant majority of the population and stimulating their interest for self-betterment. The Point Four Program in the Middle East has sought this end through helping the already increasing social integration and introducing, for example, pilot projects and audio-visual programs. The second step involves the task of improving the quality of the now-awakened people to prepare them for handling their own development efforts. This has

---

[9] Public Law 535, 81st Congress, 2nd session, Title IV, An Act to Provide Foreign Economic Assistance.

been sought through community development, health, and education programs. The third step is to equip the now-willing, able, and well-informed people with new and modern technology to increase their productivity and make their efforts more effective. This is being accomplished through various training, pilot, and community development projects.

The United States Point Four Program in the Middle East has also helped the governments and the people in planning and operating their development programs. The majority of these programs are in food and agriculture, power, industries and mining, transportation, education, health and sanitation, and public administration. United States assistance is usually supplied in the forms of direct participation in designing and operating development projects, technical advice and guidance, supplying modern tools and demonstration equipment, and—in some cases—direct financial assistance.

Efforts are also made by the United States Point Four Program to make use of private resources to further social and economic betterment in the area. For example, in 1965 three American universities were involved in developing higher education institutions in Iran, Iraq, and Jordan—the University of Pennsylvania in Iran, the University of Texas in Iraq, and the University of Illinois in Jordan. The same year four American universities were active in Turkey, four in Afghanistan, and one in the UAR.

From 1950, when the Point Four Program was first begun in Iran, through 1965, the United States has contributed $640,608,000 in cash and services to the nations of the Middle East and South Asia through this program. Today nine Middle Eastern countries and CENTO are primary recipients of this aid in the Middle Eastern and Southeast Asian region. The results of the Point Four Program in the Middle East have been tremendous. For example, under programs for rural development, by 1956 7000 village projects were completed in Iran and 2000 were under way.[10] Under programs for health improvement, also by 1956, the incidence of malaria wherever the program was applied was reduced from 90 to 10 per cent of the population. This reduction in malaria cases increased manpower by 400 per cent.[11] Similar improvements were

---

[10] USOM/Iran, Annual Report (January 15, 1956), p. 13.

[11] *Ibid.*, p. 31.

achieved in Iraq and Jordan. In education, a three-month training course at a Tehran foundry resulted in a 100 per cent increase in production.[12] Again in Iran, in two years (1954–1956), over 16,000 men were made literate through adult-education programs. In agriculture, in one project alone in Iran, demonstrating and encouraging the use of the moldboard plow instead of the traditional one in sugar-beet cultivation resulted in three times the standard yield.[13]

Food for Peace. Under the Agricultural Trade Development and Assistance Act of 1954 (PL 480), the United States has furnished the Middle Eastern countries, as well as many others, its surplus agricultural products. This program has supplemented other United States economic assistance programs in the region in two ways:

1. It has provided the fast-growing population and its increasing demand necessary food. Without this help, an increase in food imports by the Middle Eastern countries would have to be at the expense of development materials.

2. It has provided the Middle Eastern countries a source of funds which are often used on mutually agreed-upon projects.

United States aid programs under PL 480 are shown in Table 11.6. Perhaps the most important portion of PL 480 is Title I. Under this title, United States agricultural products are sold in the Middle Eastern countries. A part of the proceeds are used by the aid-receiving countries on mutually agreed-on projects. Title II covers famine relief and other emergency assistance. Title III covers donations for voluntary relief agencies. Title IV, which was added in 1959, provides for dollar-credit sales of surplus agricultural commodities, repayable in twenty years.

The Middle Eastern countries, in their efforts for economic stability and development, have also received direct assistance from various international agencies. These direct aids have been mostly provided either under economic loans or under technical assistance. Aside from such international organizations as UNICEF, UNRWA,

---

[12] ICA, *Technical Cooperation in Education* (Washington, D.C.: U.S. Government Printing Office, March 1956), p. 15.

[13] USOM/Iran, Annual Report, 1956, p. 17.

Table 11.6. Cumulative United States Aid in the Middle East under PL 480, 1955–65

(in $1,000,000)

COUNTRY	TITLE I		TITLE II		TITLE III	TITLE IV
	Sales Agreement	Planned for Country Use	Authorization	Net Expenditure		
Total	1,748.300	1,386.400	403.791	325.890	273.091	28.400
Afghanistan	1.00	0.60	82.026	59.564	1.352	—
Iran	66.40	44.70	37.305	30.791	19.031	11.800
Israel	301.60	260.30	1.492	0.474	56.497	—
Jordan	3.00	0.80	58.546	54.289	17.513	—
Syria	37.20	29.30	29.734	28.056	2.353	1.800
Turkey	525.30	365.80	31.360	25.761	20.425	—
U.A.R.	813.80	684.90	25.821	23.791	139.986	14.800
Iraq	—	—	5.986	1.820	4.268	—
Lebanon	—	—	17.458	17.034	—	—
Saudi Arabia	—	—	0.786	—	—	—
Yemen	—	—	10.096	10.005	0.033	—
UNRA (regional)	—	—	103.181	73.585	11.633	—

Source: Calculated from AID *Operations Report* (June 1965), pp. 90–102.

Table 11.7. United States Aid in Iran, 1946–65
(in $1,000,000)

	Total	Economic Aid			Military Aid		
		Total	Credits	Grants	Total	Credits	Grants
1946–65	1,549.5	837.3	391.8	445.5	712.2	—	712.2
1946–48	25.8	25.8	25.8	—	—	—	—
1949–52	33.1	16.5	—	16.5	16.6	—	16.6
1953–57	500.7	366.8	116.2	250.6	133.9	—	133.9
1958	124.9	51.9	40.0	11.9	73.0	—	73.0
1959	137.8	46.9	37.7	9.2	90.9	—	90.9
1960	127.3	38.2	—	38.2	89.1	—	89.1
1961	156.4	107.2	72.2	35.0	49.2	—	49.2
1962	102.7	69.4	26.5	42.9	33.3	—	33.3
1963	110.6	44.6	23.2	21.4	66.0	—	66.0
1964	54.0	26.7	14.2	12.4	27.3	—	27.3
1965	93.4	43.5	36.1	7.4	49.9	—	49.9

Source: Same as for Table 10.1, p. 12.

Table 11.8. United States Aid in Iraq, 1946–65
(in $1,000,000)

	Total	Economic Aid			Military Aid		
		Total	Credits	Grants	Total	Credits	Grants
1946–65	99	52.6	23.3	29.3	46.4	—	46.4
1946–48	0.9	0.9	0.9	—	—	—	—
1949–52	0.5	0.5	—	0.5	—	—	—
1953–57	38.5	13.9	—	13.9	24.6	—	24.6
1958	24.4	3.1	—	3.1	21.3	—	21.3
1959	0.4	0.3	—	0.3	0.1	—	0.1
1960	0.7	0.6	—	0.6	0.1	—	0.1
1961	1.3	1.3	—	1.3	°	—	°
1962	0.8	0.8	—	0.8	°	—	°
1963	0.7	0.7	—	0.7	°	—	°
1964	24.3	24.2	22.4	1.8	0.1	—	0.1
1965	6.5	6.3	—	6.3	0.2	—	0.2

° Less than $50,000.
Source: Same as for Table 10.1, p. 13.

Table 11.9.   United States Aid in Jordan, 1946–65
(in $1,000,000)

	Total	Economic Aid Total	Credits	Grants	Military Aid Total	Credits	Grants
1946–65	510.6	473.6	5.7	467.9	37.0	—	37.0
1946–48	—	—	—	—	—	—	—
1949–52	5.2	5.2	—	5.2	—	—	—
1953–57	54.7	54.7	—	54.7	—	—	—
1958	45.9	37.4	—	37.4	8.5	—	8.5
1959	65.7	63.5	3.7	59.8	2.2	—	2.2
1960	53.9	51.0	−1.0	52.0	2.9	—	2.9
1961	69.7	67.8	1.0	66.8	1.9	—	1.9
1962	48.5	45.9	0.6	45.3	2.6	—	2.6
1963	58.3	55.8	—	55.8	2.5	—	2.5
1964	58.5	50.4	−0.2	50.6	8.1	—	8.1
1965	46.7	42.1	1.6	40.5	4.6	—	4.6

Source: Same as for Table 10.1, p. 15.

FOA, and WHO, which have indirectly supplied assistance in the area, major international agencies involved in giving direct economic assistance to the Middle East are:

1. International Bank for Reconstruction and Development (IBRD)
2. International Finance Corporation (IFC)
3. UN Technical Assistance—regular and others (UNTAR)
4. UN Expanded Program for Technical Assistance (UNEPTA)
5. UN Special Fund (UNSF)
6. International Development Association

Table 11.10 shows, by source and agency, major assistance by international organizations in Iran, Iraq, and Jordan. It also shows total assistance from international organizations in other Middle Eastern countries.

UNITED STATES AID PROGRAMS: APPRAISAL

The United States aid programs in the Middle East have not all been equally effective. The effectiveness of each program on the

Table 11.10. **Assistance from International Organizations in the Middle East**
(in $1,000,000)

	1949–65	1949–55	1956–60	1961–65
Total Middle East	723.5	79.9	318.1	325.5
Iran	281.2	3.3	202.4	75.5
IBRD	253.2	—	194.2	59.0
IFC	0.3	—	0.3	—
UNEPTA	13.5	3.3	4.9	5.3
UNTAR	2.4	—	1.0	1.4
UNSF	11.8	—	2.0	9.8
Iraq	21.7	7.6	3.5	10.6
IBRD	6.3	6.3	—	—
UNEPTA	5.6	1.3	2.1	2.2
UNTAR	1.5	—	0.5	1.0
UNSF	7.3	—	0.9	6.4
Jordan	16.5	0.5	2.2	13.8
IDA	8.5	—	—	8.5
UNEPTA	4.1	0.5	1.8	1.8
UNTAR	0.8	—	0.4	0.4
UNSF	3.1	—	—	3.1
Afghanistan	24.5	1.6	5.2	17.7
Israel	84.5	1.4	3.2	79.0
Lebanon	36.9	0.6	29.2	7.1
Saudi Arabia	5.7	0.6	0.7	4.4
Syria	22.5	1.1	3.4	18.0
Turkey	147.2	62.0	5.2	80.0
U.A.R.	81.5	1.1	62.9	17.5
Yemen	1.3	0.1	0.2	1.0

Calculated from source for Table 10.1, pp. 149–51.

process of economic and social development is to a considerable extent dependent on its suitability to the aid-receiving country's social, political, and economic conditions. Consequently, of the existing programs, some are likely to bring better results under the region's economic and social surroundings than others.

EFFECTIVENESS OF PROGRAMS

To repeat, the United States has extended aid to the Middle East in the form of either credit or grants. Of the two forms of aid, credits by and large seem more suitable than grants as a measure of financing development projects because of certain advantages in application of credits and because of some disadvantages in the application of grants.

Credits are argued to be more suitable for helping the Middle Eastern countries for the following reasons:

1. The recipients of credit would have to include the repayment of principal and interests in their long-term plans, which often stimulates further efforts for better use of such capital.

2. Financial assistance received as a loan will have to be accounted for—more so than if it is received as a grant. The recipients often feel the fund to be their own, a future obligation. This feeling and the critical view of the country's citizens may well reduce wasteful programs or monumental projects.

3. The people in the aid-receiving country, moreover, would be likely to feel that they are obtaining help on terms of equality rather than as charity wards of the United States with all the possible political influences—real or imagined. This may help promote better understanding and relations between the United States and the Middle Eastern countries.

4. American taxpayers would feel that their foreign aid programs are based on a businesslike transaction rather than just a giveaway plan. This in turn may stimulate further the flow of American capital into the area and thus hasten progress.

5. The Communist bloc would find less basis for an anti-American campaign if United States assistance in the area is given in the form of credit, since less politics are likely to be attached to credits than to grants.

Grants, on the other hand, may tend to bring tense relations between the donor and the receiving countries. The recipients often come to look upon grants as a moral right justified by their country's past sufferings. They may thus resent any condition attached to a grant or any future reduction in its amount. In the meantime they may experience embarrassment, resentment, and suspicion of the grantor. (In fact this reaction accounts for much of the anti-American feeling overseas.) The United States, on the other hand, would probably be tempted to use grants as political means for achieving some of its strategic objectives—far more than it would have permitted itself to do if the aid was extended on a credit basis. Indeed, if the United States failed to do so, it might be criticized at home. Grants, moreover, tend to reduce the value of the capital to the recipients. Finally, they are usually looked upon with a certain amount of suspicion by most Middle Eastern people and are regarded more critically by the American taxpayer and Congress.

Today, the flow of international and even United States credits into the Middle Eastern countries, especially those suffering from exchange difficulties, has been severely limited by the extremely conservative policy of the International Bank for Reconstruction and the Export-Import Bank of Washington, D.C. Both banks lend to underdeveloped nations only in relatively small amounts to avoid the risk of default.[14] For example, of the total $32.807 billion in credit extended by the United States between 1946 and 1965, only $9.015 billion was supplied by the Export-Import Bank.[15] During the same period the International Bank for Reconstruction and Development supplied $12.4068 billion.[16] Because of this short-coming, United States grants-in-aid programs have become necessary to fill the gap. Meanwhile, any shift of emphasis from grants to credits or any effort to facilitate the flow of loans into the area will be a useful step toward better aid relationships.

The flow of credits into the Middle East, however, cannot alone solve all the region's social and economic problems. Besides, the United States has assumed a role far more basic than its role of bringing higher standards of living to the Middle East. It is believed to be responsible for developing public responsibility, promoting democracy, and bringing basic institutional reforms into the area.

[14] See discussion in Research and Policy Committee of the Committee for Economic Development, *Economic Development Abroad and the Role of American Foreign Investment* (Washington, D.C.: U.S. Government Printing Office, 1956), p. 5.

[15] Special Report Prepared for the House Foreign Affairs Committee, *U.S. Overseas Loans and Grants*, July 1, 1945–June 30, 1965 (AID Statistics and Reports Division, March 18, 1966), p. 5.

[16] *Ibid.*, p. 149.

Thus Technical Cooperation Assistance programs, which seek the above objectives, are undoubtedly the most useful approach to the region's problems. Furthermore, while the gain of the Middle Eastern countries from technical cooperation programs surpasses that of other types of programs, the cost of these programs to the American taxpayers is smaller. This is mainly because technical cooperation programs, by their nature, call for the "sharing of the benefits"[17] of American progress with other nations, rather than just giving. Sharing what American people know does not draw on their physical resources and may even benefit their economy by an exchange of information. Besides, the costs of such programs, small as they are, consist chiefly of compensation to American personnel and technicians abroad, which can hardly be considered waste. Similar arguments may well be presented for the United States Peace Corps programs abroad.

The above characteristics have made the United States Technical Cooperation Assistance programs and Peace Corps programs very popular both at home and abroad. In the Middle East in particular, these two types of programs have met with great popularity. To the sensitive and neutral-minded people of the region, a reciprocal exchange of technical information is more a sign of equal friendship than an effort by either side to use influence.

Consequently, the United States should place emphasis on credits for supplying capital and material to the Middle Eastern nations and on Technical Cooperation programs which enable the aid-receiving countries to make the best use of such capital, as in the fostering of basic and social reforms. If in a special case the extending of grants-in-aid becomes necessary, such grants should include the understanding that they are temporary. A proper clause should also be written in such a grant's agreement for its conversion to credit at a proper time.

The usefulness of United States foreign military aid programs has been questioned by some authorities for several reasons.[18] Cer-

---

[17] FOA, *Technical Cooperation Program around the World* (Washington, D.C.: FOA Office of Public Reports, 1954), p. 62.

[18] See H. R. Philly, "What Obsesses the Arab," *New Republic* (October 7, 1957), p. 8; V. M. Dean, "How to Make Foreign Aid Less Controversial," *Foreign Policy Bulletin* (June 15, 1957), p. 147; Chester Bowles, *Ambassador's*

tain regional problems, such as the development of nationalism, the existence of regional quarrels, and the underlying social problems may be aggravated rather than soothed. It is possible that United States military assistance may help bring political stability and security in the area, but it may also result in further regional frictions and disturbances by strengthening the military forces of highly nationalist governments. Moreover, in a region characterized by a great deal of political instability and social unrest, there can be no assurance that military aid (in the form of equipment and know-how) given to a friendly government would not fall into the hands of the opposition and thus be used for purposes contrary to United States objectives. Some of the recent developments in the region present a good basis for this argument.

OBSTACLES LIMITING MAXIMUM EFFECTIVENESS

The United States aid programs in the Middle East, helpful as they have been, are known to have encountered some obstacles, thus limiting their maximum effectiveness. Some of the major obstacles, with regard to origin, may be classified into three categories: (1) those resulting from the combination of the recent development of Communist-bloc economic competition and the underlying cultural ills in the region; (2) those derived from the lack of adequate cooperation among the Western nations with regard to their economic and strategic policies in the Middle East; and (3) those arising from some weaknesses in the operation and administration of the programs.

The development of economic and strategic competition by the Communist bloc in the Middle East has undoubtedly raised some obstacles to the successful implementation of United States aid policy in the area. From mid-December 1955 through 1957 the government of the Soviet Union gave, loaned, or pledged about $1.5 billion in economic aid and $400 million in military assistance to other countries. Russia had surpassed United States aid in ten

Report (New York: Harper, 1954), p. 342; J. G. Harrison, "Middle East Instability," *Middle Eastern Affairs*, (March 1954), pp. 80–81; G. V. Allen, "The U.S. and the Awakening of Public Responsibility in the Middle East," *The Evolution of Public Responsibility in the Middle East* (New York: Middle East Institute, 1955), pp. 61–62.

key countries. By 1961, this aid had amounted to $4.5 billion in grants and credits for economic development and to $2 billion in military assistance. The Communist approach generally comes with increases in technical aid programs and trade agreements. Their promises, at least as are viewed by most people of the Middle East, are based on helping the Middle Eastern nations to gain freedom from their Western oppressors. But the capitalist approach often appears to offer not national independence but a perpetual dependence on Western capital and trade. Most Communist aid goes to seven countries—Afghanistan, the U.A.R., Iraq, Syria, Cuba, Indonesia, and India—four of which are located in the Middle East.

The major threat in the Middle East, however, is not merely in the amount offered for aid by the Soviet Union or in its ability to increase the offer, but also in the existing cultural ills and social unrest in the area. That is, to many Middle Eastern people the apparently unconditional nature of Soviet aid has begun to appear a sort of opportunity that can help them achieve some of their long-desired objectives. This problem is especially aggravated because the United States, hounded by the nature of its government and ideology, cannot or will not meet Communist competition on similar ground. An additional difficulty has been caused by some Middle Eastern rulers who play both ends against the middle. They have sought to use the existing competition between the United States and the U.S.S.R. for personal benefits. This effort, while it may seem desirable from their own national point of view, may tend to make United States offers for aid even more conditional.

The lack of adequate cooperation and coordination of interests among the Western nations in the Middle East has probably been one of the major disappointments for the free world. Not all the Western nations are equally interested in improving the political stability, military strength, and economic development of the Middle East. As a result, the length to which each of these nations is willing to go to help the Middle East achieve its political and economic objectives has varied. This has often created a major critical issue. Despite the necessity for their cooperation to help improve the region and strengthen its defenses against Soviet expansion, their interests do not always run in the same direction. Several situations (such as the Suez Canal incident) have placed the United States policymakers in an embarrassing position and have affected U.S. aid policies in the area.

Finally, on some occasions, the maximum effectiveness of the United States aid programs in the Middle East is known to have been limited by:

1. Some weaknesses in design and operation, usually termed "technical errors"
2. Difficulty in finding the right personnel
3. Political situations.

The weaknesses in designing and operating aid programs are usually the result of one or a combination of the following factors:

1. The many dissimilarities between the United States (where the programs are originated) and the Middle Eastern countries
2. Lack of a custom-made blueprint for fitting the program into the receiving country's economy
3. The existence of a considerable amount of red tape and bureaucratic procedure in the operation of programs
4. Lack of adequate supervision over the use of funds and implementation of the program.

These problems have, on many occasions, either reduced the effectiveness of United States programs or have stimulated waste and misutilization of funds.

The difficulty of finding the right personnel for the right job has also resulted in some further problems. In our highly competitive market, it is difficult to obtain skilled personnel willing to go to the Middle East, where both the future job security and working conditions are lower than in the United States. But even when such personnel are found, their effectiveness is often limited by their lack of inside knowledge of the Middle East and the existing dissimilarities between the aid-receiving country and the United States, where they received their basic training.

On several occasions, the success of United States aid programs in the Middle East has been jeopardized by that country's political stand. For example, most Arab nations and Afghanistan have indicted the United States for colonialism—the result of the U.S. stand for Israeli independence and its lack of direct intervention during the Suez Canal incident.

It is difficult to point out how much the existing obstacles have reduced the effectiveness of United States aid programs in the Middle East. But an attempt to find and eliminate these obstacles can to a considerable extent make the objectives of United States aid policy in the region, as well as the objectives of the Middle Eastern nations, more attainable.

INDEX

227